BYZANTINE CIVILISATION

BYZANTINE CIVILISATION

BY

STEVEN RUNCIMAN

**FELLOW OF TRINITY COLLEGE,
CAMBRIDGE**

LONDON
EDWARD ARNOLD (PUBLISHERS) LTD.

COPYRIGHT IN ALL COUNTRIES
SIGNATORY TO THE BERNE CONVENTION
FIRST PUBLISHED, 1933
SECOND IMPRESSION, 1936
THIRD IMPRESSION, 1948
FOURTH IMPRESSION, 1954
FIFTH IMPRESSION, 1959

TO
MY GRANDFATHER

PRINTED BY THE REPLIKA PROCESS
IN GREAT BRITAIN BY
LUND HUMPHRIES
LONDON · BRADFORD

PREFACE

This book is intended to give a general picture of the civilisation of the Roman Empire during the period when its capital was Constantinople—that Orientalised Græco-Roman civilisation that is best called Byzantine. It is a lengthy period ; and during its eleven centuries many changes and modifications took place. I have tried, however, to concentrate rather on the qualities that characterised Byzantine history throughout its length. In an attempt to keep the size of the book within reasonable limits, I have passed by various aspects of the subject with undue brevity. In particular Byzantine Law and Byzantine Art have been given treatment quite disproportionate to their importance. But the former, once generalities are left behind, is a forest of intricate detail, and the latter an ocean of controversy and divergent taste, on which even generalities are very perilous. In both cases a fuller presentation would have required more pages than this book could afford. Indeed, where I have seemed too summary, I must beg my critics to be indulgent and to remember that greater generosity would have meant economies elsewhere.

The footnotes are intended to give the sources of the illustrative detail and to provide a short bibliography at the appropriate place. I have dispensed with them in Chapter II where I am dealing generally and uncontroversially with the history of the period. At the end I give the names of the more useful general bibliographies and a list of the few abbreviations that I use in the footnotes.

I wish to express my thanks to Miss R. F. Forbes for help with the proofs.

S. R.

Trinity College,
    Cambridge.
        December, 1932.

7

CONTENTS

CHAP.   PAGE

I   THE FOUNDATION OF CONSTANTINOPLE   11
Site of Constantinople—The Decay of the Roman World
—Christianity—Diocletian and the New Monarchy—Con-
stantine—The Victory of the Church—The New Capital—
The New Synthesis.

II   HISTORICAL OUTLINE   30
Historical Outline from 330 to 1453.

III   THE IMPERIAL CONSTITUTION AND THE REIGN OF LAW .   61
The Imperial Power—Its Popular Basis—Its Religious
Basis—The Empress—Regencies—The Demes—The Senate
—Law—The Law under Justinian : under the Isaurians :
under the Macedonians—Canon Law.

IV   THE ADMINISTRATION   81
The Emperor — The Imperial Family — Titles — Early
Organisation—Justinian's Reforms—The Theme System—
The Administration in the Tenth Century—The Government
of the Palæologi—Revenues—Taxation—Expenditure—Pater-
nalism—The Land Question—Justice.

V   RELIGION AND THE CHURCH   108
The Patriarchate of Constantinople—Organisation—Im-
perial Control—The Great Heresies—Schisms—The Roman
Question — Missions — Daughter-Churches — Tolerance —
Superstition—Personnel.

VI   THE ARMY : THE NAVY : THE DIPLOMATIC SERVICE .   136
The Army—Fourth Century Reforms—The *Fœderati*—
Tiberius and Maurice—The Themes—The *Tagmata*—Arms
—Strategy—Military Science—Pay—Auxiliary Corps—For-
eign Mercenaries—Decline.
The Navy under the Heraclians—Decline—Revival in the
Ninth Century—Second Decline—Palæologan Navy—Ships
—Greek Fire.
Diplomatic Organisation — Formality — Subtlety — The
Balance of Power—Diplomatic Marriages—Foreign Pretenders
—Expense.

VII   COMMERCE.   163
The Eastern Trade—Cosmas Indicopleustes—The Arab
Conquests—Ninth and Tenth Centuries—The Crusades—
Concessions to the Italians—Decline—Manufactures—Imports
—Regulations—State Control—Guilds—The Currency.

9

CHAP. PAGE

VIII TOWN AND COUNTRY LIFE 179
Ethnography — Slavs — Armenians — Constantinople — Its
Appearance—The Court—The Hippodrome—The Nobility—
Wealth—Self-made Men—The Poor—Slavery—The Middle
Classes—Eunuchs—Trade—Provincial Towns—Country Life
—Agrarian Problems—Byzantine Characteristics : Piety—
Influence of Saints—Superstition—Cruelty and Corruption—
Love of Beauty—Pessimism.

IX EDUCATION AND LEARNING 223
The Education of Boys—Constantine's University—Church
Schools—Bardas's University—Constantine IX's Law-schools
—Education under the Nicæans and the Palæologi—Female
Education — Foreign Languages — History — Philosophy —
Mathematics and Science — Geography — Medicine — The
Hospitals.

X BYZANTINE LITERATURE 240
Language—Prose—Religious Works — Historians — Hagiography — Memoirs — Handbooks — Fiction — Letters —
Poetry—Hymns—Music—Epigrams—Longer Poems—Chan-
sons de Geste.

XI BYZANTINE ART 254
Origins, Aramæan, Iranian, Hellenistic—Architecture—
The Dome—The Greek Cross—Secular Buildings—Materials
—Sculpture—Small Carvings, Metal and Ivory—Capitals—
Painting — Mosaics — Miniatures — Iconoclasm — Painting
under the Macedonians—under the Palæologi—Silk—Enamels
—Pottery.

XII BYZANTIUM AND THE NEIGHBOURING WORLD . . . 277
Influence on the Slavs—The Bulgars—The Moravian Mis-
sion—The Bulgarian Empire—Russia—Serbia—Armenia—
Georgia—Islam and Byzantium—The Turks—Byzantium and
Western Europe before the Crusades—Byzantium and the
Renaissance—Last Remains in the Christian East.

LIST OF ROMAN EMPERORS FROM CONSTANTINE I TO
CONSTANTINE XI 301

BIBLIOGRAPHICAL NOTE 306

INDEX 307

BYZANTINE CIVILISATION

CHAPTER I

The Foundation of Constantinople

The city of Byzantium was founded by sailors from
Megara in the year 657 B.C. on the uttermost end of Europe,
where the Bosphorus opens into the Sea of Marmora.
These coasts were not unknown to Greek colonists. Already
a few years before other Megarians had founded the city
of Chalcedon on the Asiatic bank opposite, winning a
proverbial renown for blindness for having overlooked the
better site across the water. Yet even Chalcedon had
advantages given to few other cities in its situation on the
Bosphorus.

Europe is cut off from South-Western Asia by two great
sheets of water, the Black Sea and the Ægean Sea ; but
between the seas Thrace juts out to meet Asia Minor till the
two continents are separated only by two narrow channels,
the Bosphorus and the Hellespont or Dardanelles, and by
the land-locked Sea of Marmora. Of these two easily
traversable channels, the Bosphorus is slightly the more
accessible from the Asian continent, as travellers to it avoid
the climb over Bithynian Olympus or Ida, and is by far
the more accessible from Europe, owing to the sharp angle
with which the Thracian Chersonnese goes out to form the
Hellespont. Thus men and merchandise journeying by
land from one continent to the other will almost inevitably

pass through a city on the Bosphorus : while ships plying between the Black Sea and the Ægean and the Mediterranean beyond, must certainly sail close by its quays. The Bosphorus stands at the crossing of two of the greatest trade-routes of history.

Chalcedon was not ill-placed, but nevertheless its founders were curiously blind, for the European shore had an advantage that the Eastern shore lacked. Just before the waters of the Bosphorus passed into the Marmora, there stretched inwards to the north-west a superb bay, some seven miles in length, curved like a sickle or a horn and known in history as the Golden Horn. Between the Golden Horn and the Marmora was a hilly promontory, in shape a very rough isosceles triangle with a blunted apex facing Asia. A city set on this promontory would not only be provided with a natural harbour where a great armada could lie in perfect security, but also would be protected by the sea on all sides against one. The only disadvantage was the climate. Throughout the winter and spring an almost incessant north wind blew across the Black Sea from the frozen Steppes, chilling the colonist used to the sheltered valleys of Greece, and proving too great a contrast to the hot sultry summers that followed. And this north wind, combined with the strong southward current of the Bosphorus, would often prevent sailing-ships from rounding the point and reaching the Golden Horn.

Possibly it was the unattractive climate that prevented Byzantium from becoming a large city for nearly a thousand years. Moreover, in the great days of Greece it was quicker and safer, considering the barbarous state of Thrace, for Asiatic merchandise to cross to Europe from Smyrna or Ephesus. But its importance as a fortress was soon realised. In the Peloponnesian War it was wooed for its command of the entrance to the Black Sea, from the corn-fields of whose northern shores Athens was fed. Philip of Macedon and his son Alexander recognised in it the main gateway to Asia. The Roman Emperors came to regard its strategic strength as a menace. Vespasian destroyed its privileges. Severus, against whose troops it held out for two years in support of the lost cause of Pescennius Niger, dismantled all its fortifications ; but Caracalla rebuilt them. Gallienus followed the example of Severus, with the result that Gothic pirates could sail with impunity down the Straits into the Ægean. So Diocletian was obliged to erect the walls once more. But its full potentialities as a fortress were not discovered till the second Licinian War of 322–3 when Licinius made it the pivot of his whole campaign against Constantine. Licinius was ruined by the loss of his fleet in the Hellespont, and his army was finally defeated at Chrysopolis ; after his surrender there was no need for the fortress to hold out any longer. But Licinius's strategy had been noted by his great opponent ; Constantine saw still further possibilities in Byzantium. Scarcely was the war over before the Emperor was conducting architects and surveyors round the city and its surroundings, and building operations began.

For some decades past, the Roman Emperors had felt the need of a new administrative centre. Rome itself was becoming uncongenial to them, with its republican and senatorial traditions, and its distrust of their new Oriental conceptions of sovereignty. Moreover, it lay very far from the two frontiers to which their attention increasingly was turning, the Armeno-Syrian frontier and the Danube. Maximian had ruled from Milan ; Diocletian had moved eastward and made Nicomedia his chief residence. Constantine had toyed with the sentimental idea of making his birthplace Naïssus or Nish his capital, and later had set to work to rebuild Troy. But once his attention had been drawn to Byzantium, its superior advantages were manifest. There was no more hesitation. The fortifications were begun in November 324, and five and a half years later the capital was complete. On May 11, 330, the city was solemnly inaugurated by the Emperor under the name of New Rome ; but men preferred to call it after its founder Constantinople.

The year 330 is the best date to take as the starting-point for Byzantine history.[1] But the foundation of Constantinople, though infinitely the most far-reaching, was only one of the reforms and changes that had already started gradually to transform the pagan Empire of Rome into the Empire that we call Byzantine. By the close of the Third Century, A.D., reforms were badly needed in the Roman Empire. This is not the place to recount in detail the causes of the break-up of the old Roman world.[2] Put briefly, these were administrative and financial chaos and feebleness, too much strength in the hands of ambitious soldiers, and a new series of dangers on the frontiers. Rome had acquired her territorial Empire by a magnificently sustained opportunism. Each captured province would be reconciled as quickly as possible by the permission to retain many of the local rights and customs. Consequently every province required a different type of administration. The state of the central government increased the diversity. The Dyarchy, so loudly advertised by Augustus, by which the Senate shared the sovereignty with the Emperor and ruled completely certain of the provinces, only added to the confusion without providing any effective check on the Emperor. The finances reflected the disorder. Taxation

[1] For the reforms of Diocletian and Constantine, see especially Stein, *Geschichte des spätrömischen Reiches*, I *passim*; Maurice, *Numismatique Constantinienne*, vol. II, introduction, and *Constantin le Grand*; Leclercq, article on Constantine in Cabrol's *Dictionnaire d'Archéologie Chrétienne*, 2262–95. Baynes, *Constantine and the Christian Church* in Brit. Academy Papers, vol. XV (with full bibliography).

[2] They are given in Rostovtzeff, *Social and Economic History of the Roman Empire*, 478–87 ; Bury, *Later Roman Empire*, I, 302–13.

was high but varied and irregular, and a considerable proportion remained in the hands of the tax-farmers. Wealth was unevenly distributed. Many millionaires could still be found, but there were whole provinces sunk in poverty. Moreover, the Empire had long been suffering from an adverse trade-balance. Already in Pliny's day the imports from India exceeded the exports annually by £600,000 and from China by another £400,000 ; [1] and the position was never righted. Throughout the early Empire the imperial coinage had been gradually depreciating, and since the reign of Caracalla the fall had been rapid : till at last the copper coins alone contained no alloy, while the silver coins came eventually only to consist of 2 per cent. of silver.

Faced with administrative confusion and continuous financial anxiety, the civil authorities were powerless. The only real strength lay with the army leaders. Rome could not dispense with her legions. There were the long frontiers to guard : police were needed for the provinces whose natural unruliness economic extortion easily inflamed. The governors of the great provinces each had a legion at their disposal ; sometimes they commanded even larger armies. This might not have been dangerous, had there been a strong central government and a fixed rule of succession to the Empire. But few imperial dynasties reached even the third generation. The throne became increasingly the prize of the strongest military leader, and ambitious generals abounded. During the Third Century there was almost invariably some province in the hands of a usurper, and the Empire was seldom in practice a united commonwealth.

The disorder was made more serious in the Third Century by new pressure on the frontiers. Since the early days of the Empire the Asiatic frontier that ran from Armenia to Arabia had provided comparatively little trouble. The

[1] See Bury, *op. cit.*

Parthian Kingdom of the Arsacids was in a slow decline. But early in the Third Century a new dynasty had arisen in Persia, the Sassanids, popular, nationalist and Zoroastrian, who for four centuries were to be aggressive enemies to Rome. They defeated four Emperors in the Third Century, even taking the Emperor Valerian into captivity ; and their strength seemed yearly to be increasing. At the same time the European frontier was in need of additional vigilance. Since Cæsar's day the governor of Gaul had a hard task to guard the Rhine frontier from the prolific West German tribes beyond, who longed to spread out from their cramping forests. But now there was pressure on the Danube. East German tribes, the Goths in particular, were settling on the further banks, and any new movement or migration on the Steppes beyond would probably incite them to cross the river. The Gothic problem was clearly a menace, and, despite the efforts of Emperors such as Claudius II, it showed no likelihood of improvement.

Such was the political background to life in the Third Century. The standards of civilisation were still high. Though the poor, slaves and freemen, found little betterment in their condition, save that many of them lived on the charity of the State, the richer classes enjoyed material comforts and luxuries surpassing anything that the world had yet seen. Roman rule had always meant an efficient programme of public works ; baths and temples, harbours and roads, all added to the amenities of life. Communications were swift, easy and safe. But all this comfort, all this security was liable to sudden and prolonged interruptions. In the frequent civil wars peaceful citizens might see themselves unexpectedly disgraced, despoiled or even condemned to death. The uncertainty led to a disillusionment with worldly things, which was to be the main feature of the culture of the age.

Culturally the Empire was divided into two. The provinces from Illyricum to the west spoke Latin as the universal language ; in those to the east it was Greek. The cleavage was as yet more apparent than real ; for while the West provided almost all the men of action, the Emperors and the statesmen, the Western men of thought followed the lead of the Greek-speaking world. Only in Africa and Gaul had Latin culture any impetus of its own. For the rest the Latins provided public works and a transcendent sense of Law which was stamped on to the East and survived even the disorder. The civilisation of the East was still the Hellenistic civilisation, a blend of Classical Greece with Semitic and Iranian conceptions ; but the part of Classical Greece had shrunk to be that of a strong tradition rather than of a vital force. The individualism which was essential to Hellenic culture could not long outlast the passing of the city-state and the fusion even of the Macedonian kingdoms into a world-empire in whose direction the Greek had no part. But art and letters still clung to the old Greek models or to their magnificent reproductions made in Augustan Rome. The artist added now only a deadly love for size and for any detail that would display the competence of his technique. Temples, statues, epic poems, all were choked with magnificence and elaboration. Only an occasional lyric or painting retained its spontaneity, and satire, the natural self-expression of a disillusioned age. The world of the Roman Empire was well educated and æsthetic ; but the great civilisation that it admired and copied was a liability now. Salvation was coming from another quarter, from the Syrian East.

Already in the Third Century architecture had begun to breathe a new splendour that was Oriental and spontaneous. But the East was to triumph against Classical tradition not so much by its conceptions of majesty as by its more purely spiritual ideas. A disillusioned age turns to religion, as an escape from the uncertainties of the world.

B

But the old religions, the pagan joy in life of the Greeks, the State-worship of Rome, failed when life was full of dread and the State in obvious decay. The East had greater comfort to offer. Since first Rome had come into contact with the East, the mystery religions of Isis and the Great Mother had spread westward, and their votaries gradually grew in number. In the secret ritual and exercise ordained by these Goddesses, the world-weary passed through into the higher reality. These cults appealed more to the sophisticated and the jaded. The soldier and man of action preferred a cult of Iranian origin, Mithraism, the worship of Apollo, the Unconquered Sun. By the Third Century Mithraism had spread throughout the Empire, embracing in its powerful organisation the vast majority of the army. It too was garnished with pomp and ceremony, but it was less quietistic. Instead it brought a sense of fellowship and discipline to combat the hopelessness and loneliness of the world. But Mithraism was faced with an even greater rival, a religion that had started obscurely in Palestine and was called Christianity.

That Christianity should be the triumphant faith was not surprising. Its message had a far wider appeal than any other. The Oriental with his apparent patience is in truth highly impatient. Unable to bear pain and sorrow he at once takes refuge in communion with higher things and escapes from the sphere of earthly sensation. The Westerner kicks against the pricks because they hurt. His comfort lies in hope and in the faith that it will not be for ever. The Hellenistic Greek was midway between. Behind his nature-worship lurked mysticism, and a love of symbolism was innate in him. All these yearnings could be satisfied in Christianity. Christianity encouraged mysticism, it preached an eschatology of hope, it was rich in symbols and had a noble ritual. Moreover, it made an especial appeal to the lowly, teaching that in the eyes of

God the slave was equal to the Emperor and ordaining brotherly love and fellowship ; and this message recommended it to philanthropists ; no other religion put charity to so practical a use. The Christian Church was admirably organised. Since the days of Saint Paul its leaders had been men of administrative ability. And it had two immeasurable advantages over its rival, Mithraism. First, it allowed women to play a prominent part in its life. The orthodox teachers might indeed deplore and denounce the complete sex-equality taught by the Montanist heretics ; but women had always been prominent in its history. As deaconesses or of recent years as abbesses [1] they could become persons of importance. Mithraism, on the other hand, was a masculine religion. We find no trace of women amongst its votaries. The second great strength of Christianity lay in the influence that from its earliest years it had allowed Greek philosophy to exercise over it. This influence gave Christian theology an intellectual content that made it acceptable to many of the ablest and most profound thinkers of the time. Neither Mithraism nor the mystery religions could produce men of the mental calibre of the early Christian Fathers, men like Origen, Irenæus, Tertullian or Clement of Alexandria, thinkers outrivalled only by their successors, the Fathers of the Fourth Century. Despite schism in the West and heresies in the East, the Christian Church was rapidly becoming the most powerful single organisation in the Empire. Of the heresies none as yet was menacing. Gnosticism, the most formidable of them, never had a very widespread public and soon split into minor sects ; and though by now Mani was producing his strange blend of Gnosticism and Zoroastrian dualism, which was to enjoy a certain vogue in

[1] Nunneries actually ante-date monasteries. In Egypt there were several in the Third Century : Smith, *Early Mysticism in the Near East*, 34 *sqq.*

the Fourth and Fifth Centuries, the centre of Manichæanism lay over the Persian frontier.

In its gradual advance Christianity had undoubtedly been helped by the legends of its saints and its well-attested miracles. For these were superstitious generations. The Augustan Age of Reason had been short-lived. Now men talked of the wonderful deeds of Apollonius of Tyana and believed in tales such as those that Apuleius had told. Fortune-telling and sorcery were highly developed. Demonology was raised to a science. All the superstitions that made Byzantine Civilisation a byword to the Eighteenth-Century historians were inherited from these days of the old Empire, though many as yet pagan were later to be hitched on to the Christian Church. Even philosophy followed the popular path. In the West Stoicism lingered to produce Marcus Aurelius before it faded, but in the East for some time past Neoplatonism alone had retained its vitality. Now, in the hands of Porphyry and Iamblichus, Neoplatonism was receiving a hectic complexion of thaumaturgy and magic, and a comprehensive polytheism. Indeed, the teachings of the Christian Fathers were probably nearer to Platonism than the doctrines aired in the schools of the philosophers.

In the year 284 the Imperial power passed into the hands of the first great constructive statesman that the Roman world had produced since Augustus—the Illyrian-born Diocletian. Diocletian was fully conscious of the state of the Empire, and he devoted his reign to a far-reaching programme of reforms. His main intentions were to centralise and introduce uniformity into the administration and to bring the army under the effective control of the government, to restore the financial situation by stabilising the imperial currency and to confirm the whole work by elevating the position of the Emperor.

Throughout the history of the Empire there had been a

tendency towards uniformity, exemplified by the gradual spread of Roman citizenship to include every free-born subject of the Empire and the recent disappearance of the last senatorially governed provinces. But the chaos that preceded Diocletian's accession made an entirely new system necessary. Diocletian considered the Empire too great for a single Emperor to rule. Since the first Cæsars it had been found necessary to have a Greek Secretary of State as well as a Latin. Diocletian carried this basic division further. He did not create two Empires, but he ordered that the Empire should have two Emperors, one to reside in each half of the Empire. To ensure peaceful accessions, each Emperor was to be aided by a Cæsar who should be his heir. Meanwhile the provinces were redivided and recast. The Empire was split into four great Prefectures, the Gauls, Italy, Illyricum and the East, under four Prætorian Prefects who were the highest officials of the State. The Prefectures were subdivided into large provinces called Dioceses, whose governor usually bore the title of Vicar and was subordinated to the Prefect : though the provinces known as Asia and Africa retained Proconsuls with the privilege of communicating directly with the Emperor. To administer this rearranged Empire a network of new civil servants was set up, and fresh powers were given to the bureaucracy.

The main characteristic of this new bureaucracy was its entire separation from the military authorities. Only on some of the frontiers were their functions at all combined, though the Prefect himself was at first a military as well as a civil official. A huge military organisation was built up at the side of civil organisation ; and it was hoped that this separation of powers would check the ambitions of disloyal generals. At the same time Diocletian founded a mobile imperial army that could be hurried to any part of the Empire in times of war or insurrection.

The reformed Empire was to be preserved by a rigid caste system. Following an idea first mooted by the Emperor Aurelian, Diocletian decreed that a son should invariably follow his father's profession, whatever it might be. Social upheavals had become so frequent, fortunes were made and lost so rapidly, that he felt that only by such rigidity could stability be maintained and there be any chance of collecting a regular revenue. It was also an advantage to recruit the army from the middle classes of society. Members of the Senatorial nobility, dangerous alike for their wealth and their oligarchic traditions, were carefully excluded from its ranks.

Diocletian's attempts to stabilise the currency were less successful. He could not bring the coinage back to the position that it had held under Augustus ; and the profusion of his attempts to issue a coinage of full weight led eventually, to his surprise, to a rise in prices. To counter this, the Emperor promulgated the famous decree of 301 which firmly fixed the price of every single commodity. The decree was not successful. It was left to Constantine to establish the Empire's money on a permanent basis.

The most lasting of Diocletian's reforms was the least tangible—his fostering of Imperial majesty. The conception of the King's divinity was endemic in the East and had been fashionable at the time of the Hellenistic monarchies. In the Oriental provinces of the Empire it had never entirely died ; the Emperor succeeded to a proportion of the divinity. But Rome with her traditional hatred of Kings never approved. Consequently Augustus was careful to establish no show of majesty. He was merely the first citizen in the Empire, an accessible if important human being. It was soon considered good for the subject peoples that defunct Emperors should be deified ; but the true Roman approved of the cynical speech of the dying Vespasian.[1]

[1] *Ut puto, deus fio*—I am becoming a god, I think.

Despite the private adulation demanded by Domitian or by Heliogabalus, this attitude had persisted in the West ; and the likelihood of sudden death that seemed part of the imperial profession had not increased the Emperor's prestige. Diocletian saw that the Emperor's authority would be greater and his life more secure were he to become a demi-god.

The newly established Sassanids of Persia surrounded themselves with a thick halo of majesty. Diocletian borrowed many of their trappings. The Emperor no longer moved freely amongst his subjects. He lived withdrawn in a ceremonious court, and eunuchs, a race despised and forbidden in the earlier days, ministered to his person. Men that sought an audience had to prostrate themselves before him and adore him. He wore a diadem now, and scarlet boots and robes of purple. In a way this was a natural development. Law was almost divine in Roman eyes and the Emperor had long been the source of law. But Rome was offended by the new outward and Oriental pomps of despotism. It was, however, Rome rather than the Emperor that suffered by the coldness. Diocletian ruled the East from Nicomedia as an accepted demi-god, and Maximian, his Western colleague, preferred to reside at Milan.

Diocletian added verisimilitude to his divinity by claiming descent from Jupiter, King of the Gods, thus easing his entrance into the Roman pantheon. Maximian decided upon a more popular if less exalted ancestor in Hercules. Constantius, the Cæsar in the West, attempted to combine his personal religion of Mithraism with Emperor-worship by becoming the descendant of the Sun-God Apollo.

But there was one large section of the community that could not give the Emperors the adoration that they demanded. The Christians, with their clear distinction between Cæsar's things and God's, were prepared to be good citizens so long as they were not obliged to pay worship to the State. But to adore a human being, even were he Emperor, was something that they certainly would not stomach. Diocletian felt that he could not permit the strongest religious body in the Empire to flout his majesty. He tried coercion, but was faced with a fanatical resistance ; and so the Great Persecution began. But the Christians remained nonconformist. It was left to the Emperor Constantine to find the solution that would blend Cæsar with God.

The reformed Empire of Diocletian barely survived his abdication in 305. The various items remained with one essential exception. He had made the Empire depend on the Emperor ; but the system of two Emperors and a fixed succession to the throne would work only if the Imperial candidates were high-minded men, free from jealousy and suspicion. The title Cæsar was a dangerous title, too high and yet not high enough. It quickly faded. By 311 there were four Emperors instead, Licinius and Maximin in the East, and Maxentius and Constantine, son of Constantius, in the West. The stage was clearly set for civil war.

It broke out first in the West. A short, brilliant campaign in 312 from Colmar to the field of Saxa Rubra by the Milvian Bridge made Constantine master of the West. Next year he helped Licinius to defeat Maximin and become master of the East. But Constantine and Licinius were each too ambitious to share the Empire. Their first war in 313 was undecisive, but in 323 Licinius was crushed at Chrysopolis, and Constantine was the only Emperor.

Diocletian's Imperial College thus ended in failure. But in other respects his work endured. Constantine retained his administrative system, and he succeeded when Diocletian had failed in establishing the currency. The old Roman monetary system could not be recovered, but Constantine set up a gold standard, the solidus, a piece of bullion stamped with his seal, rather than a coin, to which the coinage was related. The system worked well. The Imperial solidus maintained its value and its prestige unchallenged for eight centuries.

Constantine also improved and amended Diocletian's efforts in enhancing and deifying the position of the Emperor. On his southward march against Maxentius, when his future was at stake, Constantine and all his army had a vision. A shining Cross appeared in the sky before them with the legend ' Hoc vinces ' written across it ; and that night Christ confirmed the vision in the Emperor's dreams. Deeply impressed, Constantine adopted the Labarum, the cross with a looped top, as his emblem, and beneath that standard he led his troops to victory.

The miracle was timely. The visionary showed political acumen. Constantine had started his career under the ægis of his father-in-law Maximian and had been then of the House of Hercules. After his split with Maxentius he returned to the Mithraic faith of his family and became a son of Apollo. But Maxentius, like Maximin in the East, adopted a strong anti-Christian policy. His opponent ought, therefore, to woo the Christian alliance. The Christians probably included only about a fifth of the inhabitants of the Empire, but they were by far the strongest one religion, allies far more valuable than the followers of Mithraism : though the Labarum, usefully enough, was a symbol almost equally congenial to the Mithraists.

Whatever he thought in private, after the battle of Saxa Rubra it seems certain, from his coins and his decrees, that Constantine was committed to Christianity. He had crushed Maxentius as a Christian champion ; he and Licinius fought as Christian champions against the persecutor Maximin, and issued the famous Edict of Milan of 313 that gave for the first time full legal recognition to the Christian community. But Licinius remained a pagan.

In his attack on him too, Constantine was the Christian champion. Christianity and Constantine owed each other a mutual debt.

In 325 Constantine appeared as the patron of Christianity in a new manner. The Church was rent by the dispute of the Alexandrian priest Arius and his bishop on the nature of the divinity of Christ. Constantine took it upon himself to summon the bishops of the Church to meet at Nicæa at the great assembly known in history as the First Œcumenical Council ; and there under his presidency the Fathers decided that the Arian view was wrong. This First Council of Nicæa was important not only for its moulding of Christian doctrine but also as the first example of Cæsaropapisn.. Constantine intended that the Christian Church should be a State church with the Emperor as its chairman ; and Christianity in its gratitude to him did not object.

So the old antagonism between Church and State seemed to be ended. The Emperor was the head of the Christian Commonwealth. There was no need now for him to claim descent from Hercules or Apollo ; he had a new sanctity that would forgive him all his sins. The blood of his rivals, of his son and even of his wife was on his hands ; but to the world he was *Isapostolos*, the equal of the Apostles, the Thirteenth Apostle. And his spiritual prestige was enhanced by the excavating energy of his mother Helena, the former Bithynian concubine of Constantius. Constantine sent her to Jerusalem, and there, with miraculous aid seldom nowadays vouchsafed to archæologists, she found the very site of Calvary and unearthed the True Cross itself and the crosses of the thieves and the Lance and the Sponge and the Crown of Thorns and all the attendant relics of the Passion. The discovery thrilled Christendom and redounded to the eternal glory of the Emperor's mother. The names of Constantine and Helena became and remained the most reverend in the history of the Christian Empire.

But one more concrete work remained to complete the transformation of the Empire. This was the foundation of Constantinople. The Empire should have a new capital in the East, the equal of Rome in everything save age, and Rome's superior in that this would be from the outset a Christian city. The value of a new capital was obvious. The selection of the site showed genius. Here all the elements of the reformed Empire would naturally mingle, Greece, Rome and the Christian East.

Constantinople was set on Greek-speaking coasts and incorporated an old Greek city. But Constantine did more to emphasise its Hellenism. His capital was to be the centre of art and learning. He built it libraries stocked with Greek manuscripts ; still more, he filled its streets and squares and museums with art treasures drawn from all over the Greek Orient. The citizen of Constantinople walking daily through the city could never forget the glory of his Hellenic heritage.

But it was a Roman city too. For over two centuries the Court and a large proportion of the inhabitants were Latin-speaking ; and Latin was still the educated language of the Balkan hinterland. In his desire to gather together a population drawn from all over the Empire, Constantine gave the city mob the privilege of free bread and free games that the rabble of Rome enjoyed ; and the upper classes were induced, according to the legend, to transplant themselves to the Bosphorus by the gift of palaces that exactly reproduced their Roman homes. Constantinople was to be another Rome. 'New Rome which is Constantinople' remained her official title to the last ; and her citizens were always *Rômaioi*. Rome's great contributions to the new Empire were her administrative theories, her military traditions and her law. But the Constantinopolitans considered themselves as Romans by nationality, long after the Latin language was heard no more on the Bosphorus and there was scarcely a vestige of Italian blood. Even in the Twelfth Century it was the boast of aristocrats that their ancestors had come over with Constantine.[1]

The third element was the Christian East. Constantinople was to be a Christian city. The temples of old Byzantium were allowed to stand a little longer, and it seems that some were even put up for the benefit of pagans engaged in constructing the city.[2] But after the work was finished, no more were to be built. The East with its mysticism had already invaded the Roman world and taught it to regard the monarch as divine. Constantine paid respect to the Tyche, the Luck of the city, and he set up a great column of Apollo on which the statue's face was altered to be his portrait ; and there he stood with all the attributes of the Sun-God to be worshipped by pagan, Mithraist and Christian alike. Christianity was an Oriental religion. Greek philosophy had moulded it into a form acceptable to Europe, but fundamentally it remained Semitic in its conceptions. The citizen of Constantinople was fully conscious of his Greek and Roman heritage, but his basic outlook on life was different. He took less joy in the world, dwelling rather upon the eternities. This state of mind made him more receptive to ideas coming from the East than from the West ; and the history of the Byzantine Empire is the history of the infiltration of Oriental ideas to tinge the Græco-Roman traditions, and of the periodic reaction. For despite it all, the Græco-Roman traditions endured to the end. Even in the Fifteenth Century the men of Constantinople discussed the nature of their civilisation. They were the *Rômaioi* : were they

---

[1] Nicephorus Bryennius makes this claim for the Ducæ (N. Bryennius, 13).

[2] Maurice, *op. cit.* II., lxxv.

Hellenes as well ? The last great citizen of the Empire gave them the answer : ' Though I am a Hellene by speech,' he said, ' yet I would never say that I was a Hellene, for I do not believe as the Hellenes believed. I should like to take my name from my Faith, and if anyone asked me what I am answer " A Christian." . . . Though my father dwelt in Thessaly I do not call myself a Thessalian, but a Byzantine ; for I am of Byzantium.' [1] We may follow George Scholarius Gennadius, and call the civilisation made from the elements Byzantine ; and we may look for its inauguration to the ceremony of May 11, 330, when the Emperor Constantine dedicated the great city of ' New Rome which is Constantinople ' to the Holy Trinity and to the Mother of God.

[1] Gennadius, *Disputatio contra Judaeum*, ed. Jahn, 2.

CHAPTER II

Historical Outline[1]

The reformed Empire inaugurated on May 11, 330, endured for eleven hundred and twenty-three years and eighteen days. Throughout the changing Europe of those centuries one factor remained constant : a Roman Emperor reigned in autocratic majesty in Constantinople. In this Empire everything hinged ultimately upon the Emperor. Its history is therefore most naturally and suitably divided up by the dynasties that ruled in turn. At first the dynasties are short-lived. After the Roman manner they only reach the third generation. But the last eight centuries are filled almost entirely by the rule of five great families, the Heraclians, the Isaurians, the Macedonians, the Comneni and the Palæologi.

The Fourth Century is only a prelude to Byzantine history. Constantinople was not yet the indispensable centre of government. Constantius, though he added to its buildings, seldom resided there. Jovian never visited it at all. Nor was Orthodox Christianity entirely triumphant. It was still possible for Julian to revert to paganism, though the experiment showed that paganism was a dying force ; and, in spite of Nicæa, it was an Arian bishop who bap-

[1] Best short histories : Gelzer, *Byzantinischen Kaisergeschichte* in Krumbacher, *Geschichte der Byzantinischen Litteratur* (2nd edition) ; Diehl, *Histoire de l'Empire Byzantin* ; slightly longer : Vasiliev, *Histoire de l'Empire Byzantin* (most recent) ; Gfrörer, *Byzantinische Geschichte* ; Kulakovski, *Byzantine History* (in Russian), and chapters in the *Cambridge Medieval History*, vols. 1, 2 and 4.

tised Constantine on his death-bed, while Constantius and Valens definitely favoured Arianism.

Constantine the Great died in 337. His last years had been spent in peace and reorganisation. His three sons jointly succeeded him, Constantine II, Constantius II and Constans I. The brothers were quarrelsome, but by 350 Constantine and Constans were dead, and Constantius, after defeating the great usurper, Magnentius, in 351, reigned supreme till his death ten years later. During these years the external situation of the Empire was growing more serious. The Persian menace continued, and the pressure of Germanic tribes on the Rhine and the Danube became more intense, chiefly owing to the appearance on the far-off steppes of a new people from Mongolia, the Huns. On the Rhine Constantius's cousin Julian defeated a German invasion, and his exultant army, dissatisfied now with Constantius, acclaimed him Emperor in 360. Constantius died before the revolt spread, and Julian succeeded without any bloodshed.

Julian won immortal renown for his apostasy, his reversion to paganism. But the movement was a failure. The world did not want his intellectualised polytheism ; Christianity suited it better. His military activities proved equally unsuccessful. He attempted to invade Persia, but advanced too far and died on a ghastly retreat in the summer of 363. The army hastened to elect a popular Christian soldier called Jovian, who made a disgraceful Thirty Years' Peace with Persia, ceding four satrapies and the suzerainty of Armenia. Early next spring Jovian died.

On Jovian's death the army acclaimed the general Valentinian, who preferred to rule in the West and left his subservient brother Valens as co-Emperor in the East. Valens's reign is a great turning-point in European history. He himself, though mild and not incompetent, was unpopular as an Arian heretic, and had to face constant revolts ; but the crux came when in 376 the Visigoths, pressed from behind by the Huns, won his leave to settle within the Empire, and the whole nation crossed the Danube. It was the beginning of the Barbarian Invasions. The settlement was not a success ; the Goths soon quarrelled with the Imperial officials and marched on Constantinople. Valens went out to meet them, refusing to await the help sent by the Western Emperor, Valentinian's son Gratian, and met with defeat and death at Adrianople (378).

But this disaster did more harm to the West than to the East. Gratian selected his uncle's successor, the Spaniard Theodosius, whom grateful posterity called Theodosius the Great. His tactful treatment pacified the Goths and made them for a time useful servants of the State. Fervently orthodox, he heaped disabilities on pagans and heretics, and at the Second Œcumenical Council, at Constantinople in 381, forced unity on the Christian world. In 387 he made a new and satisfactory treaty with Persia, partitioning Armenia. In 392 he took over the West, after the deaths of Gratian, his brother Valentinian II and a usurper Eugenius, and for the last time one man ruled from Britain to the Euphrates. In 395 he died, leaving the Empire to his sons, the East to Arcadius and the West to Honorius. The reign of Theodosius had marked the beginning of a new era in the Roman Empire. It had become the Orthodox Empire. And with his death the East and the West were severed for ever.

The Fifth Century saw the decline of the Empire in the West, battered down by the Barbarian invasions : till after the abdication of Romulus Augustulus in 476 and the death of Julius Nepos in 480 no one in the West bore the title of Emperor. The Empire in the East fared better. Buttressed by the work of Theodosius the Great and in possession of an impregnable capital, it seemed too strong for the barbarians to attack. Visigoth, Hun and Ostrogoth each crossed the Danube, but each in the end preferred to seek his fortune in the West ; and these invasions of the West did not have much effect on the material welfare of the East, till in 439 the Vandals established themselves in Africa and launched a fleet from Carthage, thus destroying the Roman monopoly of the sea. The harbours of the Mediterranean, accustomed to security for centuries, were forced to build fortifications, and Constantinople had a Vandal question to face.

Under the Theodosian dynasty, Arcadius (395–408), Theodosius II (408–450), during whose long reign the power was mainly exercised by his sister Pulcheria, and Pulcheria's nominal husband, Marcian (450–457), despite many anxious moments the Barbarians were diverted into other channels. That this was possible was largely due to the diplomacy of Theodosius I, whose peace with Persia had proved lasting. Even so, the security was won at a price ; the Empire was defended against the Barbarians by Barbarian mercenaries and generals. At Marcian's death an Arian Alan general Aspar, was the most powerful figure in the Empire. His heresy and his birth debarred him from the throne, so he appointed an officer in his army, a Dacian called Leo. Leo I (457–474) only succeeded in freeing the Empire from its Gothic soldiery by calling on his Asiatic troops, notably the Isaurians from Asia Minor, whose commandant, Tarasicodissa, he rechristened Zeno and married to his daughter Ariadne. On his death, their infant son Leo II reigned for a few months, then died, leaving the Empire to his father Zeno. Zeno (474–491) was reigning at the time when the Western Emperors became extinct. He officially assumed control over the whole Empire, but though Odoacer and after him Theodoric the Ostrogoth were nominally his viceroys, he never sought to exercise any power in the West. When Zeno died, his widow Ariadne appointed as his successor

c

a wealthy noble called Anastasius (491–518), whose thrifty nature did much to restore the finances which had been neglected of late. With him the Leonine dynasty was ended.

The Empire had other worries in the Fifth Century besides the Barbarians. It was a vital period in the history of Eastern Christianity. For some time past there had been rivalry between the great sees of Alexandria and Antioch ; and Alexandria was further jealous of the new Patriarchate of Constantinople which had been given precedence over her at the Second Œcumenical Council. At the outset of the century there had been a quarrel between Theophilus of Alexandria and John Chrysostom of Constantinople that had resulted almost in schism. The victory was with Theophilus, though Chrysostom was later vindicated. In the 'thirties Alexandria, under the Patriarch Cyril, returned to the attack. Nestorius, the Antiochene Patriarch of Constantinople, had lapsed, it was claimed, into heresy, separating the God and the Man in Christ. The Imperial Family and the Roman See sided with Cyril ; and at the Third Œcumenical Council, at Ephesus in 432, Nestorianism was condemned. But its opponents went too far. A doctrine of the single nature of Christ was promulgated by an obscure archimandrite Eutyches and accepted by the Alexandrian school. To settle the question, the Emperor Marcian convened the Fourth Œcumenical Council at Chalcedon in 451. Marcian was politically anxious to keep on good terms with Rome ; and Pope Leo the Great was strongly opposed to the movement. Under Imperial influence Eutychianism or Monophysitism was condemned as a heresy.

The Council of Chalcedon was the turning-point in the history of the Empire in Egypt and Syria. The Monophysite Christology suited the Oriental temperament ; and soon Monophysite churches, united in their opposition to

Chalcedon, spread over the provinces. Moreover, the heresy became the rallying point of the many provincials with grievances against the Imperial bureaucracy ; it was the expression of the growing feelings of nationalism and secessionism. From the bitterness sown at Chalcedon was reaped the easy Arab conquest of Syria and Egypt nearly two centuries later The Armenian Church also rejected the decrees of Chalcedon, though its objections were constitutional rather than dogmatic. And even in Constantinople itself the heretics were numerous.

The Emperors of the Leonine dynasty climbed down from the Chalcedonian position. Zeno issued a brave attempt at a compromise in his Henoticon which satisfied no one and caused a breach with Rome, which Anastasius, an unacknowledged Monophysite, left unhealed. But the South-East was still unsatisfied.

Meanwhile Paganism had died out. Theodosius II in 431 had heaped further disabilities upon the pagans, and in 438 he claimed that none were left in the Empire.

Throughout the century Constantinople had grown in size and wealth. So far had the city extended beyond the walls of Constantine, that in 413 the regent Anthemius, under Theodosius II, built new walls from the Marmora to the Golden Horn, some two miles to the west of the old enceinte to include these suburbs, while in 439 the Prefect Cyrus built sea-walls to connect with the new land-walls ; and the whole fortification was repaired after an earthquake in 447. The work was done in sixty days owing to fear of a Hunnish invasion. Cyrus, an Egyptian poet, had the further distinction of being the first Prefect of the City to issue orders in Greek and not in Latin.

The Sixth Century is dominated by the figure of Justinian. On Anastasius's death, a subtle and dishonourable intrigue elevated to the throne an illiterate Illyrian soldier, Justin. Justin brought to the court his nephew Justinian, who very soon acted virtually as regent and on Justin's death in 527 became Emperor. Justinian's reign (527–565) is the climax of the Christian Roman Empire. The Barbarian kingdoms in the West, with the exception of Frankish Gaul, had fallen into an early decadence. Justinian made it his task to recover Africa from the Vandals and Italy from the Ostrogoths and even Spain from the Visigoths. War with Persia broke out again and continually his armies had to concentrate on the East. But thanks to the genius of his generals Belisarius and Narses and the skill of his diplomats, the Eastern frontier was maintained, Africa and parts of Spain were conquered and the long resistance of the Ostrogoths in Italy was broken down. Once more the Mediterranean was a Roman lake. Justinian turned his attention too to internal affairs. The administration was reformed and tightened up, and he was still more efficient as a legislator. Early in his reign he collated and revised the existing codes of Roman Law and issued his great Code (533), a monument of jurisprudence ; and for the rest of the reign he busily added *Novels* to supply any deficiencies. But the Emperor, besides being a conqueror and the source of law, must also be the embodiment of majesty. To this end Justinian worked hard to beautify his capital and make it more sumptuous. He was an indefatigable builder, and for him was erected the greatest triumph of architecture in the world, Saint Sophia, the Church of the Holy Wisdom, the temple that made Justinian boast that he had surpassed that other lawyer-monarch, Solomon.

In all his work Justinian had till 548 the help of the most remarkable woman of the time, his wife, the former actress Theodora. Her courage, her clarity and unscrupulousness were invaluable to him, and her power even surpassed his own. But on one question of policy they were divided. Theodora was a Monophysite, and she used her influence to secure the triumph of her heresy. She was unsuccessful, but while she lived the Monophysites enjoyed the security of her strong protection and encouragement. Had her will been done, Egypt and Syria might have remained loyal provinces of the Empire. But Justinian, with his Western ambitions, feared to displease the Orthodox West. Besides, he considered himself a theologian and was unconvinced by Monophysitism. But he hoped to find some compromise that he could force upon all Christendom. He and Theodora agreed that everyone, even Patriarchs and Popes, should follow the Imperial theology. Pope Vigilius, who had ventured to regard himself as the repository of orthodoxy, was punished by a long imprisonment at Constantinople, during which he subscribed first to Theodora's dictates and then to Justinian's. But it was only after Theodora's death that Justinian gave full rein to his passion for theology and evolved formulæ that would satisfy the Monophysites without infringing the decrees of the Council of Chalcedon. In 553 the Fifth Œcumenical Council condemned at Justinian's orders the abstruse heresy of the Three Chapters that he himself had artificially created a few years before, and completed the humiliation of the Papacy. But his gestures towards the heretics were ill-received ; they would not modify their heresy, preferring persecution. He wandered further and further into Christological subtleties in his search for a solution, growing more convinced of the wisdom of Theodora's politics if not of her faith. At last in 565 he stepped himself into undeniable heterodoxy, and died that year branded by the vast majority of his subjects as an Aphthartocathartic heretic.

Justinian's religious policy had, for a time at least, established the Emperor as a theological dictator, providing a precedent of Cæsaropapism for later theologian Emperors to quote. But in its main object it had failed. The Eastern provinces remained ill-disposed and the West suspected him. The dissatisfaction might not have been dan-

gerous, had not the provincials and indeed all the citizens
of the Empire a worse cause for grievance. The taxation
reached limits beyond endurance. The glories of Justinian's reign, the foreign conquests, the great buildings,
were extremely costly and financially quite unproductive.
Anastasius's hoard was quickly used up ; and Justinian
had to employ as ministers those that were most competent
at extortion, however dishonest their methods might be.
Already in 532, the sinister abilities of his favourites, the
lawyer Tribonian and John the Cappadocian, provoked the
famous Nika riots, which burnt down the city and would have
cost the Emperor his throne but for the firmness of the
Empress. The hated John remained in power till 541
when Theodora could bear him no longer ; but his successors were equally oppressive. Later in the reign nature
added to the difficulties of Justinian's government ; earth-
quakes, a series of famines, and the great plague of 544
further diminished the revenues. There had been a revival
of commercial prosperity during the first decades of the
century, and Justinian himself did much to foster trade.
But it was nipped in the bud. The profits were never
allowed to fructify ; the tax-gatherers came too soon.
The subjects of the Empire grew increasingly weary and
resentful.

Justinian achieved much. He beautified the world and
he gave it its finest code of laws ; his conquests revived
Roman civilisation in the West ; his Cæsaropapism saved
his Eastern successors from a Canossa. But it taught two
bitter morals : that the East and the West could not
be reconciled, and that good finance is the basis of successful government. By ignoring these rules Justinian did
irreparable injury to the Empire.

Incidentally his reign marked the further decline of
Latin. He himself was Latin-speaking and issued his great
code in Latin. But apart from that no Latin literature

was produced at his court, and his later *Novels* were issued in Greek.

Justinian was succeeded by his nephew Justin II, who had married Theodora's niece Sophia. They emulated in vain their great predecessors. On the east the Persian Wars were marked with disaster ; on the north a new barbarian tribe, the Avars, pressed down ; on the west another, the Lombards, invaded a worn and apathetic Italy. Under the strain Justin's sanity collapsed. Sophia bought peace with Persia and selected a general, Tiberius, to succeed her husband. In 574, in a brief lucid interval, Justin adopted Tiberius as his son and crowned him Cæsar. In 578 Tiberius succeeded as Emperor.[1]

With Tiberius a new era began. The imperialism of the House of Justin had broken down. Tiberius saw that it was the East that must be saved from the wreckage. The bulk of Italy was abandoned to the Lombards. The Viceroy retired behind the inviolable marshes round his capital Ravenna, and the southern coastline was preserved. Rome won semi-independence under the Popes, though an Imperial commissioner still resided in the palace of the Cæsars. Meanwhile, unnoticed, Imperial Spain lapsed back to the Visigoths. Tiberius practised tolerance towards the heretics, and concentrated on driving off the Persian and the Avar. In a brave attempt to restore the public morale, he remitted a year's taxation, and it seems that he tried to use popular support against the Imperialistic Roman aristocracy. But he died in 582, his work quite unfinished, with the Avars triumphant on the Danube frontier and the Slavs pouring in around them. His successor, his son-in-law Maurice (582–602), pursued the same policy. He kept the Avars at bay, and triumphed against Persia ; he attempted to put the Empire in a better defensive state by giving the military more power in the provincial adminis-

[1] Justin crowned him eight days before he died.

tration ; a rigid economy repaired to some extent the
Imperial finances. But his austere realism put too great
a strain on his subjects. His soldiers, their pay reduced,
could not stand the rigours demanded of them. In 602
the army revolted. Maurice was killed, and the army
leader Phocas became Emperor in his stead.

The reign of Phocas (602–610) was a nightmare of disruptive anarchy and tyranny, foreign invasions and internal
risings : till at last Heraclius, son of the governor of Africa,
sailed to Constantinople as a deliverer, and founded a
dynasty to last for five generations.

With the reign of Heraclius the Roman Empire turns
the corner to Byzantinism. It was dominated by a long
war to the death against the Persians, a war that was
truly a crusade. The Persians in the course of it sacked
Jerusalem and invaded Egypt, and with Avar help almost
captured Constantinople itself ; but in the end the Kingdom of the Sassanids was crushed for ever (628). About
the same time the Avar Kingdom began to crumble, and
Heraclius established his suzerainty over the Slavs that now
filled the Balkan peninsula. But the wars had been costly
and exhausting, and the Monophysite provinces had suffered in particular. Heraclius, like his predecessors, sought
to win Monophysite friendship by a theological compromise. He adopted the idea that Christ had only one
energy or at any rate only one will. But this Monotheletism, though it met with a certain success in Constantinople, and even Pope Honorius I subscribed to it, did not
satisfy the Monophysites. Their present political grievances and their loyal hatred of the decrees of Chalcedon
kept them permanently disgruntled ; and anyhow it came
too late. In 636, the year in which the Emperor signed
the *Ekthesis*, the document embodying the new confession,
a battle had been fought in Syria that lost that province
for ever for the Empire.

Early in the century the tribes of Central Arabia had won political unity and religious inspiration from a certain Mahomet. The aridity of their climate forced the Arabs to periodic expansion, and now with this new strength and fervour they burst on the civilised world. In 634 they first invaded Palestine. In 636 at a battle on the River Yarmak they routed the great army that Heraclius managed to scrape together from his weary Empire, and all Syria lay at their mercy. In 637 at Kadisaya they overwhelmed the troops of the Sassanids, finally ending the Persian Kingdom at the battle of Nihawand four years later. In 638 they captured Jerusalem. In 641 they invaded Egypt. The overtaxed, persecuted heretics made no attempt to preserve the Imperial dominion. In Syria and Egypt alike they welcomed the change of masters, considering the theology of Islam closer to their own than that of Chalcedon. Only Alexandria resisted. But in 647 that stronghold of Hellenism finally fell and its libraries were consigned to the flames. At the time of the death of Heraclius (641) the Empire was reduced, with a few isolated outposts, to Asia Minor and the Balkan coastline, the province of Africa and Sicily. With the exception of Africa, this made a Greek-speaking entity, and an entity religiously dependent on the Patriarchate of Constantinople. The amputation of the great heretic provinces was in the end to ease the Empire's troubles. But the outlook was black enough.

The decades following the death of Heraclius are the darkest in Byzantine history.[1] The Arab menace was unending. All the energy of the Empire was needed to keep the Taurus, the northern limit of their expansion. Continually the Arabs would cross the range to ravage Asia Minor. And they built a fleet. In 673 they established themselves in the Sea of Marmora and yearly till 677 raided the walls of Constantinople. Early in the next

[1] Even the chronology is somewhat doubtful.

century they were planning a great expedition to give the *coup de grâce* to the Empire by the capture of the Capital. Meanwhile they expanded westward. In 670 they began to attack the province of Africa, and in 697 Carthage fell to them. Thence they moved towards Spain. In the Balkans the Slavs caused perpetual disorder. Saint Demetrius had more than once to come miraculously to save his city Thessalonica from their attacks. In 679 a new element of chaos was introduced by the invasion and settlement south of the Danube of a warlike Hunnish tribe known as the Bulgars. Religiously the Heraclian Emperors supported Monotheletism for a while, then veered round and summoned the Sixth Œcumenical Council to Constantinople in 680 to condemn the heresy. An appendix to this Council, the Synod *In Trullo* drew up what was to remain the constitution and rule of the Byzantine Church.

The Emperors of the Heraclian dynasty, though all were gifted men, were none of them equal to the hard task of government in those times. Heraclius left his throne to his sons Constantine III and Heracleonas, but the attempt of the latter's mother Martina (her husband's niece) to rule was a failure. Constantine died after a few months and Heracleonas fell shortly after ; and the former's son Constans II (641–668) succeeded. The bulk of Constans's reign was occupied with wars against the Arabs. In the end Constans despaired of saving the East and went to live in Sicily, with the intention apparently of re-establishing Imperial rule in Italy and making Rome his capital. But he was murdered at Syracuse before his plans were matured. The reign of his son Constantine IV, Pogonatus or the Bearded (668–685), was equally filled with war. On the whole he maintained the defences of the Empire, though he permitted, owing to an attack of gout, the invasion of the Bulgars. Constantine's successor was his young son Justinian II, a brilliant unreliable tyrant with a taste for blood. After ten years of his oppression Constantinople rose against him, slit his nose and banished him to Cherson in the Crimea. But he escaped from his prison there, and after ten years' adventures among the barbarians, he returned to Constantinople with Bulgar help. In the meantime a soldier Leontius had reigned from 695 to 698, to be replaced by a sailor Apsimar, renamed Tiberius III, who fell on Justinian's reappearance. But Justinian's tyranny now knew no bounds. The Chersonites, his former gaolers, fearing his vengeance, revolted under a general Bardanes, or Philippicus, who in 711 succeeded in dethroning Justinian, and putting his family to death. Philippicus however was an indolent man in everything except heresy—he was a fervent Monothelete. After two years he fell in a palace plot and was succeeded by a civil servant Artemius, who took the name of Anastasius II. The Empire had fallen into chaos, and the Arabs were mustering in Asia Minor. But Anastasius's attempts to restore vigour to the army cost him his popularity. The revolt of a regiment brought an obscure and unwilling provincial tax-collector, Theodosius III, to the throne (716). Theodosius clearly was unable to deal with the situation. Next year, in face of the Arab menace, the greatest general of the Empire, Leo, surnamed the Isaurian, with scarcely any opposition took over the government.

It was the destiny of the Isaurian Emperors to save the Empire from the Saracens and to perfect its transformation into the best defensive organisation that Christendom has known. Leo III (717–740) triumphantly preserved the Capital through the great Arab siege of 717–718, and in his later wars beat the infidel back to the Taurus frontier. He turned to the administration, repaired the finances and developed the system of themes ; each theme or province was put under a military governor, whose government was, however, well supervised from Constantinople. His son

Constantine V, rudely surnamed Caballinus or Copronymus [1] (740–775), was an even more remarkable man. His general-ship and diplomacy temporarily crushed the Bulgars, and repeated his father's success against the Arabs, helped by the decline of the Ommayad Califate. His financial and administrative energy completed his father's work. But both father and son became the villains of Byzantine history owing to their religious policy.

In 726 Leo III published a decree forbidding the worship of images, and followed it with a general destruction of icons representing Christ and the saints. His original motive was probably theological ; but the movement soon acquired a political basis, as an attack on the Church— particularly on the monasteries, whose growing power was aided by their possession of holy pictures. Under Con-stantine V, who himself was a theologian with heretical Unitarian tendencies, this anti-monachal aspect became very definite. The monks were at the forefront of the Iconodules, the Image-worshippers. Iconoclasm had a certain success in Asia Minor and among the soldiers, who were mostly Asiatics ; but it met with a passionate resist-ance, especially in Europe. In Constantinople there were riots and risings, and one great rebellion on the accession of Constantine V. In Italy it was so unpopular that the Lombards found little opposition when they overran Ravenna and the last Imperial districts, till by 751 nothing was left to the Emperor north of Calabria. It led to a breach with the Papacy that had far-reaching results. The Popes sought new allies in the Franks, while the Empire lost its last Latin interests and became a purely Greek-speaking whole.

After Constantine V there came his son Leo IV, called the Chazar as his mother had been a princess of that Turkish race. He reigned only five years (775–780) and

[1] The Stable Boy or Called from Dung.

was succeeded by his ten-years-old son, Constantine VI,
under the regency of the Empress-Mother, the Athenian
Irene. Irene, a European, was an Iconodule, and in 787
she made peace with Rome and summoned the Sixth
Œcumenical Council to Nicæa to restore Image-worship.
The restoration delighted the Church and the bulk of the
common people, but was disliked by the Asiatic soldiery :
who further resented the rule of a woman, especially when
the Arab power was reviving under the Abbasid Califs
of Baghdad. But the young Emperor did not possess the
ability to stand up against his mother, and his character
inspired no respect. In 797, after a long sequence of
quarrels, Irene at last seized her son and blinded him and
for five years reigned alone (797–802). It was during this
feminine rule that Pope Leo crowned Charles the Great
Emperor of the West.

The Isaurian dynasty was followed by a period of short
reigns punctuated by rebellions ; and as the military
party regained power, Iconoclasm returned. Irene was
dethroned by her treasurer, Nicephorus I (802–811), an
excellent financier but a poor amateur soldier, who lost
Crete to Arab pirates and had to face a sudden renewal
of the Bulgar power as well as the Saracen wars. Nicephorus
was killed in a battle against the Bulgar prince Krum ;
and his son and heir Stauracius was so badly wounded that
he died a few months later, to be succeeded by his brother-
in-law, the rich civilian Michael I Rhangabe (811–813).
Michael I fell in a military revolt organised by his traitorous
general Leo, an Armenian. During Leo V's reign (813–820)
Iconoclasm was reintroduced, as a political, anti-clerical
rather than a theological movement. But Leo was murdered in 820 by another soldier, Michael, a Phrygian from
Amorium.

The Amorian or Phrygian dynasty founded by Michael II
lasted nearly half a century. Michael II (820–829) was

an eager Iconoclast and further enraged the Church party by marrying as his second wife a nun, Euphrosyne, daughter of Constantine VI. He was succeeded by his son Theo-philus (829–842), an Iconoclast like his father, but less extreme. He was a good administrator and a fervent patron of culture, and his reign saw a renaissance of secular learning and artistic magnificence, largely influenced by the civilisa-tion of the Abbasids of Baghdad. His wars against the Arabs were not, however, uniformly successful. After his death in 842 his widow Theodora became regent for their young son Michael III. Like the last Empress-regent Irene, Theodora was an Iconodule, and in 843 she restored Image-worship, to the delight of the vast majority of her subjects. The religious peace, added to the political recon-struction of the Isaurians and of Theophilus, brought a new period of prosperity to the Empire. But the prudent rule of Theodora was followed in 856 by the extravagance of Michael, who won from his habits the surname of the Drunkard. He, however, chose able advisers in his uncle Bardas and then a slave-boy called Basil ; and eventually the latter, after causing the death of Bardas, in 867 murdered his benefactor the Emperor and assumed the Imperial power. During Michael III's reign there was a new breach with Rome, caused by the clashing ambitions of the Pope Nicholas the Great and the Patriarch Photius, a quarrel intensified by the conversion of the Bulgars and the central European Slavs.

Under Basil I and his descendants, known usually if misleadingly as the Macedonian dynasty [1] (867–1057), the Empire reached the zenith of its mediæval glory. The internal organisation of the Empire was strong enough for the Emperors to be able to indulge in a programme of expansion, while the more orderly condition of the whole

[1] Basil was born in the Macedonian Theme, near Adrianople. By birth he claimed to be an Armenian.

Western world led to a growth of commerce from which Constantinople was quick to benefit. Basil I (867–886) was a capable general : under his command the tide of the Saracen wars at last turned in favour of the Empire, though the results at first were small. In the West the Arabs had recently overrun Sicily and South Italy. Basil left Sicily to its fate, but his general, Nicephorus Phocas, restored the Imperial power in South Italy to a height unknown for three centuries. Under his son [1] Leo VI (886–912), surnamed the Wise, these military successes were not continued. There was an unsuccessful war against the Bulgarians ; a greater disaster was the sack of Thessalonica, the second city of the Empire, by Arab pirates from Crete in 901. Both Basil and Leo followed the same internal policy, aimed at strengthening the royal prerogative and opposing the independent tendencies of the Patriarchs Photius and Nicholas Mysticus. To dissociate themselves from the hated Iconoclasts, Basil began and Leo completed a new codification of the laws, issuing a code, the *Basilica*, that remained in force till the end of the Empire. Leo raised trouble for himself by marrying twice as often as the religious law permitted in the quest of a male heir ; it was only his fourth wife that gave him a son. Leo succeeded in establishing the boy's legitimacy, despite ecclesiastical opposition, but after his death his matrimonial prodigality was formally condemned.

Leo was followed on the throne by his brother Alexander (912–913), who had been co-Emperor since his youth, and now reigned jointly with Leo's young son Constantine VII, surnamed Porphyrogennetus, ' Born in the Purple Chamber.' [2] On Alexander's death after a year's misrule, and a further year's misrule under a regency council

[1] Leo's paternity was doubtful. His mother was Michael III's mistress.

[2] For this surname, see p. 70.

dominated by the Patriarch Nicholas Mysticus, the government was taken over by Constantine's mother Zoe (914–919). Meanwhile the Bulgarians under their Tsar Symeon invaded the Empire. Zoe's vigorous attempts to defeat them met with disaster and caused her downfall. Her place was taken by her admiral, Romanus Lecapenus, who raised himself to the throne and soon took precedence over Constantine, whom he married to his daughter. Romanus I (919–944) ruled the Empire well. He made a satisfactory peace with the Bulgarians ; and his general, John Curcuas, launched the Empire on the voyage of spectacular conquest in the East that marked the next hundred years. But Romanus's attempt to found a dynasty failed, though he crowned three of his sons. They in the end dethroned him, but within a month of his fall Constantine VII was in sole control of the Empire.

Under Constantine VII's rule (945–959) and that of his son Romanus II (959–963) the Eastern conquests continued. Crete was recovered and even Aleppo taken for a while by the general Nicephorus Phocas, grandson of Basil I's general. When Romanus II died leaving two young sons, Basil II (963–1025) and Constantine VIII [1] (963–1028), his widow, the temporary regent Theophano, married Nicephorus Phocas, who assumed the crown. Nicephorus II's reign was made glorious by the recovery of Cilicia, Cyprus and the great city of Antioch, but in 969 he was murdered with his wife's connivance by his cousin John Tzimisces, who took his place. John I (969–976) was an equally able general, who conquered half Bulgaria, defeated a Russian invasion, and marched his armies as far as the outskirts of Jerusalem and Baghdad. On his death Basil II was left supreme.

The Empire had been organised by the Isaurians as a

[1] Sometimes numbered IX, as Romanus I crowned a son Constantine Emperor.

defensive unit and consequently great powers had been given to the military. During the recent wars the army leaders were supplied by the landed aristocracy. Meanwhile the increased security of the Empire gave a new value to land as a source of wealth. The strength derived by the great families first as estate-owners and secondly as soldiers began to make them a menace to the central government. Both Romanus I and Constantine VII had foreseen this and had legislated, insufficiently, against the amassing of landed estates. Under John I the revolt of the Phocæ had shown the trouble that one great family could cause to the Emperor. During the first decade of Basil II's personal rule the intertwined rebellions of Bardas Phocas and Bardas Sclerus illustrated the danger still more clearly. Basil's eventual victory was largely caused by luck, but he took advantage of it to strike hard at the aristocracy. Thanks to his energy it was for a while crushed. After this victory Basil, though he indulged in a few campaigns to enlarge the Empire's boundaries on the east, spent the bulk of his career fighting in the Balkans. The Bulgarians had revived during the rebellions of the Bardæ, and their Tsar Samuel ruled from the unconquered Macedonian mountains an Empire that stretched again to the Black Sea. In 981 Basil had vainly attempted to check them. From 996 to 1018 he warred almost continuously against them, till at last they were utterly conquered ; the whole peninsula from the Danube southward obeyed the Emperor once more, and his grateful subjects surnamed Basil Bulgaroctonus, the Bulgar-slayer. Meanwhile his passionate thrift and austerity filled the Imperial treasury, which had been somewhat depleted by the expensive wars of his predecessors. By the end of Basil's reign the Empire had never since the days of Heraclius been so far-flung, and had never been so prosperous.

On Basil's death the decline began. His brother Con-

D

stantine VIII reigned ineffectively for three years (1025–
1028), then died leaving three middle-aged daughters,
Eudocia, a pock-marked nun, Zoe and Theodora. For the
next decades the husbands and protégés of Zoe ruled the
Empire. The first of these, Romanus III Argyrus (1028–
1034), was worthy but extravagant, vain and weak. After
his death under suspicious circumstances, Zoe hastened to
marry a handsome young Paphlagonian, who ruled for
seven years (1034–1041) as Michael IV. Michael was able
and vigorous—he successfully put down a serious Bulgarian
rebellion—but he was an epileptic. Continual ill-health
forced him to be a mere opportunist. On his death Zoe
was induced to adopt and crown his nephew Michael,
surnamed the Calfat or Chandler from his father's profession. Michael V had schemes of reform that involved
the fall of his benefactress Zoe. The dynasty was however
too well loved to be overthrown by a chandler. A popular
rising in Constantinople dethroned Michael and established as sole sovereigns Zoe and her sister Theodora (1042).
But the sisters were jealous of each other, and to lessen
Theodora's power Zoe remarried an elderly debauchee,
Constantine Monomachus. Constantine IX (1042–1054)
was not incompetent but lazy and corrupt, and did nothing
to stop the growing power of the Church and of the aristocracy. The Patriarch Michael Cerularius behaved almost
as an Eastern Pope, and in 1054 manœuvred the final schism
of the Eastern Churches with Rome. Under Constantine
the Empire's area was increased by the annexation of
independent Armenia ; but at the same time Norman
adventurers began to overrun Byzantine Italy and Sicily,[1]
and the attempts of the Imperial armies to retain those
provinces met with failure. On Constantine's death in
1054 (Zoe had died in 1050) the aged Theodora assumed

---

[1] Sicily, lost to the Arabs in the late Ninth Century, had been half-
reconquered early in the Eleventh.

sole control and ruled for two years with surprising firmness. In 1056 the Macedonian dynasty was extinguished.

These years had seen Byzantine culture raised to an unprecedented height. In the person of Psellus, historian, philosopher and court-politician, clever, learned, inquisitive, unscrupulous, cynical yet religious, we can see it at its most characteristic. But at the same time prosperity had upset the balance of the stern centralised militarist organisation of the Empire. The end of the great dynasty let loose the disruptive elements. From 1056 to 1081 there was a period of chaos in which the Church and the civil bureaucracy fought for power with the landed military aristocrats. Unfortunately this chaos coincided with the attacks of newly-come enemies on the Eastern and Western frontiers. The Normans completed their conquest of Southern Italy by the capture of Bari in 1071 and then crossed the Adriatic to the Balkan coasts. The Seljuk Turks gathered on the borders of Armenia preparing to invade Asia Minor. Meanwhile the growth of the Italian maritime republicans was beginning that revolution in commercial geography that was consummated by the Crusades and struck heavily against the financial hegemony of Constantinople.

Theodora had appointed as her successor an elderly civilian, Michael Stratioticus ; but after a year Michael VI was dethroned by the militarists, led by the noble, Isaac Comnenus. Isaac I reigned two years ; then, unexpectedly, he abdicated in favour of his finance minister Constantine Ducas, an aristocrat allied with the Church and the civil bureaucracy rather than with the militarists. Economy and fear of military revolts made Constantine X (1059–1067) cut down the army and disorganise it at this very unsuitable moment. After he had died, leaving a young son, Michael VII, his widow, Eudocia Macrembolitissa, changed his policy and gave herself and the throne to an army leader. Romanus IV Diogenes. Romanus restored order in the army, but in 1071 he went out to meet a great onrush of the Seljuks in Armenia. Thanks to his careless strategy the Empire underwent at Manzikert a disaster from which it never was to recover. 1071, the year of the fall of Bari and the Battle of Manzikert, is the turning-point in Byzantine history.

Romanus IV had been captured at Manzikert. On the news of the battle reaching the Capital, Michael VII, now just grown up, assumed the government and ruled, vainly trying to restore order, restrain the nobles and expel the Turks. Meanwhile the Turks overran all Asia Minor and showed a determination to establish themselves there. They were a primitive people, destructive, pastoral and not agricultural. Wherever they settled cultivation ceased, roads and aqueducts fell into ruin. The consequent and very rapid decline of Asia Minor into a desert made the task of its recovery far harder for the Empire : while the loss of the province robbed the Empire of its main recruiting ground and its main granary. The question of supplies had to be reorganised, and more and more reliance had to be put on foreign mercenaries. The financial strain grew greater.

In 1078 Michael VII was forced to abdicate in favour of a soldier, Nicephorus III Botaniates (1078–1081) ; but he in his turn was dethroned by a far abler soldier, Alexius Comnenus, Isaac I's nephew, who had by a timely marriage secured the alliance of the civilian Ducas party. Alexius I (1081–1118) saved the Empire. He had to fight continually on every front ; but his wars and his subtle diplomacy kept the Normans from the Balkans, drove back barbarian invaders from the north and held the Seljuks at bay. In 1096 the movement known as the Crusades thrust new problems on the Emperor. The Crusaders, though the bulk of them was inspired by religion, were led by politicians who coveted Constantinople quite as much as the Holy

Land. The situation was well handled by Alexius. He utilised Crusading arms to win him back land from the Seljuks, notably their capital Nicæa, then sent the Westerners on to menace Islam on its flank. In the end the Crusades, opening a new direct trade-route from Syria to the West, would do the Empire inestimable harm commercially; and the tricky diplomacy in which both sides indulged wildly exacerbated the friction between the Empire and the Latin West, a friction already emphasised by the religious schism. But for the moment the Crusaders had served Alexius's purposes. The salvation had, however, been bought at a price; the financial cost was more than the Empire could bear. The help of Venetian ships had been bought by commercial concessions, taxation was raised, a weight so crushing that the rule of the Seljuks seemed almost less oppressive; and Alexius was led to tamper slightly with the currency. After maintaining its value throughout all the disturbances of seven centuries, the Imperial coinage lost its position as the one reliable medium of exchange. Constantinople was no longer the financial centre of the world.

Under the capable rule of Alexius's son, John II (1118–1143), the decadence barely showed. John's military exploits won more land back from the Seljuks and awed the Crusaders; but though concessions to foreigners were withdrawn the expenses of government could not be reduced. Beneath the glittering surface of the reign of John's son, Manuel I (1143–1180), worse disintegration set in. Manuel was attracted by Western ideas, and he began to rely upon Western arms, particularly on the ships of the Italian republics. But this naval support meant more commercial concessions; and concessions given to Venice were demanded and secured by Genoa and Pisa. Constantinople remained to the last a great factory of the world's luxuries, but her customs' revenue dwindled and her overseas trade disappeared. On the other hand, it had seemed during John's reign and Manuel's early years that Asia Minor might be wholly recovered from the Seljuks ; but Manuel's great defeat at Myriocephalum in 1176, a disaster that he himself rightly compared to Manzikert, meant that the Turks were to be established there for ever.

The regency of Manuel's widow, the Latin Maria of Antioch (1180–1183) for their son Alexius II, meant chaos. In 1183 his cousin, Andronicus Comnenus, seized the power, and soon had the young Emperor murdered. Andronicus I's reign (1183–1185) was a reaction against the Latins. His accession was marked with a great massacre of the Italian merchants in Constantinople, and he withdrew all concessions. His administration of the provinces was conducted with competence and exemplary justice, but in Constantinople his arbitrary despotism roused him enemies, and the threatened vengeance of the Westerners added to his difficulties. In 1185 he was overthrown by riots in the capital and was replaced by a distant relative, Isaac Angelus.

The rule of the Angeli, Isaac II (1185–1195) and his brother Alexius III who deposed and succeeded him (1195–1203), was a tale of melancholy weakness, of more disorder and poverty in the Empire and more concessions to the Italians. Bulgaria won her independence ; Cyprus revolted. Finally in 1203 a Crusade from the West intended for the Holy Land was diverted by Venetian greed to Constantinople. Its appearance for a while replaced its nominees Isaac II and his son Alexius IV on the throne, but in 1204 a riot broke out which gave the Crusaders their excuse for capturing and sacking the City.

It is hard to exaggerate the harm done to European civilisation by the sack of Constantinople. The treasures of the City, the books and works of art preserved from distant centuries, were all dispersed and most destroyed. The Empire, the great Eastern bulwark of Christendom, was broken as a power. Its highly centralised organisation was ruined. Provinces, to save themselves, were forced into devolution. The conquests of the Ottoman were made possible by the Crusaders' crime.

Venice and the Latin princes divided the spoil. A Latin Emperor was set up in Constantinople. Latin lords overran the Greek peninsula, spreading a restless romanticism over that long-quiet province. Venice took islands and built colonies along the coastline and won concessions that captured for her the whole Eastern trade. But the attempt to take over the whole Empire failed. Imperial Asia Minor remained in Greek-speaking hands. In Nicæa Alexius III's son-in-law Theodore Lascaris established a court that soon became the headquarters of the Empire in exile. At Trebizond a Comnenus declared his independence and in Epirus an Angelus, who soon acquired Thessalonica from its Latin lords. These three self-styled Empires disputed the claim to be the Roman Empire in exile, but Nicæa's was always the most generally accepted and in the end triumphed. The Empire of Thessalonica fell before the Nicæan in 1246 and the Angeli were reduced to the Despotate of Epirus, which in the end acknowledged the suzerainty of the Emperor. The Empire of Trebizond remained unconquered till it was extinguished by the Ottomans in 1461 ; but, isolated in the East by the Nicæans and the Seljuks, the Grand Comnenus could never make a convincing claim to be œcumenical Emperor.

In this rivalry the Nicæan victory was due to the high abilities of her Emperors. Theodore I Lascaris (1204–1222) and his son-in-law John III Vatatzes (1222–1254) organised the Empire into an efficient and profitable concern, and both were good soldiers and consummate diplomats. Under John III's son, Theodore II (1254–1258), an ill and morbid intellectual, the Empire still grew despite the discontent of the aristocracy, whom he persecuted. When his infant

son, John IV (1238–1259), succeeded, the aristocracy rose
and murdered George Muzalon, the humble-born agent
whom he had appointed in his will, and gave the power
to their most prominent member, Michael Palæologus.
But it was only a change of masters. On New Year's Day,
1259, Michael assumed the crown, and soon afterwards
the boy emperor was blinded.

Meanwhile in Constantinople the Latin Empire ' of
Romania ' was sinking in poverty and decay. Baldwin of
Flanders, the first Emperor, was quite unequal to the task.
The Empire was organised on strict feudal lines, and he
was little more than its premier baron. He might, however,
have won the support of his subjects against his vassals
had he not alienated them by forcing on them the hated
Latin Church. In 1205 Baldwin was killed in a war against
the Bulgarians. His successor, his brother Henry (1205–
1216), was more conciliatory towards the Greeks and under
his rule it seemed for a time that the Latin Empire might
emerge as a power. But it was too late ; the Greeks had
learnt to seek religious freedom at Nicæa. The Latin lords
and the Venetians, out for their own profit, were useless as
supports for the Empire, and after his death it speedily
declined. He was succeeded by his sister Yolande and her
husband Peter of Courtenay. But Peter was killed in
Epirus in 1217 before ever he reached Constantinople.
Yolande governed for two years (1217–1219), then resigned
the power in favour of her second son Robert (the eldest
wisely refused it). Robert was deposed for incompetence
in 1228 and was succeeded by his brother Baldwin II, under
the regency of the ex-King of Jerusalem, John of Brienne
(1225–1237), an old man of more gallantry than brains.
It had been suggested that the regency should be offered
to the Bulgarian king, to secure his help against the Greeks ;
but the Latin clergy could not bear the idea of a schismatic
regent and prevented the plan. Under Baldwin II the

plight of the Empire of Romania grew worse. He spent
most of his reign touring the West seeking help. He had
no money, and pawned his palace-roofs, his relics and his
son to the Venetians. Constantinople was steadily depopulated by poverty and famine. It was a merciful deliverance
when in 1261 the troops of Michael Palæologue forced
their way into the city, and Baldwin, the Latin Patriarch
and the Venetian podestá hurried to the harbour and sailed
away to the west.

But the harm was irrevocable. Michael entered a half-
ruined depopulated city. It was a valuable recovery, for
no one in the Near East can afford to let his enemies hold
Constantinople, and it was glorious for the prestige of the
Empire. But it brought problems and expenses that were
too much for him to bear. The Genoese had been his
allies ; they must be paid with commercial privileges which
reduced the Empire's revenues. The Latins found a
champion and would-be avenger in Charles of Anjou, now
King of the Two Sicilies ; he had to be out-manœuvred
by a movement for Union with the Latin Church, a movement which infuriated the Emperor's subjects without
restraining Charles. The Imperial coinage, stabilised by
the thrift of the Nicæan Emperors, began to fall again ;
and Michael, unable to afford the system of paying his
frontier forces with gifts of tax-free land, abolished such
holdings in Asia, and so weakened his defences. On
Michael's death in 1282 the Empire showed the barrenness
of its political revival. The only positive achievement of
the reign besides the capture of the capital had been in the
Peloponnese, where the victory of Pelagonia in 1259 had
placed the pivotal fortresses of Mistra, Monemvasia and
Maina in the Emperor's hands.

The long reign of his son Andronicus II (1282–1328)
saw a slow decline. The Sicilian Vespers in 1282 had
ruined the power of Charles of Anjou, and Andronicus

could safely break off the negotiations for Church union. But a new menace was growing on the East. Mongol invasions of Asia Minor in the Thirteenth Century had brought in their train fresh Turkish tribes. One of these settled on the Imperial frontier and was organised during the last decades of the century into a strong militarist power by its chief Osman, after whom it was known as the Osmanli or Ottoman Turks. After Michael's abolition of the frontier soldiery, Andronicus's military forces were not strong enough to deal with them. He had to rely on foreign mercenaries, and in a foolish moment hired a band of adventurers known as the Catalan Grand Company (1302). But they soon turned against their employers, blockaded Constantinople for two years (1305–1307), introduced the Turks into Europe (1308) and eventually retired to ravage Macedonia and Frankish Greece. Meanwhile in Europe the Bulgarian Empire of the Asen and the Serbian Empire of the Uroš were continual sources of danger. Internally the reign though active culturally was a story of financial embarrassment and revolt. From 1321 to 1328 Andronicus was fighting his grandson and heir Andronicus III, and only the old Emperor's death brought peace.

Under Andronicus III (1328–1341) the same story continued. The Ottoman Turks had captured Brusa in 1326 ; in 1329 they took Nicæa and in 1337 Nicomedia. Under Stephen Dušan (1331–1355) the Serbian Empire reached its zenith and menaced Constantinople. Andronicus's death, leaving a child, John V, as Emperor, brought civil wars in a struggle for the regency between the Empress-mother, Anne of Savoy, and the usurper John VI Cantacuzenus. The latter, a brilliant man forced to be an opportunist, won in 1347, but fell in 1355 before John V's son Andronicus IV. John V returned to power in 1379, was ousted for a while by his grandson John VII in 1390, but died on the throne in 1391. Things had been growing steadily worse. In the Peloponnese, indeed, the Imperialists gradually recovered the whole peninsula from the Franks, but elsewhere it was a different story. It was clear now that destruction was coming from the Turks. In 1356 they began to settle in Europe. In 1357 they captured Adrianople and soon made it their capital. The battles of the Maritsa in 1371 and of Kossovo in 1389 placed Bulgaria and Serbia in their hands. By 1390 their power reached the Danube, and the Empire held only Constantinople, Thessalonica and the Peloponnese, the Despotate of Mistra.

John V had toured Italy vainly seeking help, to be detained as a debtor at Venice. But under his younger son and successor Manuel II, Western Europe grew conscious of the danger, and sent an army to the Balkans. It was destroyed at Nicopolis in 1396. In 1397 the Turks besieged Constantinople. But the hour was not yet come. The Turks were attacked from the East by Timur the Tartar, and in 1402 the Sultan was defeated and captured by the Mongols at Angora. It was an opportunity to eject the Turks from Europe. But the Empire was not strong enough, the Serbs were traitors, and the West would not co-operate. By 1413 Timur's Empire was broken up and the Turks had quite recovered. Meanwhile Manuel, like his father, set out to find allies in the West, journeying even to Paris and London—equally vainly.

Manuel's tact and popularity amongst his subjects and at the Turkish court preserved the Empire unharmed so long as he ruled, but in 1420 he handed over the government to his son John VIII, dying five years later. In 1422 John provoked the Turks to make an attempt against Constantinople, but a rebellion made the Sultan raise the siege. In 1423 the governor of Thessalonica, fearing a Turkish attack, sold the city to the Venetians ; but the Turkish attack came seven years later and succeeded. John VIII, following the family tradition, travelled hopefully to Italy. There in 1439 at the Council of Florence he pledged his Imperial authority to the Union of the Churches, a union disowned by the vast majority of his subjects. As a reward a new Western expedition invaded the Balkans, to be crushed by the Turks at Varna in 1444.

In 1448 John died, and his brother Constantine XI succeeded to the doomed Empire. The end came in 1453. After a hopeless but heroic defence of seven weeks, on May 29, the City fell into the hands of the Infidel. In 1460 the Turks overran the Peloponnese. In 1461 they extinguished the Empire of the Comneni of Trebizond. The blend of Imperial Rome and Christian Greece became a thing of the irreparable past.

CHAPTER III

The Imperial Constitution and the Reign of Law

That the Byzantine Empire should have endured for eleven hundred years was almost entirely due to the virtues of its constitution and administration. Few states have been organised in a manner so well suited to the times and so carefully directed to prevent power remaining in the hands of the incompetent. This organisation was not the conscious and deliberate work of a single man or a single moment. Fundamentally it was a heritage from the Roman past, but continually it had been adapted and supplemented throughout the centuries to suit their varying requirements.[1]

The Empire was an absolute autocracy. The dyarchy that Augustus had set up with the Senate as his partner, had not lasted long. The last trace of it only disappeared, it is true, at the end of the Ninth Century ; but since Diocletian's day the Emperor had in fact reigned alone. He was the ultimate authority in the Empire. He could appoint and dismiss all ministers at his will ; he had complete financial control ; legislation was in his hands alone ; he was commander-in-chief of all the Imperial forces. He was, moreover, head of the Church, High Priest of the Empire. His policy and his whims moulded the destiny of the millions of his subjects. During the Early Empire his title had been Imperator, or Augustus.

[1] See Bury, *The Constitution of the Later Roman Empire* in *Selected Essays*, ed. Temperley, 99 *sqq.*

Augustus survived as a title till the very end, but Imperator, with its military suggestion, gradually gave place, as the Empire became Orientalised, to Autocrator, with its more absolute implication. But from Heraclius's days onwards the usual name given to the Emperor was *Basileus*, the old Greek name for a King, which in recent years had been applied only to the King of Abyssinia, when people remembered him, and to the great rival of the Emperor and his model as an autocrat, the Sassanid King of Persia. And it is significant that the title Basileus first appears as borne by the Emperor in 629, just after the final defeat of the Persians.[1]

Though there was no constitutional check on his power, the Emperor's autocracy was nevertheless limited. He always recognised his obligation to respect the fundamental laws of the Roman people ; [2] and, deep down, there lingered the idea that sovereignty was the people's, and the people had only delegated their power to the Emperor. Justinian in the *Lex De Imperio* expressly states that the people have transferred their sovereignty to the Emperor.[3] It is improbable that this law was well known in later centuries, but the idea lingered on. In 811 the dying Emperor Stauracius, torn by the quarrels of his wife and his sister for the succession, threatened to give the Empire back to the people—to found a Christian Democracy—but the scheme was considered quite impracticable.[4] But the ultimate sovereignty of the people did manage to express itself. In the first place the throne was elective ; in the second there was what Mommsen has called ' the legal right of revolution,' a right that the Patriarch

---

[1] See Bréhier, *Les Origines des Titres Imp.*, *B.Z.*, vol. 15, 161 *sqq.*, esp. 171–2.

[2] E.g. *Digest*, I, iii, 31 ; *Basilica*, II, vi, I.

[3] See Bury, *op. cit.*, 112.

[4] Theophanes, 492.

Nicholas Mysticus in the Tenth Century was not afraid to voice.[1]

The electors to the Empire were the Senate, the Army and the People of Constantinople. Every Emperor had to be acclaimed by these three bodies and then undergo the rite of coronation. He then was absolute so long as his rule gave satisfaction ; but if he proved incompetent, it was open to any of the electors to proclaim a new Emperor. Usually it was the army, or a section of the army, that would do so, as in the case of Phocas, of Leo the Isaurian, Leo the Armenian, and many others down Byzantine history ; and if the Emperor so appointed could induce the Senate and People of Constantinople to accept him his usurpation was legitimised. Sometimes however the Emperor would be dethroned as the result of a palace conspiracy. In that case the usurper would intrigue to appear as the candidate of the Senate and would have himself acclaimed as soon as possible by the troops resident in Constantinople, as in the case of Nicephorus I or Michael I. If the Empire was vacant in times of peace, it was usually the Senate's proclamation that announced the new Emperor, but the Senate in those cases invariably acted as the tool of some general or some faction, as when in 457 it appointed Leo I at Aspar's dictation.[2] Occasionally, however, the People of Constantinople would take matters into their own hands. In 944 it was the clamour of the People that brought Constantine VII into power.[3] In 1042 it was the People that dragged Theodora from her convent to reign alongside of her sister Zoe.[4] In 1185 it was popular riots that overthrew Andronicus I and set up Isaac Angelus in his stead.[5]

[1] Nicholas Mysticus, *Epistolae*, *M.P.G.*, vol. CXI, 210.
[2] Malalas, 369.   [3] Liudprand, ed. Becker, *Antapodosis*, 142.
[4] Psellus, *Chronographia*, ed. Renauld, I, 101 *sqq.*
[5] Nicetas Choniates, 448 *sqq.*

But the elective principle had in practice one great modification. It was part of the Emperor's sovereignty that he
could co-opt other Emperors. Therefore there need never
be a gap in the Empire. The electors had to give formal
assent by acclamation, but the assent was never withheld.
The great majority of the Emperors succeeded because they
had been already crowned in their predecessor's lifetime ;
and the sequence was further preserved as it was thought
that in the absence of an Emperor, the Empress could dispose of the throne. There was no limit to the number of
Emperors that might co-exist. Under Romanus I there
were five. Under Constantine IV the army demanded
three, thinking with admirable piety that the Emperor
should follow the example of his prototype, the Deity.[1]
But only one Emperor exercised the power, the *Autocrator
Basileus*.[2] The others were sleeping-partners, but, on the
Autocrat's death, the Emperor next in seniority automatically succeeded to the Imperial authority. It was
possible thus to establish dynasties, which would last as
long as their representative was competent to rule—and
even longer. The case of the Empress Zoe shows how
dynastic sentiment could grow in this elective monarchy
even when its object was clearly unworthy.

After an Emperor had been elected or co-opted he had
still to be crowned.[3] This gave a religious sanction to his
authority so that he could truly perform the functions of
God's viceroy on earth. The idea of a diadem and a
coronation came from the Persians, whose King was crowned
by the Magian High Priest. But when Diocletian borrowed
the practice, being already Pontifex Maximus, he dispensed
with a priest's help ; and his Christian successors followed

---

[1] Theophanes, 352.

[2] The phrase appears first in Philotheus, *Cleterologium*, in Constantine
Porphyrogennetus, *De Ceremoniis*, I, 712.

[3] See Sickel, *Das Byzantinische Krönungsrecht*, B.Z., vol. 7, 511 *sqq.*

his example. The coronation was performed by some eminent representative of the electors. Valentinian I was crowned by the Prefect of the City. Gradually it was felt that the Patriarch of Constantinople was the most suitable representative, as holding the highest office under the Crown. Marcian was probably and Leo I certainly crowned by the Patriarch.[1] Henceforward this was the rule. The only exception was the last Emperor, Constantine XI, but his case was altogether unusual as he was crowned at Mistra.[2] But throughout the Patriarch acted as the most eminent citizen of the Empire, not as a Priest. Phocas indeed was the first Emperor to be crowned in a church.[3] Consequently when the coronation was of a co-Emperor, the existing Emperor performed it, though the Patriarch might assist, particularly when the existing Emperor was a minor.[4] The Patriarch might occasionally demand concessions from the Emperor before consenting to crown him. But in that case he was acting officially as the people's representative. His only legitimate weapon against the Emperor was the threat of excommunication, and even its legitimacy was questioned. However, certain promises were at times demanded from an Emperor before his coronation. Anastasius, whose orthodoxy was suspect, had to guarantee in writing to maintain the existing ecclesiastical arrangements and to show no malice against his former enemies ; and later Emperors with reputations for heterodoxy were obliged to make similar declarations.[5] Under the Palæologi there was a regular coronation oath to which Emperors swore. They promised to observe the decrees of the Œcumenical Councils and the various accepted Church doctrines and rights, and to rule justly

---

[1] Bury, *op. cit.*, 104.   [2] *Ibid., loc. cit.*
[3] Simocatta, 334.
[4] Constantine Porphyrogennetus, *op. cit.*, I, 191 *sqq.* ; Cedrenus, II, 296.
[5] Bury, *op. cit.*, 114.

E

and mildly and to anathematise everything anathematised by the Church.[1] After the Fifth Century it would have been impossible for a declared heretic to become Emperor.

The coronation, since the Seventh Century, took place in Saint Sophia and was witnessed by the Senate and representatives of the army and the people who acclaimed the new Emperor in the church and outside. Earlier it had taken place at the Hebdomon, outside the City. The ceremony, fully described by Constantine VII,[2] was followed with a few alterations by the Palæologi, who introduced the Western custom of unction.[3] Sometimes there were additional ceremonies to strengthen the rights of minors. On Good Friday, the day before he was crowned, the governors of themes, ministers, all persons of senatorial rank, and all the soldiers in the Capital, and representatives of all classes of citizens, especially of the guilds, were made to take a solemn oath of allegiance to the boy-Emperor, Constantine VI.[4]

It was felt that the coronation gave the Emperor his position as a demi-god, as the Viceroy of the Almighty. The Emperor was very consciously the head of the Christian Church. ' I am Emperor and priest,' wrote Leo the Isaurian to the Pope, and he claimed to be the deputy ' whom God has ordered to feed his flock like Peter, prince of the Apostles ' ; and the Pope agreed so long as the Emperor was orthodox.[5] By the time of Basil I it was customary to tonsure the Emperor's son and heir soon after his birth, as though to ordain him.[6] Justinian I won the

---

[1] Codinus, *De Officiis*, 87.

[2] Constantine Porphyrogennetus, *loc. cit.*

[3] For the question of unction see Brightman, *Byzantine Coronation Ceremonies* in *Journal of Theological Studies*, vol. 2, 383–5, but also Sickel, *op. cit.*, 547–8.　　　　　[4] Theophanes, 449.

[5] Mansi, *Concilia*, vol. 12, 976 ; *Ecloga*, trans. Freshfield, 66–7.

[6] Constantine Porphyrogennetus, *op. cit.*, 620–2.

right of the Emperor to make doctrinal pronouncements ;
and already it was his function to preside at the Councils
of the Church or to appoint a chairman in his place.[1]
The Patriarch was in practice his nominee. Even the
Popes, so long as the Exarchate of Ravenna lasted, were
only elected after the permission of the Imperial Viceroy
had been obtained.[2] His theocratic position led the Emperor to consider that he received the Empire from God.
' You received the crown from God by my hand,' said Basil I
to his heir Leo VI.[3] This did not mean that the *Lex De
Imperio* was forgotten. The people still were electors and
could take the Empire away ; but the people were the
Christian Commonwealth. The Emperor derived his power
as representative of the Christian Commonwealth and was
by his coronation appointed its High Priest. He could
therefore claim with reason to be in a direct relation with
God, the source of all power. The idea was in accord with
the mysticism of the times, and no one in the Empire would
have challenged it. In this position, it was necessary for
the Emperor to maintain a high prestige. In his presence
everyone must prostrate himself, even the foreign ambassadors. He might in the end be dethroned, but till then
lèse-majesté was a very serious crime. The servant-girl who
spat accidentally out of an upper window on to the coffin
of the Empress Eudoxia as it journeyed from the Palace to
its sepulchre, was put to death on the very tomb (412).[4]
It was to further this prestige that the innumerable formal
ceremonies were evolved that Constantine VII described,
and that ingenious Emperors like Theophilus called in the
co-operation of art and science, seating himself on a throne

---

[1] Gelzer, *Die Verhaltnisse von Staat u. Kirche in Byzanz, H.Z.*, *New Series*,
vol. 50, 193 *sqq.*
[2] *Liber Pontificalis*, 1, 363–4.
[3] Basil I, *Paraenesis ad Leonem, M.P.G.*, vol. 107, xxxii.
[4] Nicephorus, *Breviarum*, 7.

that rose to the ceiling and surrounded with singing birds and roaring lions made from gold.[1]

These many ceremonies and all the work that he must superintend as head of the Church and State, kept the Emperor fully occupied and made it necessary for him to be both conscientious and active. A eunuch was physically disqualified to be Emperor, and anyone blinded was felt to be unable to rule, though Isaac Angelus returned blind to the throne. A boy might become sole Emperor, but in that case there would be a regent. It might have seemed that the task was beyond a woman, especially as a woman could not in theory be a priest nor in practice lead an army. Nevertheless there was no constitutional bar in a woman exercising the autocracy. The position of the Empress, the Augusta,[2] was unusual according to modern notions. The existence of a female counterpart to the Emperor was needed for ceremonial purposes,[3] but the Empress was not necessarily the Emperor's wife. She had to be specially crowned and acclaimed : though unless she was crowned along with the Emperor, the ceremony took place in the Palace, not in a church. Almost invariably the Emperor's wife was raised on her marriage or on his accession ; but the number of Empresses was unlimited, and might include other Imperial relatives. Pulcheria, the sister of Theodosius II, was crowned early in her brother's reign. Theophilus and Leo VI crowned daughters,[4] Alexius I his mother.[5] The coronation gave the Empress a share in the sovereignty ; she even took some part in the Government. Theodora was present at Justinian's councils,

[1] See below, p. 157.

[2] *Augusta* was always the formal title, though from the Seventh Century onwards *Basilissa* was the usual colloquial term.

[3] Theophanes Continuatus, 364.

[4] Theophanes Continuatus, 107–8.

[5] The actual coronation is nowhere described, but she bore the title of Augusta.

though she apologised for speaking at them.[1]   If there were
no Emperors the *Imperium* was all vested in her, and she
could nominate the successor to the throne.   Thus Pulcheria
nominated Marcian and Ariadne Anastasius ; thence the
successive husbands of Zoe derived their rights.   Her
sovereignty also was shown in the case of a Regency.   If
the Emperor were incapable of governing, through youth
or illness, and there were no other Emperors, the Empress
exercised full sovereignty as a matter of course.   Pulcheria
ruled for her young brother, Sophia for her mad husband
Justin II till a Cæsar was appointed : [2] and throughout the
whole history of the Empire, the Empress-mother, if one
existed, was regent during part if not all of the minority
of each child-Emperor.   But what if there were no Emperor
and the Empress did not choose to nominate one ?   The
position was uncertain.   Irene, after she had deposed and
blinded her son, determined to reign alone.   It was something of an innovation, and in official documents it was
thought best to call her Irene the Emperor ; [3] but there
was no constitutional opposition to it : and she fell eventually owing to her ill-health rather than to her sex.   Her
cousin, Theophano, the wife of Stauracius, aimed at suc-
ceeding her husband, but failed.   However, in 1042, we
find two Empresses, Zoe and Theodora, jointly exercising
the sovereignty—the unique instance of the autocracy being
divided.   But when Zoe appointed an Emperor, the two
ladies automatically gave place to him.   However, after
his death Theodora returned to full power and could
nominate a successor on her death-bed.   It was never
considered that these female reigns were illegal.

But were the Empress-regnant or the Empress-regent

[1] Procopius, *De Bello Persico* (Loeb edition), I, 230.

[2] See Bury, *Later Roman Empire from Arcadius to Irene*, II, 76 *sqq.*

[3] *Irene Pistos Basileus*—Zachariae von Lingenthal, *Jus Graeco-Romanum*,
III, 55.

incompetent, a revolution would dispose of her. Irene fell when she could no longer control her ministers, the regent Zoë Carbopsina when her political policy ended in disaster. On an occasion such as the latter, when there was an emergency during a minority, an ingenious solution was evolved. Certain Emperors on their death-beds appointed regency-councils. Theophilus appointed two officials to act with Theodora, and Alexander seven regents under the chairmanship of the Patriarch.[1] But such councils were unsatisfactory. From the Tenth Century it became a frequent habit during a minority for a strong general or admiral to occupy the throne as Emperor-regent, enjoying full autocracy and precedence but preserving the rights of the legitimate Emperor. The Emperor-regent would usually half-legitimise himself by marriage with the Imperial family. Romanus Lecapenus, the first of them, married his daughter to the Emperor, an example followed by John Cantacuzenus. Nicephorus Phocas and Romanus Diogenes each married his predecessor's widow, with whose help each secured the throne. John Tzimisces would have done so too, but the Church protested—the lady was Theophano, his accomplice in the murder of Nicephorus Phocas—so he married the Emperor's aunt instead. These usurpations were accepted but considered temporary. When the Lecapeni and the Cantacuzeni attempted to found dynasties, the disapproval of the public ruined the projects. The legitimate Emperor, the Porphyrogennetus, born in the Purple Chamber where the accouchement of the Empress took place, was felt to have a right that must not be ignored. The constitutional powers of the electors to the Empire, the Senate, the Army and the People, did not entirely disappear at the election of the Emperor. The Army necessarily kept a large practical influence ; but both the Senate and the People inherited vague theoretical rights from the past,

[1] Theophanes Continuatus, 380.

that in the earlier centuries of the Empire found a definite expression.

The People of Constantinople had been organised, at some date unknown to us, into four divisions or *demes*,[1] called Blue, Green, White and Red ; and gradually the latter two were merged in the former. These can best be described as self-governing municipal bodies, further divided into civil and military bodies, the former called Politicals governed by a Demarch, the latter Peratics governed by a Democrat. The Politicals probably saw to such civic duties as keeping up the public gardens or taking precautions against fires ; the Peratics were certainly expected to act as a territorial garrison to the City. The Circus of Constantinople fell at some time into the hands of the Demes, and all the Circus events resolved into competitions between partisans of the Blues and of the Greens, both of whom acquired enormous circus organisations, while all the population of the Circus-loving City took one side or the other. The Demes, as the bodies through which the City expressed itself, became extremely powerful towards the close of the Fifth Century, and during the Sixth Century frequently threatened the State. Fortunately the Blues and the Greens were jealous of each other, and would adopt competing views ; the Greens for example favoured Monophysitism in opposition to the Orthodoxy of the Blues. It was possible therefore for the Emperor, anxious to suppress bodies over which he had no control, to play off one against the other. But occasionally they would combine. Together with the army, they insisted on Justin I having the throne. In 532 Justinian's heavy taxation and city-rates united them against him in the Nika Riots. Justin II, in the

---

[1] For the demes, see Bury, *Appendix* 10 *to Gibbon, Decline and Fall,* vol. 4, 531 *sqq.*, idem, *Later Roman Empire,* 1, 84 *sqq.*, 11, 11 *sqq.* ; and especially Uspenski, *Circus Factions and Demes in Constantinople* (in Russian), *V.V.*, vol. 1, 1 *sqq.*

hands of the aristocracy, attempted to keep them down, but Tiberius found it wiser to encourage them and play them off against the aristocrats. Maurice fell largely because he offended them through attempting to impose further military duties on the Peratics. Their constitutional position is shown by the way that Justinian has officially to parley with them and listen to their opinions in the Hippodrome. During the Seventh Century the power of the Demes faded, and after the accession of the Isaurians the Politicals became purely nominal organisations, used to represent the People on ceremonial occasions. The Demarchs of the Blues and the Greens appeared as sinecured officials in the Court hierarchy. The Peratics, on the other hand, became the nucleus of the Palace guards and City garrison from which the Imperial as opposed to the Provincial army was formed. With the decline of the Demes, the People of Constantinople lost their one constitutional means of expression. They could only show their wishes henceforward by riot and unrest.

The Senate, on the other hand, never utterly disappeared, though its heyday in Constantinople was in the Sixth and Seventh Centuries.[1] The Senate of Constantinople was never like the old Roman Senate. Even when in 359 it was given the privileges that the Roman Senate enjoyed —thus becoming an official elector—it remained different in its composition and devoid of the other's tradition. Its very name was less venerable ; in the Greek language it was translated not *gerousia* but *sugklêtos*, the assembly. The Senate of Constantinople consisted of all present and past holders of offices and rank above a certain level and their descendants. It was thus a vast amorphous body comprising everyone of prominence, of wealth and of a responsible position in the Empire.

[1] See Bury, *Later Roman Empire*, I, 12 *sqq.*, Buckler, *Anna Comnena*, 274–6 ; Diehl, *Le Sénat et le Peuple Byzantin*, in *Byzantion*, vol. I, 201 *sqq.*

The actual powers of the Senate were undefined.   Members of the senatorial classes enjoyed certain rights and advantages, stated by old Roman law and mostly confirmed by Justinian.   In an attempt to keep their ranks respectable, they had been forbidden to marry actresses, till Justinian, betrothed to the comedienne Theodora, made his uncle Justin I repeal the measure.   But actually the power of the Senate lay in the fact that it was a semi-constitutional body expressing the views of the wealthier and more powerful elements in the State.   As such, when the Emperor was weak, it seemed the most serious authority in the Empire. During the late Sixth and the Seventh Centuries it was particularly prominent.   Justin II was a tool in its hands. Heraclius, who won the throne as its candidate, treated it with great deference.   When he went to the Persian Wars he left his ten-years-old son as regent under the tutelage of the Patriarch and a Senator, who, it is true, was also *magister officiorum* : [1] while in 614 an Imperial embassy to Persia was sent in the Senate's name in the belief that that carried more weight than the Emperor's.[2]   A few years later Constans thanked the Senate formally for its help against the Empress Martina and asked for its co-operation in future.[3]   But at the close of the Seventh Century it declined.   The tyranny of Justinian II was largely directed against it : and though Leo the Isaurian's triumph represented the triumph of the aristocracy, Leo himself as Emperor would brook no interference from the Senate.   Its powers fell into desuetude, till at last they were abolished by Leo VI, who in doing so was only legalising the existing state of affairs.[4]   It itself lingered on as a body whom the Emperor could call as a respectable witness to his actions.   Thus Theodora when she abdicated the Regency in 856 summoned the Senate to see how full she

---

[1] Theophanes, 303.   [2] *Chronicon Paschale*, 706 *sqq.*
[3] Theophanes, 342.   [4] Leo VI, *Novella no.* 47.

had left the Treasury, and Basil I when he assumed the
government eleven years later, opened the Treasury again
in its presence to show its emptiness.[1] To the very end of
the Empire the Senate was present on practically every
important occasion in Constantinople, such as the interview
of Romanus I with Symeon of Bulgaria.[2] Alexius I consulted
it at times on matters of policy ; [3] and its formal consent
was demanded at the coronation ceremony : while ' to join
the Senatorial ranks ' was the usual phrase to describe a
young nobleman coming of age.[4] But its political importance never re-arose. The new aristocracy of the Eleventh
Century was more a military aristocracy and preferred to
act through the army.

There was however one check on the Emperor's constitutional authority far more powerful and more lasting than
either the Senate or the Demes. This was the Law.[5] The
Emperor was the source of all Law, yet, paradoxically, the
Law remained something above him. Because no human
authority could call him to account Justinian was urged
by Agapetus to be the more careful to observe the laws.[6]
Leo the Isaurian declared that it was the Emperor's duty
to maintain the things laid down in the Scriptures, the acts
of the Church Synods, and Roman Law ; [7] and Basil I
acknowledged the sovereignty of Law in even stronger
words.[8]

With the law occupying so reverend a position it was
essential that it should be carefully and clearly codified.
An era of codification had begun with Diocletian. About

---

[1] Theophanes Continuatus, 171, 255.   [2] Ibid., 407.
[3] Anna Comnena, *Alexiad*, trans. Dawes, 363.   [4] Ibid., 83.
[5] See Zachariae von Lingenthal, *Geschichte des Griechisch-Römischen
Rechts* ; Siciliano Villanueva, *Diritto Bizantino* ; Cambridge Medieval
History, vol. 4, chapter xxii.
[6] Agapetus, Pope, *Epistolae*, M.P.G., vol. 66, 38–40.
[7] *Ecloga* in Leunclavius, *Juris Graeco-Romani*, 1, 83–4.
[8] *Basilica*, preamble.

the year 300 two lawyers, Gregory and Hermogenianus, made successive compilations of the legislation of the last century. A century later Theodosius II embarked on a scheme of a general codification of all Roman law ; but he never actually went further than to issue a series of Imperial constitutions, which however only covered a comparatively small ground. At last Justinian, irritated by the repetitions and contradictions, the obscurities and obsolescence of much of the existing law, determined to reorganise the whole body. Ably assisted by his Quæstor, the lawyer Tribonian, he appointed ten commissioners to draw up as quickly as possible a code embodying the existing legislation. This was issued in 529. Next, sixteen commissioners were appointed to compile from the two thousand works of the great jurists of the past every passage that was still relevant and useful for the present, and thus, too, to preserve for all time the opinions of the best authorities on the legal foundations on which the Roman State was built. This vast compilation, known as the Digest, was published in 533, and was to remain the ultimate authority on all legal questions. Meanwhile for students a manual was issued that same year, embodying the latest features of the Imperial legislation ; and in 534 a new and improved edition of Justinian's code was made. Even so, his legislating activity was not over. From 534 to the end of his reign he published a long series of supplementary laws, his Novellæ. But by the end of his reign Roman law had been completely revised and brought up to date.

The law that Justinian promulgated was still Roman law. Even his amendments were Roman rather than Christian in spirit. Despite the enmity of the Church, divorce and slavery both were retained. Justinian considered himself to be guided by ' humanity, common-sense and public utility ' ; and the ' humanity ' was essentially practical. Justinian abolished the *noxae deditio*, by which children could be sold as slaves by their parents in compensation to anyone whom they had wronged, because ' according to the just opinion of modern society harshness of this kind must be rejected.' Women's rights, which Justinian particularly advanced, such as the rights of a wife to property equal to her dowry and of a widow to the guardianship of her children, which were improvements on the old Roman system, were made more in the spirit of the Empress Theodora than in that of Saint Paul. It is a remarkable tribute to the sacrosanctity of Roman law amongst the Byzantines that, fanatically pious as they were, it was long before they allowed it to be seriously affected by the wishes of the Christian Church.

Justinian further strengthened his legal work by reforming the law-schools. Many of the schools were closed. It was felt that only by concentrating the teaching of law at the Universities of Constantinople, Berytus and Alexandria, could the authorities be certain of maintaining the standard of the law-degree. A few decades later the Arab conquests resulted in legal knowledge in the Empire being practically restricted to the Capital.

Justinian had intended his juridical reforms to be so thorough that no further commentaries were to be necessary. His embargo on them was not however carried out, and several legal works seem to have been written during the next century. But his civil code remained in force till the reign of Leo the Isaurian. Leo the Isaurian was a pious man. In the sphere of theology his piety led him into the Iconoclastic heresy ; in the sphere of law it led him to humanise the whole code. During the troubled Seventh Century the study of law had lapsed, and there was room for a new code. In 739 Leo issued his *Ecloga*, designed, he said, to introduce Christian principles into the law.

In criminal law the Christianity was displayed by a general restriction of the death-penalty, and the substitution of mutilation in its place.[1] In civil law it was displayed in particular by its marriage laws. Christian marriages alone were recognised ; the grounds for divorce were reduced to four,[2] though not utterly abolished as the Church desired, and the prohibited degrees of relationship were raised from four to six : second cousins were forbidden to marry. The *Ecloga* also improved still further the status of women ; the wife had an equal share with her husband in their joint property and the guardianship of their children : while the children were further emancipated from the *Patria Potestas*. The Church won the control of the guardianship of orphans.

About the same time three unofficial handbooks appeared, covering supplementary branches of the law : the *Military Code*, the *Nautical or Rhodian Code* and the *Farmer's Code*, each illustrating the customs and requirements of the time.

The next great period of legislative activity followed the accession of Basil the Macedonian. Basil, to undo any work done by the hated Isaurians and at the same time to weaken the Church, prepared to revert back to Justinianean law. Early in his reign he published a handbook, the *Procheiros Nomos*, to replace the *Ecloga* till his commissioners prepared a full new code ; and a little later he had compiled a revised handbook, the *Epanagoge*, which however was never completed nor issued. It was left to his son Leo VI to issue the whole amended law in the *Basilica*, which remained henceforward the authoritative work on Imperial Law : though Leo supplemented it with several *Novellae*.

The Macedonian legislation was consciously a return to Justinian. But actually much of the Isaurian work remained. The criminal code developed further the com-

[1] See below, p. 219.
[2] The wife's adultery, the husband's impotence, attempted murder by one spouse of the other, and leprosy. *Ecloga*, trans. Freshfield, 78–9.

parative mildness. In civil law, though the rights of the husband and father were partially revived, in practice the family arrangements of the *Ecloga* were retained. Basil was less accommodating towards the Church. Orphans were taken from its care, and its bugbear, divorce, was made easier.

After the *Basilica* no new code was issued. The task of lawyers was helped only by a series of epitomes, beginning with the full and interesting *Ecloga Legum* published in 920 and culminating in the muddled, ill-compiled *Hexabiblion* of Harmenopulus, published in about 1345. The legislative activities of the Emperors consisted of isolated measures, mostly directed against the great landowners or in favour of or against the Church. The Church at last was beginning to make herself felt in law. In Leo VI's own reign she defeated him on the question of repeated remarriage.[1] Constantine VII allowed her one-third of the property of childless intestates. Nicephorus II's attempts to restrict legacies to her failed. Under the Comneni she won the right to hear more cases in her courts, and the tendency towards widening ecclesiastical jurisdiction grew. In consequence canon law became increasingly studied. There had already appeared the *Syntagma*, a compilation of canon law ascribed to Photius, but the great work on the subject was the *Exegesis Canonum* of Balsamon, Patriarch of Antioch under Manuel I, published about 1175. This work, like the *Basilica*, remained—and still remains—authoritative in the East ; and it too was followed by a series of epitomes, none of any great importance except the *Syntagma Canonum* of the monk Matthew Blastares, written in 1335.[2]

A knowledge of law was considered essential for every Imperial official. But the facilities for acquiring it did not

---

[1] The *Tomus Unionis* of 921 forbade fourth marriages and censured Leo's. Theophanes Continuatus, 398.

[2] See Leunclavius, *Juris Graeco-Romani*, 1, 1 *sqq.*

always exist. How long the law-schools encouraged by
Justinian remained open we do not know, nor how much
law was taught at the University founded by Bardas in the
Ninth Century we cannot tell. In the Eleventh Century,
when Byzantine learning was at its height, the Emperor
Constantine Monomachus found legal knowledge so poor,
that he started in 1045 a special school for law, which
provided an excellent education and probably lasted till
1204.[1] The facilities for studying law under the Palæologi
are unknown to us.

Roman Byzantine law was a changing thing ; and its
fundamental conceptions and its later amendments were
alike often unknown or misunderstood by the citizens of
the Empire. But it remained nevertheless an essential part
of the Imperial constitution, the one authority to which the
Emperor himself must bow. The law-courts even took
precedence of the Imperial Court. The Senator who dined
with the Emperor Justin II instead of answering a case in
the courts was flogged for his contumacy.[2] In the Fourteenth Century the young Andronicus, summoned as a
rebel before his grandfather the old Emperor, won the
sympathy of all the onlookers by appealing to be judged
by that which lay beyond the Emperor, by the Law.[3]

The Imperial Constitution, the Emperor, elected by the
Senate, the Army and the People of Constantinople, to be
the Viceroy of God but to rule according to Roman Law,
was in many ways illogical and incomplete, but it had the
supreme and essential merit that it worked. Its efficiency
is remarkably illustrated by the fact that while in the
West innumerable writers arose to discuss the difficult
problems of Church and State, of Emperors and Kings
and Popes and their inter-relations, for centuries Byzantium
did not produce a single political theorist. The constitution

[1] See below, p. 227.   [2] Cedrenus, 1, 682.
                [3] Cantacuzenus, 1, 69.

worked too well for abstract discussions to be needed. It was only in the last years of the Empire, when it was clearly dying, that theorists arose with schemes to put the world right : that the Zealots of Thessalonica planned a city-state that would, it seems, combine the theocratic ideals of Mount Athos with the mercantile practices of the Italian republics, and that Gemistus Plethon dreamed to build in the Peloponnese a commonwealth guided by Platonism and the glories of Ancient Greece.

CHAPTER IV

The Administration[1]

The Emperor's time was fully taken up with his duties. Almost daily there was some ceremony for him to attend, a feast of the Church, the reception of some ambassador, the investiture of some minister, a visit in state to the Hippodrome. In between them he had to interview his secretaries and officials and preside over his councils. Usually too he would lead his army himself; Constantine V and Nicephorus II, for instance, would every summer campaign on one of the frontiers. The Emperors who did not try to be soldiers were very few indeed. Thus the Emperor had little time for his personal pleasures. If, like Michael III, he sought to enjoy himself, he soon lost control over the administration and fell. Leo VI and his son Constantine VII, neither of them soldiers, managed to write several books while on the throne; but we cannot tell how much of the labour was done by secretaries. It was difficult for the Emperor to leave Constantinople. Cecaumenus, who in the Eleventh Century wrote a treatise of advice to an Emperor, recommended that he should travel and inspect his dominions.[2] But he really had not the time; and Constantinople so controlled the whole Empire that it was unwise to leave it except at the head

[1] See Bury, *Later Roman Empire*, II, 334–48 ; idem, *Imperial Administrative System in the Ninth Century* (*British Academy* supplemental Papers, I)—the most important work on the subject.

[2] Cecaumenus, ed. Vasilievski, *Noutheteticos*, 101.

of an army. Cecaumenus remarks elsewhere that the
Emperor who holds Constantinople always wins the Civil
War.[1]

For practical purposes the Emperor was assisted in his
main decisions by a small council, a sort of unofficial
sub-committee of the Senate. Occasionally we see it in
operation, as in that famous meeting during the Nika
Riots when Theodora's speech saved the throne for Justinian,[2] or when in 812 Michael Rhangabe discussed
whether he should declare war on Bulgaria because of the
Bulgar attack on Mesembria. At this council the spokesmen
all seem to have been ecclesiastics, the Patriarch, the
Metropolitans of Nicæa and Cyzicus and the Abbot of
Studium.[3]

The Emperor was at the head of everything. Behind
him came all the dignitaries and officials of the Empire,
ranged strictly according to their rank. In the Empire,
as in England to-day, there were titles—they were not,
however, hereditary—that gave the wearer precedence, but
no duties ; while most great offices of State bore with them
a certain rank. Some of these honours, however, could be
openly bought, and then commanded a certain salary,
being in fact a form of Government security. The dignities
and offices varied during the centuries of the Empire's
existence ; and we have only three full accounts of them,
one of the Fifth Century (the *Notitia Dignitatum*), one of
the early Tenth (the *Cleterologium* of Philotheus) and one of
the Fourteenth (the *De Officiis*, wrongly ascribed to Codinus).
From these and from less precise references in other sources
it is possible to evolve a rough idea of the Imperial administration, though we cannot trace in detail the various changes
and developments. The tendency throughout was for

---

[1] Cecaumenus, ed. Vasilievski, *Strategicon*, 74.
[2] Procopius, *loc. cit.*
[3] Theophanes, 498 ; Theophanes Continuatus, 13.

official posts to become honorary with the bureaucratising
of the administration : while the titles, thus increased in
number, gradually sank in the scale of precedence and new
titles would be created at the top.

The members of the Imperial Family occupied no office
as such. Their power was restricted by their unofficial
influence—an influence of whose dangers Cecaumenus
warned his Emperor.[1] They were seldom employed in the
administration except as soldiers ; but they were usually
given high titles. The heir-apparent was almost invariably
crowned Emperor in his predecessor's lifetime, but originally
Diocletian had intended him to bear the title of Cæsar.
Gradually, however, this title had grown less definite. The
Cæsar was crowned, but his crown had no cross on it, and
he ranked below the Patriarch.[2] The rank was therefore
a suitable one for a high prince of the blood, a regent or
even an heir-presumptive. Tiberius, when regent for the
mad Justin II, bore the title of Cæsar,[3] Heraclius and Constantine V appointed their second and third sons Cæsars,
probably with a view to their peaceable succession should
their delicate elder brother die,[4] and Theophilus to his son-
in-law Alexius Musele ; he had no son at the time and
clearly intended Alexius to be his heir. But Alexius's wife
Maria died and he retired to a monastery ; so Theophilus
crowned his next daughter Thecla Empress, that her
future husband might succeed. However, eventually his
son Michael was born.[5] Michael made his uncle Bardas,
the virtual regent, Cæsar ; Romanus Lecapenus assumed
the rank as a step to the throne, Nicephorus Phocas gave
it to his old father.[6] Under Alexius I it descended a place ;

[1] Cecaumenus, *Noutheteticos*, 98–9.
[2] Philotheus, in Bury, *Imperial Administrative System*, 145.
[3] Bury, *op. cit.*, 36.   [4] *Ibid.*, *loc. cit.*
[5] See Bury, *Eastern Roman Empire*, 465–8.
[6] Genesius, 97 ; Theophanes Continuatus, 397 ; Leo Diaconus, 49.

the new title of Sebastocrator took precedence. Under the Palæologi the highest princely title was Despot,[1] which however usually had a territorial significance. Cæsar was reduced to the third rank. The other titles reserved to Imperial relatives till the days of the Comneni were Nobilissimus and Curopalates. The latter, however, was given as an hereditary title to the King of Iberia by Leo VI and was thrown open to non-royal holders in the Eleventh Century.[2] Alexius I invented new titles, ranking below the Cæsar, the Sebastus, the Protosebastus and the Panhypersebastus : [3] while ambitious fathers-in-law of the Emperor could havè the title of Basileopator.[4] The bearers of these titles and their wives were permitted to dine at the Imperial table, as was also the Zoste Patricia, the chief Lady-in-Waiting, who was usually, it seems, a member of the Family.[5] The surname Porphyrogennetus, given to the children of the Empress, whose confinement always took place in the Purple Chamber of the Palace, apparently carried no official rank, though its prestige was enormous.

The highest title [6] open for all was for many centuries that of Patrician, founded as a very restricted order by Constantine the Great. Gradually the numbers of Patricians increased ; certain of them were given precedence as Anthypati Patricians, and by the Tenth Century there was a higher title, the Magister. But the Magistri too grew more numerous, and Nicephorus II invented the title of Proedrus over them.[7] Beneath the Patricians there were in the Tenth Century eleven other titles. By the time of the Palæologi these have mostly disappeared. The numerous titles then in use were former names of offices. Of almost

---

[1] Codinus, De Officiis, 6.

[2] Bury, Imperial Administrative System, 33–5.

[3] Anna Comnena, 78–9.   [4] Theophanes Continuatus, 357, 394.

[5] Under Theophilus, it was the Empress's mother. Ibid., 90.

[6] For titles, see Bury, op. cit., 20–36, 121–4.

[7] See Diehl, Le Titre de Proèdre in Mélanges Schlumberger, I, 105 sqq.

all of them we are told that they used to have functions but now have none.[1] Eunuchs had special titles reserved for them. Where the name of the title was the same, the eunuch took precedence. Thus the eunuch Patrician ranked above the ordinary Patrician.[2] In the Tenth Century there were eight titles for eunuchs. All titles had their special insignia ; the Spatharius, for example, had a gold-handled sword, the Patrician an ivory inscribed tablet, the Magister a white tunic embroidered with gold.[3]

The order of precedence was complicated in that offices as well as titles carried rank. In the Fourth Century the Empire had been divided into four vast Prefectures, ruled by the Prætorian Prefects. They were the highest members of the Government ; they enjoyed viceregal powers, with complete administrative, financial, and judicial authorities. They could even legislate on minor matters. Provincial governors were appointed and dismissed by them, subject to the Emperor's approval, and the administration of the dioceses and provinces into which the Prefectures were sub-divided was under their control, though the Proconsuls of the provinces of Africa and Asia were supervised by the Emperor and he might communicate directly to the vicars or governors of the Dioceses. They had, however, no control over the army, though military officers had to bend the knee on their entrance.[4] The capitals, Rome and Constantinople, were each under a Prefect of the City, a definitely civilian post, next in rank to the Prætorian Pre-fects, responsible for the policing and order of the City and the free doles of bread. At the Court itself, round the Emperor's person, there was the supreme legal minister, the Quæstor of the Sacred Palace, the two chief financial ministers, the Count of the Sacred Largesse who admin-istered the public revenues and expenditure and the Count

---

[1] Codinus, *De Officiis*, 35 and *passim*.   [2] Philotheus, 146.
[3] Bury, *loc. cit.*   [4] Idem, *Later Roman Empire*, I, 25 *sqq.*

of the Private Estates, who, as his name suggests, saw to
the vast personal properties of the Emperor. But the chief
minister at the Court was the *Magister Officii*, the head of
the whole civil service, director of the State Post, controller
of the Secret Service, master of the Imperial ceremonies,
and, as the minister responsible for the reception of ambassadors, Foreign Secretary of the Empire. The Emperor
had also attached to him a number of secretaries, the
Magistri Scriniorum, ministers of State, whom the *Magister
Officii* supplied with clerks from his various bureaux.
Eunuchs seem as yet only to have been employed in waiting
on the Emperor. The whole civil service in Illyricum and the
East (that is, the Empire ruled from Constantinople) has
been estimated as numbering 10,000 in the Fifth Century.
The army was organised separately under the *Magistri
Militum*. There were five for the Eastern Empire under
Theodosius I.

This early system of administration did not last for very
long. Barbarian invasions during the Fifth Century restricted the size of the Empire, while the distribution of
wealth amongst the provinces altered. Justinian attempted
to reorganise the machinery. The government had become
very corrupt. During the Fifth Century the system known
as the *Suffragia* was employed in the provinces : the provincial governor bought his post with sums that went partly
to the Emperor and partly to the Prætorian Prefect ; he
then recouped himself over-amply out of the local taxes.
Justinian, urged on by Theodora, abolished the sale of
offices and gave the governor a salary on which he was
obliged to live. The law forcing him to remain in his
province fifty days after leaving office to answer charges
was revived, and an official, the *Defensor Civitatis*, was
elected locally, as a check on him and to try petty law-
cases. The provinces were re-divided in 536–7. A curious
system united rich provinces with poor, in order that the

former might pay for the latter. Thus Caria, the Cyclades and Cyprus were combined as a unit with the much-ravaged districts of Lower Moesia and Scythia. Justinian did not introduce uniformity. The governors of Pontica (because of the robbers there) and Cappadocia (because of the vast Imperial domains there) were given special disciplinary powers. On the other hand local law, such as the Armenians', was discouraged—partly perhaps because according to Armenian Law the eldest son inherited all his father's property, whereas the Emperor liked to break up large estates. Justinian followed Diocletian's precept of tying people to their fathers' professions, particularly to the land.[1] He even appointed a special official, the Quæsitor or Quæstor, who saw that no provincials entered Constantinople except on business and that the idle in the City were made to work in the State bakeries or factories.[2] More spectacular but less important was Justinian's abolition of the Consulate. Since the early days of the Empire two consuls had been appointed yearly, in a nominal continuance of the old republican system ; but the dignity was honorary, and extremely expensive. The year was still called by the names of the consuls. All that they had to do was to distribute largesse and pay for games and spectacles. It cost a Consul nearly £90,000 for his year of office ; and almost invariably the Imperial Treasury had to pay as no private person could afford it. Justinian tried to make the alms-giving voluntary, but no one was brave enough not to be generous ; so after 542 he appointed no more consuls.[3] For some decades years were dated from the last consulship ; but Justinian introduced a new system of dating by the Emperor's regnal year—a system probably copied from the Vandals—and by the year of the Indiction, the cycle of fifteen years started by Diocletian

---

[1] Bury, *op. cit.*, II, 350. [2] *Ibid.*, II, 337.
[3] *Ibid.*, II, 346 *sqq.*

for the purpose of tax assessment. The Indictional dating was henceforward employed throughout the Empire's history : but later the *Annus Mundi* (the world was created in 5508 B.C.) was given along with or instead of the Emperor's regnal year.[1]

The troubles that the Empire suffered in the late Sixth and the Seventh Centuries necessitated a new organisation. Justinian had already toyed with the idea of militarising the provincial governors. On his reconquest of Africa he appointed a man to combine the posts of Magister Militum and prefect there. Italy he put under a viceroy known as the Exarch, who soon became a military official with civil powers. But such appointments were only made for provinces in danger of wars and invasions. The Persian and Arab wars of the Seventh Century showed that no province was out of danger ; even Asia Minor, the heart of the Empire, had to be put in a perpetual state of defence. It became customary to quarter certain regiments or *themata* permanently in certain districts ; and the general of the regiment would be given civil powers over the inhabitants of the district. Gradually the districts came to be known collectively as *themata* or themes, and each bore the name of its particular regiment.[2] Thus by the close of the Seventh Century there were large areas in Asia Minor known as the Bucellarian theme, the Anatolic theme, the Opsician theme, the Thracesian theme, and so on, after the regiments of the Bucellarii, the Anatolics, the Obsequii and the Thracesians. Leo the Isaurian perfected the system, subdividing the Asiatic themes and extending it to Europe. These later themes, not having a regimental

---

[1] Bury, *op. cit.*, II, 348.
[2] For the Theme system, see Gelzer, *Die Genesis der Byzantinischen Themenverfassung ;* Uspenski, *Sketch of Byzantine History* (in Russian), 144–52 ; Stein, *Studien zur Geschichte des Byzantinischen Reiches*, 117–40 ; Brooks, *Arabic Lists of the Byzantine Themes*, *J.H.S.*, vol. 21.

origin, were given geographical names : though occasionally
historical development caused the geography to err ; thus
the Macedonian theme was reduced by Bulgar invasions to
the district round Adrianople, while the themes in Macedonia itself, instituted a little later, were called the Thes-
salonican theme and the theme of Strymon ; and Calabria
was in the Tenth Century called the Sicilian theme, as it
had been part of it before the Arabs conquered Sicily.
When the conquests of the Ninth and Tenth Centuries
added fresh territory to the Empire, themes would be
created to suit the new requirements.

At the end of the Ninth Century, when we have Philotheus's description of the Imperial organisation and two
Arabic lists of the themes, there were twenty-five themes,
divided into two groups, the East and the West. The
former was composed of the Asian themes, including Thrace
and ' Macedonia,' but excluding the so-called Maritime
themes, the Cibyrrhæot and Samian themes on the Ægean
coast, the latter of the other European themes including
the maritime themes, Cherson (the Crimea), Dalmatia, and
' Sicily.' The generals or Strategi of the former group
were given a fixed salary from the Central Government
and ranked above those of the latter group, who drew
their salaries from the local taxes. The Strategus of
Cherson was in a class of his own.[1] The chief of them was
the Strategus of the Anatolic theme, whose office descended
from that of the Magister Militum of the East. He always
enjoyed special precedence, and during the Eighth and
early Ninth Centuries his was the chief military post. The
themes were subdivided into two or three *Tourmai*, and
these turms into three *Moirai* or *Drouggoi*. The Strategus
had eleven classes of officials in his bureaux, to help him
with the civil as well as the military government. His

---

[1] He was lowest in rank (Philotheus, 147) ; see Constantine Porphyrogennetus, *De Administrando Imperio*, 178–9, 244 *sqq.*

powers in local affairs were almost unlimited, but he was appointed and degraded at the Emperor's pleasure, it was possible to lodge complaints against him, while the Chartularius in his bureau, who paid all the soldiers and officials, and the thematic tax-gatherers took orders directly from the central government. Moreover, legal cases of any importance were heard at the Capital. Additional Strategi, called *ek prosôpôn*, could be sent anywhere during an emergency.[1]

Though the provinces were ruled militaristically, the central government remained civil. The central military officers, the Domestics and the Stratarchs, took no share in the administration. This was controlled by two great classes of officials, the Kritai and the Secretikoi.[2] The Magister Officii had vanished : only the empty title of Magister bore witness to his former greatness. The most important of the Kritai was the Prefect of the City, the Eparchos.[3] This office was as old as Constantinople itself, and always enjoyed a high precedence. It was one of the few offices that a eunuch could not hold. The Prefect was supreme in the City after the Emperor, and was usually named as regent of the City during the Emperor's absence. He was responsible for law and order. His bureau had two divisions, that of the Symponus, who controlled the guilds and supervised the various mercantile regulations and the civic duties of the inhabitants, and that of the Logothete of the Prætorium, who was at the head of the administration of justice and of the prisons. Both were supplied with an ample and varied body of officials. The Prefect was aided by the Quæstor,[4] who blended the old post of the Quæstor with that of Justinian's Quæstor. He was partly legislative, drafting new laws, partly the head of a court of appeal against magistrates and the nobility,

---

[1] Bury, *Imperial Administrative System*, 39–47.
[2] *Ibid.*, 69–105.   [3] *Ibid.*, 69–70.   [4] *Ibid.*, 73–5.

partly the Public Trustee, sealing, opening and seeing to
the execution of wills, and supervising the administration
of the property of minors. As such, cases of forgery came
within his jurisdiction. He also found work for the able-
bodied unemployed, and saw that no one visited the
Capital without a reason. Under him was a large body
of subordinate officials. The third great Kritês, the official
known as the official *epi tôn deêseôn*, dealt with petitions to
the Emperor. He had a bureau but no court.[1]

The Secretikoi were mainly financial ministers.[2] The
two main divisions of the public and private purse had
been supplemented. In the Sixth Century there had been
seven Treasuries, the fisc, that is, the old Sacred Largesse
or Public Purse, the chests of the two Prætorian Prefects
and the Quæstor of Moesia and Syria, and three chests for
the Privy Purse. During the next centuries further ramifica-
tions took place, and the finances were controlled from a
number of bureaux, placed under the supreme control of
the Sacellarius, whose office had been that of the Count
of the Private Estates and probably was raised by Leo the
Isaurian. Under him were the four Logothetes, *tôn Dromôn,
tôn genikôn* (the central tax-collector), *tôn stratiôtikôn* (pay-
master of the troops) and *tôn agelôn* (manager of the
Imperial estates), and the various provincial tax-collectors
(*epoptai*), the officials in charge of the State factories (the
epi tôn eidikôn), of the mines (Count of the Lamia), the
aqueducts (Count of the Water), the customs officers (the
Commerciarii) and all the Curatorii who administered the
privy purse and the State charities, and the Imperial
Secretaries, the Protoasecretis. Most important of these
offices was that of the Logothete of the Dromus, who was
Postmaster-General, head of the Foreign Office, and controlled the communications between other ministers and
the Emperor, whom he saw daily. He was sometimes

[1] Bury, *Imperial Administrative System*, 77-8.   [2] *Ibid.*, 78-105.

called simply the Logothete ; and in the late Eleventh and the Twelfth Centuries under the name of Grand Logothete he was principal Secretary of State. Under the Comneni the Sacellarius was replaced by the Grand Logariastes.

Offices about the persons of the Emperor and Empress and about the Palaces were reserved for eunuchs : [1] a custom that had begun in Diocletian's day and had developed since. Each Palace was under its Papias, the Papias of the Great Palace being assisted by a Deuteras who saw to the ceremonial robes and furniture of the Court. We are never actually told the numbers and duties of lesser members of the Household. The Emperor and Empress each had their Controllers of the Table and of the Wardrobe. But the chief of the eunuchs was the High Chamberlain, the Paracoemomenus, who in the late Ninth and the Tenth Centuries was the chief minister of the Empire. Samonas under Leo VI, Theophanes under Romanus I and Basil for almost all the latter half of the Tenth Century, were practically Grand Viziers. The office was not always filled, and once it had been held not by a eunuch but by Basil the Macedonian, under Michael III.[2] The advantage of having eunuchs in high confidential positions was obvious. They had no descendants for whom to intrigue : and an unwritten but unbreakable law debarred them from the Imperial throne. The employment of eunuchs, characteristic in particular of the Empire at its zenith in the Tenth Century, was one of its most useful weapons against feudal devolution.

There were certain offices, called *Axiai eidikai*, that could not be classified. Most important of these were the Rector, of whose duties we cannot tell, and the Syncellus, an Imperial official who acted as liaison-officer between the Emperor and the Patriarch, apparently inquired into cases

---

[1] Bury, *Imperial Administrative System*, 120 sqq.   [2] *Ibid*, 115–16.

of suspected heresy [1] (heresy was a crime against the State), and usually succeeded to the Patriarchate. Rome and the Eastern Patriarchs might have their Syncellus too, and Constantine IX appointed one for the Armenian Catholicus —his nephew and successor-designate.[2] The other bearers of the *axiai eidikai* were aides-de-camp and personal secretaries of the Emperor. One of them, the Protostrator, rose to a high position later.

This central administrative system lasted practically unaltered till it was rudely ended by the Crusaders' capture of the City in 1204. The provincial system was necessarily more elastic, changing with the changing boundaries of the Empire. On the Eastern frontier there were several small districts under martial law called Clissuræ, where the great military border barons, like Digenis Akritas, ruled almost unchecked. As the frontier was pushed back, these Clissuræ rose to be themes, and their Strategi had to be fitted into the Imperial hierarchy.[3] When Antioch was recaptured it was placed under a special military governor known as the Dux or Duke. Difficult provinces like the Longobard Theme would be reorganised. About the year 975 the Strategus of Longobardia was raised to the new office of Catepan and given viceregal powers over the Calabrian theme and the Italian vassal-states.[4] The same title was given a few years later to the governor of the newly conquered Armenian theme of Vaspurakan.[5] When Basil II conquered Bulgaria, he founded two themes there, Bulgaria and Paristrion, the first being under a Pronoëtes. But, in accordance with the precepts quoted by Constantine

---

[1] *Vita S. Symeonis Novi Theologi*, ed. Hausherr, *Orientalia Christiana*, vol. 12, 101 *sqq.*

[2] Philotheus, 146 ; Matthew of Edessa, ed. Dulaurier, 79 *sqq.* ; Bury, *op. cit.*, 116–17.

[3] See below, p. 141.

[4] See Gay, *l'Italie Méridionale*, 343 *sqq.*

[5] Cedrenus II, 494. The province was usually called Media.

Porphyrogennetus, the Bulgarians were allowed to keep their national methods of justice and taxation.[1] In the Greek peninsula the presence of Slavs and Albanians made the government of the themes of Hellas and the Peloponnese particularly full of problems. It was only under Irene that the Peloponnese was at last effectively controlled, and even in the Tenth Century there were tribes there that only paid an annual tribute and suffered no further interference from Imperial officials. When the tribute was raised under Romanus I, they revolted, and the old scale had to be restored. It is doubtful when they were finally absorbed.[2]

The conquests of the Seljuks restricted the area of the Empire, and under the Comneni the themes had to be rearranged. The remodelled themes were smaller, and their governors now were called Dukes. It is possible that their powers were somewhat restricted.

The fall of Constantinople in 1204 wrecked the whole machinery of government. Of the administrative system of the Nicæan Emperors we have very little information. They attempted to establish in Nicæa a central bureaucracy copied from that of Constantinople ; but they were poor and economical, so it was all carried out on a humbler scale. The question of provincial government did not at first arise ; each provincial centre had become a political capital. When the Nicæan Empire extended to Europe, the conquered territories seem to have been held as under a military occupation. The return to Constantinople meant a certain return to grandeur. The *De Officiis* gives a list of all the functionaries with their duties and insignia in the middle of the Fourteenth Century. But probably it was an ideal picture ; the Treasury of the Palæologi grew emptier and emptier, and actually, it seems, many of their offices were

[1] See Schlumberger, *Epopée Byzantine*, II, 418–43.
[2] See Runciman, *Romanus Lecapenus*, 72–4.

left unfilled. Many too of the older offices were now empty
titles ; the Prefect, the Quæstor and many of the logothetes
are quoted amongst others as having no duties. A few
unfamiliar names of offices appear ; these, such as that of
the Grand Tzausius, seem mainly to be posts about the
Emperor's person. The administration, such as it was,
was conducted by the Grand Logothete, assisted by the
minister for the army, the Grand Domestic, and the minister
for the navy, the Grand Duke.[1] In practice it seems that
the Patriarch played the part of a minister. Under
Andronicus II the Patriarch Anastasius regarded economics
as his business and even attempted to revive for himself
the duties of the Prefect of the City.[2]

The Empire of the Palæologi really only contained territory that could be governed from Constantinople and
Thessalonica, with the addition of the Morea or Peloponnese. The name Theme lingered on for the district round
Thessalonica, but from the middle of the Fourteenth Century
both Thessalonica and the Morea were put under Despots,
younger members of the Imperial family. These Despots
seem to have had absolute powers in their provinces but
to have taken an oath of allegiance to the Emperor, by
whose diplomatic agents they were represented abroad.
Finally a Despot of Thessalonica handed over his province
to Venice ; but the Despotate of the Morea, despite the
perpetual turbulence of the local nobility, who had learnt
bad habits of feudalism from the Franks, outlasted the
Empire itself ; and the Despot's residence, Mistra, possessed to the end the intellectual amenities of a capital.[3]

The vast bureaucracy by which the Empire was administered was naturally very costly ; and the additional charge

---

[1] Codinus, *De Officiis*, 23, 38.
[2] Bratianu, *L'Approvisionnement de Constantinople* in *Byzantion*, vol. 6,
642 *sqq.*
[3] See Zakythinos, *Le Despotat Grec de Morée*, *passim.*

of a standing army and diplomatic expenses made a large
revenue essential. We have, however, no means of assess-
ing the amount of the Imperial revenue at any period of
the Empire's history. It has been estimated at such various sums as 105–120 million gold francs under Justinian
and 640,000,000 gold francs in the Tenth Century.[1] The
former figure is certainly far too small. Benjamin of
Tudela says that Manuel Comnenus drew a yearly income
of 106,000,000 gold francs from Constantinople alone.[2]
This was undoubtedly an exaggeration, and most Western
contemporaries were even wilder in their statements. We
can only tell that the income was enough for Anastasius,
who was a thrifty financier, to accumulate a reserve of
355,600,000 gold francs for the Treasury during a reign
of twenty-seven years, for the Empress Regent Theodora
to leave 140,000,000 francs in the Treasury, and Basil II,
after a costly reign though he kept Court expenses low,
250,000,000 francs.[3] The whole question of how the
revenue was made up and the details of the expenditure
are equally wrapped in mystery and controversy. Byzantine historians contain many oblique references to it, but
nothing that enables any definite calculation.[4] Direct
taxation came under two headings, taxes on land and taxes
on persons. The fundamental land-tax, the *zeugaratikion*,
was based according to the value of the land as it was
assessed every fifteen years, the first year of each indiction.
All property, even the Imperial estates, were liable, though

---

[1] The former estimate is Stein's, the latter Paparrhigopoulos's ; see
discussion in Andreades, *Le Montant du Budget*.

[2] Benjamin of Tudela, trans. Adler, 13.

[3] See Andreades, *op. cit.*

[4] For the fullest discussions, see Dölger, *Beitrage zur Geschichte der
Byzantinischen Finanzenverwaltung (Byz. Arch.,* 1927) ; Ostrogorsky, *Die
Ländliche Steuergemeinde* in *Vierteljahrsschrift fur Sozial- und Wirtschaftsges-
chichte,* vol. 20, 108 *sqq.* ; and Andreades's review of these two books
in *B.Z.,* vol. 28, 287 *sqq.*

under Irene and Manuel Comnenus monasteries were exempted. The details of the assessments were kept in the catasters or registers—there was a full register at the Central office and local ones at the provincial capitals. It is uncertain how much they were kept up to date ; Basil I is said to have tried in vain to have a new assessment made. This tax was originally paid in kind but later in cash. The difficulty of the Imperial Government was to see that the revenue did not fall if a landowner or tenant failed. For centuries the system called *epiboli* prevailed. The whole local community was responsible for seeing that the requisite amount was reached. But Nicephorus I, the one professional financier to become Emperor, reformed the system. The widespread distress in his time made the burden too great for the village community. Nicephorus introduced the *allelengyon* by which the taxes on a defaulting farm had to be paid by the nearest prosperous neighbour, a system that was unfair but effective. Michael the Amorian repealed it and reverted to the *epiboli* ; but Basil II, desirous of striking at the rich landowners, reintroduced it, though it again was revoked in the Eleventh Century. Large estates had always to pay an equal amount, even if certain portions were temporarily unfertile. If, however, the estates were divided up, the esoteric obligation ceased. There were additional taxes or rather levies on beasts, goods and implements, for military purposes, and obligations of billeting.

The question of the capitation tax is particularly obscure. There was a tax called the Kephaletion or head-tax, possibly restricted to non-Christian subjects.[1] The *Kapnikon* or hearth-tax is scarcely clearer to define. All we can say is that at the time of Nicephorus I there was a *kapnikon*, of 2 miliaressia (or 2·40 gold francs) per head ; Nicephorus insisted on its strict payment, and taxpayers exempted by

[1] See Andreades, *op. cit.*

Irene had to pay the arrears.   Michael II won popularity
by reducing it.[1]   According to the Arab Ibn Hauqal in
the Tenth Century there was a charge of 2 dinars for each
house in maritime themes and 10 dinars for every father
of a family in other themes, used for naval and military
expenses.[2]   A Cypriot text says that the Cypriots had to
pay for their defence in the Tenth Century by a hearth-
tax, apparently of 1 nomisma (14·40 francs) for the towns
and 3 nomismata for the country districts.[3]   Nicetas Acominatus, punning about the tax, says that at the close of the
Twelfth Century the Corfiotes preferred the fire of foreign
slavery (to the Normans) to the smoke of the tax.[4]   Of
the tax called the *aerikon* which Justinian introduced and
which brought in 3,000 lbs. of gold we know nothing, though
it is mentioned again in the *Tactica* of Leo VI.   Probably
it was some sort of land-tax on town property ; but every
Byzantinologist supplies a different explanation.[5]   There
was also a system of death-duties, introduced by Augustus,
for inheritance not from an ancestor, apparently repealed by
Justinian, but reintroduced later to include direct inheritance.   Nicephorus I, who enforced it strictly, also invented
a tax on unearned increment, by counting it as treasure-
trove, of which the State was entitled to a share.[6]   The
indirect taxation consisted of customs-duties, harbour-dues,
market-dues, tolls, and for a time receipt-stamps.   Of the
first alone we have reliable information ; they had been
raised in the Fourth Century to the uniform rate of $12\frac{1}{2}$

[1] Theophanes, 486 : Theophanes Continuatus, 54.

[2] Quoted in Vasilievsky, *Materials for a private History of Byzantium* (in
Russian), 369.

[3] Makhairas, ed. Dawkins, 8, notes, 48 ; Andreades, *Le Montant du
Budget, passim.*

[4] Nicetas Choniates, 97.

[5] Ostrogorsky, *loc. cit.* ; Andreades, in *B.Z.*, vol. 28, 309 ; Dölger,
Das Aerikon, B.Z., vol. 30, 450–6 ; Bury, *Later Roman Empire*, II, 350.

[6] Theophanes, *loc. cit.*

der cent., and apparently stayed there. Import duties
were levied at Abydos on the Hellespont or Hieron on the
Bosphorus, export duties at Constantinople. To prevent
smuggling in slaves, a special tariff of 2 nomismata (28·80
francs) was arranged by Nicephorus for slaves from the
south sold anywhere in the Empire west of Abydos. The
customs-duties must have brought in considerable sums.
Irene's flirtation with Free Trade, abolishing the dues at
Abydos, affected her revenues very seriously, and Nicephorus reverted to a tariff policy, keeping down prices
more subtly by restricting the currency in circulation.[1]
When under the Comneni the Italian republics won the
right to import with a duty of only 4 per cent., the Emperor
lost heavily in revenue quite apart from the blow to the
trade of the Empire.

There were occasional super-taxes, such as the *dikeraton*,
the extra $\frac{1}{12}$ that Leo the Isaurian introduced to repair
the walls of Constantinople ; and tax-collectors occasionally
raised the taxes to enlarge their commission.[2] The State
also made money from the State factories and the silk
monopoly, and by selling titles. It controlled the corn-
trade, and some Emperors, such as Nicephorus II, were
accused of making a personal profit out of it. Nicephorus I
also ingenuously forbade usury and all money-lending, and
then lent from the Treasury, charging an interest of $16\frac{2}{3}$
per cent., but his successors did not pursue the method.[3]
Under the Palæologi, when things were desperate, John
Cantacuzene attempted to collect a voluntary levy from
all classes, for war expenses ; but scarcely anyone was
able or willing to contribute.[4]

The whole system of taxation, by giving the Emperor a

[1] See Bury, *Eastern Roman Empire*, 212 *sqq.*
[2] Bury, *Later Roman Empire from Arcadius to Irene*, II, 424 *sqq.*
[3] Idem, *Eastern Roman Empire*, *loc. cit.*
[4] Cantacuzenus, III, 38–40.

constant supply of cash, and thus enabling him to maintain his huge bureaucracy and his standing army, put him
in a far stronger position than any Western monarch or
the Calif. But the high taxes meant that his subjects
were continually dissatisfied and also put them in a weak
position when commercial rivals appeared ; they had not
the ready capital for new enterprises. And when the whole
financial system broke down under the Comneni, the burden became intolerable ; the rule of the Seljuks or the
Normans seemed almost preferable.[1]

Of the details of expenditure we are equally ignorant.
There is no means of telling how much the upkeep of the
army or the civil service cost the Treasury. The only
figures given are those of the salaries of some of the high
officials in the Tenth Century. Constantine VII, in the *De
Ceremoniis*, mentions the sums due yearly to the Strategi of
the Themes under Leo VI. The Strategi of the Anatolics,
the Armenians and the Thracesians received the handsome
sum of 40 lb. of gold (43,200 gold francs), the Opsician,
Bucellarian and Macedonian Strategi 30, and so on down-
wards, the frontier strategi being given less, as they collected
frontier dues, and the Europeans nothing, as they lived on
the local taxes.[2] The Italian Ambassador Liudprand saw
the Emperor Constantine VII paying out the small salaries
of the title-holders one year. The ceremony took place on
the days just before Palm Sunday. The Magistri, twenty-
four of them, each received 24 nomismata (345·6 francs)
and 2 *scaramangia* or ceremonial robes, the Patricians 12
nomismata and 1 scaramangion, and the other titles 7, 6,
5, 4, 3, 2, and 1 nomisma according to rank. Salaries of
less than 1 nomisma were paid out by the Paracoemomenus.[3]
The doyen of the law faculty—the University was a State

[1] Nicetas Choniates, *loc. cit.*, and 50 ; Cinnamus, 22.
[2] Constantine Porphyrogennetus, *De Ceremoniis*, ii, 696–7.
[3] Liudprand, *Antapodosis*, 157–8.

institution—received in the Eleventh Century 4 lb. of gold
a year, as well as certain perquisites.[1]

The administrative machinery of Byzantium was expensive and cumbersome, but it was sufficiently elastic and, so
long as the Empire's finances remained sound, extremely
efficient. It needed to be large, for every detail in the
life of the Empire was considered to be the Government's
business. The idea of *laissez-faire* was undreamt of. Education, religion, everything to do with trade and finance, all
were under State control. A Tenth-Century handbook
exists that explains the duties of the Prefect of Constantinople.[2] It was his province to superintend all the commercial activities of the City, fixing prices, wages and hours,
licensing the opening of new shops, watching that the
export by-laws were followed. He had too to see to the
proper observance of Sundays. Provincial life was regu-
lated with equal care. To facilitate taxation and general
stability, travel and migration were discouraged. The local
authorities had to issue passports for *bona-fide* travellers,
the Quæstor of Constantinople to see that visitors to the
City came only for a good reason. The City had to be
fed, and relief work was necessary during the famines that
periodically devastated the countryside. The able-bodied
unemployed had to be found work, so charitable institutions had to be run. Such all-embracing watchfulness and
interference kept the bureaucracy fully occupied.

This paternalism also found scope in the supervision
that the Government exercised over religion. Since the
Fifth Century a good citizen had to be orthodox, and
heresy was a crime against the State. The heretic philosopher John Italus and the Bogomil leaders under Alexius I
were persecuted by the civil authorities. Where heresy was
widespread in a district, State officials would come and
forcibly remove the population of whole villages to other

[1] See below, p. 227.   [2] See below, p. 175.

parts of the Empire where they would be swamped or, it was rather hoped, converted by their new neighbours. Thus the Mardaïtes, Syrian Monothelites, were moved from the Lebanon in the Seventh Century to the shores of Asia Minor, and thus the Armenians, particularly Paulician heretics, were continually being settled in Europe throughout the Ninth Century. The Government was justified in taking action against heretics, for heresy was usually a political movement. Monophysitism in Egypt and Syria was inspired by enmity against the Imperial tax-collector rather than against the theology of Chalcedon : though Orthodoxy was embroiled in that some of the heavy taxes were levied to repay a loan from the Church of Constantinople to Heraclius. The Armenian Church existed largely as a focus for Armenian separatism from the Empire. This system of forced migration in whole villages was useful also to break up any *bloc* of unruly peoples in the provinces : apart from the question of heresy. The Slavs of Macedonia would be less formidable if they had Armenians settled amongst them. So the balance necessary for stability would be preserved.

The ideals of Byzantine administration might be called almost socialistic. Everyone was to be a good citizen of the State. Worship of the State, of the Emperor as its head and symbol, of the Law that created it, was considered the essential basis of society ; and, indeed, it was this rigid religion that preserved the Empire through so many centuries. Byzantium produced many ambitious statesmen, but very few of them forgot their duties to the State. Even Basil the Macedonian or Basil the Paracoemomenus or John Cantacuzene, though they might win crowns or wealth for themselves by neglecting to be overscrupulous, always put the interests of the Empire before their own.

There was, however, one class that would not fit in

permanently to this State-worship. That was the landed aristocracy. The existence of great landowners had provided a problem to the old Roman Emperors, but the trouble that lasted from the Fifth to the Eighth Centuries when no province was free from barbarian devastation or immigration had destroyed the value of land and broken up most of the estates. But by the middle of the Ninth Century the Asiatic provinces and a century later the European were more or less secure, and land became, in view of the Government restrictions on trade, the most profitable investment. A class of aristocrats arose, deriving vast wealth from estates that they continually sought to increase. The free small-holder tended to be bought out and either became a tenant or disappeared. This upset the taxation-system and also the system of army recruiting, which was bound up with land-tenure ; moreover, the wealthy nobleman with a huge retinue of servants and retainers, whom he armed, was an obvious menace to the State. The administration drew a clear distinction between the wealthy—the *dunatoi* or powerful—and the poor—the *penêtes* ; and on the whole it attempted to confine the aristocrats to military affairs, keeping the civil service democratic and free. Throughout the Tenth Century the Emperors were preoccupied in legislating against the power of the magnates to buy up the land of the poor. Romanus I forbade them to acquire any land in a village community, and he and Constantine VII and Basil II spent time and energy enforcing and elaborating such measures. Basil II was particularly vigorous ; like Henry VII of England he found on a tour that his hosts were too powerful and firmly reduced and punished them, and even took steps against self-made landowners.[1] Old families increased their domains and new families arose. But the government failed. Even Basil II's reintroduction of the *alle-*

[1] See below, p. 198

lengyon tax which was used to mulct landowners could
not destroy their power ; and already Nicephorus II,
himself a member of a great landowning, family, had been
a black-leg to the Imperial policy. By the middle of the
Eleventh Century the landowners, amongst whom the religious hierarchy now had to be included, were strong
enough to capture the government, amid chaos that caused
the Seljuk victories. Henceforward, though foreign invasions and conquests restricted their lands, the aristocrats
really commanded the administration. Entrance to the
civil service depended less upon merit than upon family
influence ; and the loss of so much territory meant that
new families scarcely had the scope to arise. The aristocracy closed its ranks. In the provinces it was already
tending to devolve into semi-feudal independence, when
the Latin conquest came and all at once completed the
devolution. The Emperors still waged war against the
Magisters and the stronger Comneni and Nicæan Emperors
deliberately kept them in check. But Michael Palæologus,
in the Thirteenth Century, and John Cantacuzenus, in the
Fourteenth, showed their strength. At Thessalonica in the
Fourteenth Century the movement known as that of the
Zealots was largely provoked by their arrogance and
attempted to challenge their power, but it was in vain.
In the very evening of the Empire the aristocracy, which
had lost its lands long since to foreign conquerors, became
almost an hereditary civil service, and as such was of value
to the Government. But the harm had already been done.
Yet even to the end the Government service remained open
to all ; the meritorious plebeian could still climb to prominence. And to the end the administration retained an
efficiency unknown in Western Europe. The taxes might
be burdensome or unproductive, but they were collected ;
and the Emperor's wishes, issued from his secretarial bureau,
were disseminated throughout his shrinking dominions and,

except when they outraged public opinion, they were respected.

The Government was aided in its task by the innate reverence for Law that Byzantium inherited from Rome, and its efficiency was further illustrated by the administration of justice. The Emperor was the ultimate judge, and it was possible always to appeal to him. Certain Emperors would hear appeals in person : Justinian liked to exercise this function, while Theophilus received suitors during his weekly procession through the City to Blachernæ. But usually petitions were received and prepared for the Emperor by the minister *epi tôn deêseôn*.[1] It had been, however, part of the viceregal powers of the Prætorian Prefects that in their districts there was no appeal from them. It is probable that the Italian Exarch inherited this right. In Constantinople the Prefect of the City (or his successor the Great Drungarius) and the Quæstor divided the administration of justice. In the provinces there were judges at the capital of each theme who heard cases of local interest or minor importance, but more momentous suits were taken to Constantinople, to a High Court of twelve judges. A law-suit was one of the few accepted excuses for a visit to Constantinople, and pious Emperors like Romanus I would build hostels for litigants during their stay in the City. Cases in which ecclesiastics were involved were heard in the ecclesiastical courts, who could hear any civil case if both parties wished it. Alexius I extended the sway of the ecclesiastical judges to hear cases to do with marriage and with bequests to charity. It must be remembered in this connection that the Church was a department of the State and that Alexius in particular controlled it very firmly. Under the Palæologi when the Patriarchs played an increasingly large part in the administration, the Church courts grew in scope till by the Turkish conquest they were

[1] See above, p. 91.

widely enough organised to take over the whole jurisdiction
of the Christian populations.

The punishments in criminal cases were either fines and
confiscation of property or mutilation. The death penalty
after Leo III's time was reserved for treason, desertion to
the enemy, murder and unnatural vice, and even so was
seldom carried out.[1] Under John II it was never once
employed.[2] Mutilation was considered a humane substitute, and one justified by the words of Christ about pluck-
ing out offending eyes and cutting off offending limbs. It
was only widely introduced by Leo III, but thenceforward
it was frequently employed. We are apt nowadays to
think it a revoltingly barbaric custom ; but the fact remains that most people preferred and prefer mutilation to
death. The punishments were further mitigated by the
right of asylum in churches, a right from which after Leo III
few classes of criminals were excluded.[3] Constantine VII
even allowed it to a murderer, provided that he became a
monk ; in which case half his property went at once to
the murdered man's heirs and half to his own, though
some might go with him to his monastery.[4] Even treason
was less and less visited with death. Usually monastic
seclusion, providing the offender with present detention and
future salvation, was considered enough, though it was
wiser to add mutilation. Imprisonment, which was costly
and unproductive to the State, was practically unknown.
The State prison, the Prætorium, was only used for offenders
awaiting trial.

How far corruption interfered with the administration of
justice it is difficult to estimate. Till Leo III published
his *Ecloga*, one might say that there was officially one law

---

[1] *Ecloga*, trans. Freshfield, 106, 111–14.
[2] Nicetas Choniates, 63 : John never even employed mutilation.
[3] *Ecloga*, 105–6.
[4] *Jus Græco-Romanum*, III, 276.

for the rich and one for the poor ; and stories like that of the Seventh-Century widow oppressed by the noble Vutelinus [1] suggest that though justice was done if the case penetrated through to the proper courts, influence could often delay it. Leo III in the preface to the *Ecloga* complains that bribery and corruption were becoming frequent. But throughout most of Byzantine history there are singularly few complaints about the administration of justice ; and from this silence we must conclude that the Byzantine, compared at any rate to his neighbours and contemporaries, had little cause to be dissatisfied.

[1] Nicephorus, 8.

CHAPTER V

Religion and the Church

The practical efficiency of the Imperial Constitution and the administration might have deprived the citizens of the Empire of the delights of political discussion and controversy, had not an ample field been open to them in religion. To understand Byzantine history it is essential to remember the unimportance of life in this World to the Byzantine. Christianity triumphed in a disillusioned age because it promised a better world to come and provided a mystic escape from the world here and now. But the right eternal bliss, the right ecstasies, could only be won by treading the path of perfect orthodoxy. Consequently tiny points of theological doctrine were infinitely more important than grand questions of secular policy, for the latter only concerned this world, and the former had eternity at stake. The worldly instincts of comfort and self-advancement could never, it is true, be suppressed ; and financial worries, the burden of over-taxation, always could rouse strong if negative feelings. But the main attention of the Byzantine was very reasonably concentrated on those little details that would open or close to him the gates of Heaven.

Constantine the Great, by adopting Christianity as a State religion, made this preoccupation the affair of the State and practically raised the Emperor to be the guardian of the Keys, the Pastor of the Flock, like Peter, Prince of the Apostles, as Leo the Isaurian claimed.[1] The Em-

[1] *Ecloga*, trans. Freshfield, 66-7.

peror's position as such was never seriously challenged in the East. To the last, the Church remained a department of the State. But it had its disadvantages ; the Emperor would frequently be drawn into controversies and struggles from which a less Erastian ruler might have been free.

The genius of the early Christians had decided that the Church, to achieve the widest possible influence, must model itself upon the organisation of the secular state ; and since the days of the Apostles the central sees of Christendom had been placed in the three capitals of the Mediterranean world, Rome, Alexandria and Antioch, other cities and towns having their bishops and hierarchs according to their civil importance. When Diocletian reorganised the State, the Church followed suit. The hierarchy was rearranged to fit the new provinces. The foundation of the new capital by Constantine revolutionised the ecclesiastical no less than the secular administration. Byzantium had been a minor bishopric under the jurisdiction of the Metropolitan of Heraclea, a position clearly unsuitable for the new Christian capital of the world. The Bishop of Byzantium soon was raised to be the Patriarch of Constantinople. But within the Church the older sees were jealous and obstructive, and the heretic and pagan Emperors of the House of Constantine were not able to enforce the new authority of the State. It was only under the orthodox Theodosius I that the new ecclesiastical status of Constantinople was publicly recognised. The Second Œcumenical Council gave the Patriarch of Constantinople second position amongst the Patriarchs, ' because Constantinople is New Rome.' [1] The Bishop of Old Rome took precedence, but the Alexandrian and Antiochene Patriarchs and their later-created confrère of Jerusalem came after him. The provinces over which the see of Constantinople now ruled

[1] Mansi, *Concilia*, vol. 3, 560.

were Asia Minor and the greater part of the Balkan peninsula.

Rome never recognised the claim of Constantinople to the second place, mistrusting the possible conclusions of the argument ; [1] and Alexandria accepted it under protest, always hoping for opportunities to assert her own independence and her stricter orthodoxy. Throughout the history of the heresies of the next centuries there is always the subsidiary motif of the jealousy of the Patriarchs, Rome trying to assert an authority over Constantinople, and Alexandria seeking to prove herself the only vessel of orthodoxy.

Fate, however, played drastically into the hands of Constantinople in the Seventh Century. The Patriarchs of Alexandria, Antioch and Jerusalem suddenly found themselves bishops *in partibus*. The Saracen conquests, helped on by their own hatred of the authorities of Constantinople, robbed them of half their flocks and almost all their importance, turning them into the slaves of an infidel master. Meanwhile barbarian invasions isolated Rome, leaving her, free from any strict secular control, to develop her own notions of theocracy. The Empire became coterminous with the Patriarchate of Constantinople, except for certain districts under the Roman see, which were transferred to Constantinople by Leo the Isaurian. Henceforward the Patriarch of Constantinople was unquestioned head of Eastern Christendom, his jurisdiction embracing the whole of Christendom's most powerful Empire. For positive power even the Roman pontiff, for all his greater independence, might well envy him. But the Patriarch paid for his authority. He was never for long allowed to forget that he was the servant of the Emperor.

[1] She recognised it only during the Latin occupation of Constantinople. when the see was firmly under her control (Mansi, *Concilia*, vol. 22, 991).

The recapture of Antioch at the close of the Tenth Century scarcely affected the situation. For Antioch by then was sufficiently humbled to count merely as an archbishopric with special rank and semi-autonomous privileges. The Cypriote Church enjoyed a long-established claim to autonomy, but this, however, was not very important.

The organisation of the Church of Constantinople to the last remained a copy of the secular state : [1] though it is not possible to say how exactly the great dioceses corresponded with the Themes of the Empire. Its constitution had been laid down by the Council *in Trullo* in 681 and never was seriously altered afterwards : under the Patriarch came the metropolitans and archbishops of the big cities and the provincial centres. Under them came the various bishops, each of whom controlled his local clergy down to the humble village priest or pope. But there was a great difference between the local clergy and the higher ranks. Whereas the village pope ought to be married, so as to keep him from the distractions of sexual temptation and housekeeping worries, the higher clergy, the bishops and their superiors, were all recruited from the monasteries. The monasteries were of various kinds. The humblest were under the local bishop or some local lord, but others were under higher ecclesiastics, others admitted the authority of the Patriarch alone, others, still higher, only that of the Emperor. Of the last named, the most famous example was the monasteries of Mount Athos, where from the end of the Tenth Century there was a self-governing republic of monasteries, of various foundations and even of various nationalities, with the Emperor as their suzerain. The monasteries obeyed with varying strictness the rule that Saint Basil drew up in the Fourth Century enjoining study and labour. But there were also Lauræ, communities of

[1] For the organisation, see Le Quien, *Oriens Christianus* ; Pargoire, *L'Eglise Byzantine*, 199 *sqq.*

hermits, more exclusively quietistic and therefore rather
more admired. These too might have privileges of government similar to the monasteries. The isolated local hermit
or Stylite saint came, strictly speaking, under the authority
of his local bishop, than whom he was probably infinitely
more powerful, such was the veneration given to uncomfortable piety. The women's convents followed the same
lines as the men's. Both the secular church and the monasteries were extremely rich. In the Tenth Century the
Bishop of Patras could afford to equip for the wars a far
larger contingent than any layman in the theme ; [1] and
the frequency of the legislation directed from the Tenth
Century onward against monastic inheritance shows what
powerful landowners the monasteries were becoming, while
the later Iconoclastic movement was largely anti-monastic
in its intentions. But the monasteries grew in power, and
their Abbots, their Higumenes and Archimandrites, particularly those of the monasteries within Constantinople,
were often men of vast political importance. Theodore of
Studium ranked as one of the great statesmen of the day. [2]

The whole organisation was controlled very strictly from
the Patriarchal court. In the correspondence of the great
Patriarchs we find letters written often to some quite unimportant ecclesiastic, giving orders or making complaints
about minor questions of policy or discipline. The Patriarch was clearly kept admirably informed about everything that passed within his Church, and his will was
enforced throughout. [3] But the Patriarch himself was under
the control of the Emperor. Nominally he was elected by
the body of the bishops. Actually the Emperor nominated
him, and could always depose by packing a synod subservient to his will. The only weapon that the Patriarch

[1] Constantine Porphyrogennetus, *De Administrando Imperio*, 243.
[2] Ferradou, *Les Biens des Monastères en Byzance*, *passim*.
[3] See, e.g., the correspondence of the various Patriarchs.

could use against the Emperor was excommunication. Sometimes, as in the case of Polyeuct and the murderer John Tzimisces, the threat was enough to cow the Emperor ; [1] but a Patriarch who, like Nicholas Mysticus, carried it out even though the Emperor was manifestly breaking God's laws, soon found himself deposed and treading the path to exile.[2] The Emperor exercised his control through his minister the Syncellus.[3]

On the whole the Imperial control worked smoothly. The Emperors did not interfere much in Church affairs, recognising, as John Tzimisces said when creating Basil Patriarch, that ' God has ordained two powers,' the Emperor for the State, the Patriarch for the Church.[4]   Certain energetic Patriarchs chafed under the Cæsaropapism, but even Photius fell, not so much for having defied the Emperor as for carrying on too breathless an ecclesiastical policy, Chrysostom for having censured the morals of the Court, which he reasonably regarded as coming within his sphere, and other dethroned Patriarchs such as Germanus or Arsenius chiefly for resisting what they regarded as ecclesiastical or doctrinal misdemeanours on the part of the Emperor. Michael Cerularius alone, who wore the purple boots and claimed to make and unmake Emperors, aimed at freeing the Church entirely from State control ; but his ambitions were regarded as bombastic and impracticable.[5] The Emperors nearly all took their duties conscientiously, and appointed suitable Patriarchs. Basil I was cynical enough to plan to raise his own young son to the Patriarchal throne, but the boy died before he had been there long ; [6] and Romanus I followed his example by elevating his young son Theophylact, a good-tempered youth with

<hr>

[1] Cedrenus, II, 380.   [2] See above, p. 47.
[3] See above, p. 92.   [4] Leo Diaconus, 101–2.
[5] See Bury, *Roman Emperors* in *Selected Essays*, 210–14.
[6] Theophanes Continuatus, 354, states that Basil made him Syncellus. He became Patriarch after Basil's death.

a passion for the stable. But Theophylact, who attempted to lessen his boredom by introducing miracle-pantomimes into Church services, though he fulfilled many of his duties adequately, caused a scandal by his obvious apathy ; and such an experiment was not repeated.[1]

At times, particularly when the Imperial control was firmly exercised, there was a certain amount of bribery and simony. Saint Luke the Stylite wheedled a sum of 100 *nomismata* (1,420 gold francs) out of his parents on the plea that he was trying to secure the vacant Bishopric of Sebaste.[2] This was probably when the Church was under the creatures of Leo VI, whose ministers were notoriously corruptible.

Since the Fifth Century the Empire had regarded heresy as a crime against the State ; consequently it was the State authorities and not the Church that took action against it. As a rule, such action was taken when the heretics were politically dangerous, like the Bogomils who preached disobedience to the State, or in responsible positions like the Professor John Italus. If the suspected heretic were an ecclesiastic, it seems, to judge from the life of Saint Symeon the New Theologian, that the Syncellus, after asking him test questions, reported him to the Patriarch, who took action. But there was a right of appeal to the Emperor —the Patriarch gave way when Symeon's powerful friends threatened to bring the case before Basil II.[3]

Heresy consisted officially in the rejection of any of the canons of the Œcumenical Councils. An Œcumenical Council, an assembly under the presidency of the Emperor, where every inter-communicating church was represented, was the inspired body whose decisions were binding on Christendom. From early times the Roman bishop, as senior bishop, would make doctrinal pronouncements and

---

[1] Cedrenus, II, 332-4.   [2] *Vita S. Lucae Stylitae*, 208.
[3] *Vita S. Symeonis Novi Theologi*, 140-1.

Justinian established a similar position for the Emperor, but a General Council was needed to secure the acceptance of such pronouncements in the East throughout the whole life of the Empire.

The Seven Œcumenical Councils were considered, along with the Holy Scriptures, to be the basis of the Orthodox faith. Each had been convened to settle some particular point of theology and pronounce against some particular heresy. The doctrine of the Trinity is a difficult doctrine and the doctrine of the Incarnation makes it no easier. The path of correct Christology was very narrow, and even the best-intentioned theologian might slip to one side or the other. Christianity had triumphed over paganism in the midst of one of her own civil wars, when the Arians, by denying the full divinity of Christ, were trying to establish a more unitarian conception of the Godhead. The First Œcumenical Council, the Council of Nicæa, had anathematised them ; but throughout the Fourth Century Arianism enjoyed a popularity in smart circles in Constantinople. It was not till after the Second Œcumenical Council of 381 that it died in the East—in the West, as the religion of the Goths, it survived for centuries. The triumph of orthodoxy had been the triumph of Alexandria, under Athanasius. Throughout the Fifth Century Alexandria sought to follow up her victory by forcing her more particular theology on Christendom.

Her opportunity came when the Patriarch of Constantinople, Nestorius, divided the nature of Christ into two, the human and the divine. This was an unpopular move, because it logically led to an attack on the beloved patroness of Constantinople, the Virgin Mary, who was threatened with the loss of her title, the Mother of God. Alexandria united with Rome and the Byzantine populace against him. The Third Œcumenical Council, of Ephesus, pronounced against him, swayed by the personality of the Alexandrian

Patriarch, Cyril. A few churches in Northern Syria there-upon seceded, and formed independent bodies under the protection of the Persians. Their theology and practices showed a Puritanism that their founder would scarcely have admitted. They were vigorous missionaries, journey-ing even to China ; and till the other day they survived in the mountains of Kurdistan.

But Alexandria overreached herself. Her next Patriarch, Dioscorus, plunged for the Eutychian or Monophysite view of Christ. Rome disapproved, and the Imperial Court preferred to humour Rome. The Fourth Œcumenical Council, of Chalcedon, condemned Dioscorus. The Mono-physites became heretics and the objects of persecution.

The theological issues at stake in the Monophysite con-troversy were comparatively small—the difference between One Nature and Two Indivisible Natures—but the political issues were enormous. For nearly two centuries Mono-physitism as a problem dominated Imperial history. At the Fifth Œcumenical Council at Constantinople in 553 Justinian admitted his failure to promulgate a compromise. The Sixth Œcumenical Council, at Constantinople in 680, denounced the compromise known as Monothelitism favoured by the Heraclian Emperors. But by then it was late ; the Monophysite churches had seceded, and the bulk of their flocks had perverted to Islam.

The Eighth Century was filled by the Iconoclastic con-troversy.[1] Northern Syria was a home of Puritanism. Nestorianism had been popular there as a puritan move-ment. Its opposite, Monophysitism, also won favour there under the puritan leadership of Jacob Baradæus. And now a Northern Syrian, Leo, surnamed the Isaurian, sought to enforce Puritanism on the Empire. Basically Iconoclasm was a Christological question : could the divinity of Christ

[1] See Bréhier, *La Querelle des Images* ; Ostrogorsky, *Studien zur Geschichte des Byzantinischen Bildestreites.*

be depicted? If not, was it not idolatry to worship pictures of Him? It was easy to prove Iconoclastic theology
to be either Monophysite or Nestorian; and subtle dis-
tinctions were drawn in the nature of worship; but Iconoclasm really failed because it threatened to deprive the
people of the pictures they loved. Just as Nestorius had
seemed to attack the Virgin, now Leo and his successors
were insulting Christ and all the Saints. Iconoclasm only
succeeded so long, because it was ably led, and supported
by the army, mostly Asiatic by birth, and by all who disliked the growing power of the Church and the monasteries. The Seventh Œcumenical Council, at Nicæa in
787, condemned Iconoclasm; and though it was revived
in the next century, the movement was largely political
and short-lived.

After Iconoclasm, the Church was troubled by no serious
internal heresy. It was still possible for the unwary to fall
into error, like Demetrius of Lampe who returned from a
tour in Germany in the Twelfth Century laughing because
the Germans said that the Son was equal to but lower
than the Father. His opinion of the absurdity of this had
a considerable success until the ecclesiastical authorities
pointed out that he was failing to understand the subtleties
of the Trinity.[1] But there was no further serious attempt
to upset the Christology of the Seven Councils. Theological
controversies centred more round the theology and usages
of mysticism. The Greek Church had always favoured
mysticism and been proud of her mystic writers like ' Dionysius the Areopagite ' and Maximus the Confessor, whose
works were freely read throughout the Empire's history;
but she was puzzled as to the theological import of the
mystic's ecstasy. We see the problem exercising the authorities early in the Eleventh Century, in the life of Symeon
the New Theologian; and it was not finally settled till

[1] Cinnamus, 251 *sqq.*

after the Hesychast Controversy in the Fourteenth Century, when the Quietist extremists, led by the Athonite Palamas, finally induced the Church to admit that the mystic was truly visited by the very light that shone on Mount Tabor.[1] The main heresies that the Empire had now to combat were heresies outside of and against the Church, heresies in the Manichæan tradition. Manichæanism itself never won a strong hold within the Empire ; but in the Ninth Century a Dualist sect, known as the Paulicians, established itself among the Armenians of the Upper Euphrates, forming there a religious republic.[2] Basil I crushed it politically and sought to suppress it by settling the Paulicians in driblets along the Bulgarian frontier. But there they inspired and combined with a Bulgarian heretical movement called by the name of its founder Bogomil.[3] The Bogomils did not much trouble the Empire till after the conquest of Bulgaria ; but thenceforward, holding as they did that all things of the flesh, including labour, obedience to authority and the procreation of children, were equally wicked, they were a problem that had to be faced. Alexius I even found a nest of Bogomils in the Capital itself, and tried and executed its leaders with pardonable severity.[4] The Bogomil question was, however, only solved for the Empire when the Empire lost the bulk of its Balkan provinces at the end of the Twelfth Century.

Schism would, however, still frequently divide the Church. In the earlier days schism had been the natural consequence of heresy. The introduction of Iconoclasm, for example, provided the Empire with a vast body of displaced nonjuring clergy as well as their officially appointed successors, and there was no peace between them. From the Ninth

[1] See Tafrali, *Thessalonique au XIV Siècle*, 170 *sqq.*
[2] Conybeare, *Key of Truth*, introduction, *passim.*
[3] Runciman, *First Bulgarian Empire*, 190–6.
[4] Anna Comnena, 384 *sqq.*, 412 *sqq.*

Century the schisms became more personal in origin, usually resultant from the attempts of an Emperor to over-step his rights. Thus when the Patriarch Ignatius was unwarrantably deposed by Michael III and the Cæsar Bardas, half the clergy went into exile rather than acknow-ledge his successor Photius ; and at the Council of 879, designed to make peace between the two Patriarchs, many sees were represented by two bishops. The schism was only healed by the death of Ignatius, after his restoration.[1] A similar schism was made a few years later, when Leo VI, having outraged the law and moral sentiment by marry-ing a fourth wife, deposed the Patriarch Nicholas who had excommunicated him. Half the Church followed Nicholas, half felt with his successor, the saintly Euthymius, that the Emperor was justified.[2] The third such schism took place under Michael Palæologus, who deposed the Patriarch Arsenius for a variety of trumpery excuses, because the Patriarch would not condone the murder of the rightful Emperor John IV. Arsenius kept his supporters ; and in the end Michael had half to climb down, seeking absolu-tion after Arsenius's death from the Patriarch Joseph.[3]

But there was one problem that troubled the Orthodox Church throughout its whole history, causing sometimes schisms, sometimes appearing as a question of heresy ; that was the problem of its relation with Rome.[4] The root of the problem lay in the jealousy of the old for the newer capital. In the days of the Apostles it was obvious that Rome, the secular capital, was best fitted to be the reli-gious capital ; and Peter, Prince of the Apostles, ended

[1] Bury, *Eastern Roman Empire*, 180–209 ; Ruinaut, *Le Schisme de Photius* ; Hergenröther, *Photius, passim*.

[2] Runciman, *Romanus Lecapenus*, 41 *sqq*.

[3] Chapman, *Michel Paléologue*, 99 *sqq*.

[4] See Hergenröther, *Photius, passim* ; Norden, *Das Papsttum und Byzanz, passim* ; Bréhier, *The Greek Church*, in *Cambridge Medieval History*, vol. 4, 241–73, 594–626 and bibliographies.

his career as Bishop of Rome. When Rome ceased to be
the political centre of the world, her Church clung to her
Petrine origin as the reason for her exalted position. Un-
generously she would not even have allowed Constantinople
second place, because Constantinople claimed it as New
Rome and she only admitted the claim of an apostolic
foundation—though why Mark's see of Alexandria should
always have precedence over Peter's of Antioch was never
clearly explained.

The great heresies of the Fifth and Sixth Centuries embittered the situation, and showed the already divergent
attitudes. The protagonists were Alexandria and Constantinople, and each side would appeal to Rome for help.
Rome maintained that her view must prevail unquestioned.
Constantinople would accept what Rome promulgated if
an Œcumenical Council endorsed it ; Alexandria preferred
to secede rather than desert her own theology. But Constantinople, in the power of the lay Imperial authorities,
continually sought for a compromise with the Monophysites, which Rome, with no political interests at stake, was
determined not to endure. In the end, though the power
of the lay authorities had caused Pope Vigilius to promise
every sort of compromise, while Pope Honorius I unwisely
made an heretical Monothelite pronouncement *ex cathedra*,
Roman inflexibility triumphed ; the Christology that Pope
Leo I had dictated in his *tomus* in the Fifth Century was
universally accepted as an essential part of orthodox faith.
But while Rome came to consider that it was Leo's pronouncement that made it orthodox, Constantinople accepted
it because three Œcumenical Councils had done so. Meanwhile, as Constantinople grew more uniquely the great
Christian city, her bishops grew more self-confident and
arrogant. Finally in 595, provoked by the claims of Rome,
the Patriarch John the Faster took the title of Œcumenical
—world-wide. The Pope, Gregory the Great, was natur-

ally indignant and cried that Antichrist must be at hand.
No see, he declared, had any jurisdiction over another,
but all were equal before God.[1] Rome, however, did not
retain this view in later years. Meanwhile, further anti-
pathies and openings for misunderstandings were provided
by the linguistic question. Rome, by now, contained
scarcely anyone who knew Greek, while at Constantinople
Latin was increasingly forgotten.

The Iconoclastic Controversy led to an open breach between Rome and the Imperial Government. Hitherto the
Papacy had acknowledged the overlordship of the Emperor.
Till the Seventh Century indeed, permission had to be
obtained from Constantinople before a new Pope could
be elected ; but Constantine IV declared that the consent of the Exarch at Ravenna would be enough.[2] During
the Eighth Century the combination of the Controversy
and the Lombard wars made the Romans decide to dispense with this act of allegiance. The Popes, reasonably
provoked by the Emperor's confiscation of their revenues
from Sicily and Calabria, looked now to find allies in the
West, among the Franks. But there were many circles in
Constantinople that disliked to break with Rome. Many
felt with the Patriarch Germanus that no such innovation
as Iconoclasm should be made without an Œcumenical
Council, and later the Iconoclast Patriarch Paul resigned
in 784, conscience-stricken at ' the church being ruled by
tyranny and severed from the other chairs of Christendom.'
And it was to Rome as the foremost of these chairs that the
dissentients appealed. Some of them even went further ;
Theodore of Studium in his dislike of Erastianism maintained that Rome, being conveniently free from Imperial
control, should decide on matters of doctrine : while it
was almost universally felt the Petrine see ought anyhow

[1] Gregory the Great, *Epistolae, M.P.L.*, vol. 77, 738 *sqq.*
[2] *Liber Pontificalis*, I, 363–4.   [3] Theophanes, 409, 457.

to be consulted. But already while Theodore wrote, Rome threw away her chance of establishing herself in the East by an act of great political unwisdom.

Pope Leo crowned Charlemagne at a time when the Churches were again in communion ; and the coronation made it impossible for the Imperial Government to trust the Papacy any further. Constantinople inevitably saw it as an act of treachery. Scarcely was the Iconoclastic controversy ended when a new quarrel broke out ; Pope Nicholas I attempted to intervene, encouraged by the defeated side, in a dispute within the Constantinopolitan Church. When a new Patriarch was elected to any of the great sees, it was customary for him to circularise a declaration of faith to his compeers and to ask for their endorsement. Nicholas refused to endorse the enthronisation letter of the Patriarch Photius, not because of his faith, but because his election was doubtfully legal. But Photius was his match. In a few months each pontiff had solemnly excommunicated the other, and a little later Photius, to his scandalised delight, caught out the Pope subscribing to a heresy.[1]

The theological import of the addition of the word *Filioque* to the creed is not very great, but the fact remained that it was an addition to the doctrine of the Seven Councils ; and Rome herself had formerly condemned it. To tamper with the creed was unpardonable in the eyes of Constantinople and the Churches of the East, whom Photius carefully informed of the Roman iniquities. The difference might be slight, but it was there. Rome, by calmly introducing it, cut herself off from the body of the Orthodox. Henceforward, though theologians might declare that *Filioque* was implicit in the creed, it was this word, rather than all the differences in usage, that made a lasting peace between Rome and Constantinople impos-

[1] See references on p. 119, note 4.

sible. Rome would not give it up, maintaining that what she said was correct ; and Constantinople would not accept what she considered heresy, merely because it was promulgated by Rome.

The Photian dispute was exacerbated by a struggle to secure dominion over the nascent Church of Bulgaria—a struggle from which Constantinople emerged victorious.[1] But peace, tactfully unprecise, was made after the second fall of Photius ; and for over a century and a half the Churches were in full communion and the word *Filioque* was ignored. The Emperor Leo VI even called in the doctrinal authority of the Pope to pit it against that of the Patriarch on the question of fourth marriages.[2] During these years Rome was in feeble hands and Constantinople was at the zenith of her glory. The Byzantines did not concern themselves about Rome. When the Papal embassy addressed Nicephorus II as Emperor of the Greeks, the Imperial Court showed its contempt by imprisoning the ambassadors and ignoring the message contained in the Papal letter.[3]

But the Cluniac revival in the Eleventh Century led the renewal of the Petrine claims for world-jurisdiction ; and a breach with Constantinople was inevitable. The Patriarch Eustathius attempted in 1024 to avert it by asking the Pope to recognise the Byzantine claims to autonomy, Rome retaining her precedence. Pope John XIX would have agreed, had not his Cluniac advisers prevented him. But relations remained friendly ; John XIX agreed with the Patriarch's suggested reform of the South Italian Church, while chapels following the Latin rite were encouraged at Constantinople.[4]

[1] Runciman, *First Bulgarian Empire*, 99 *sqq.*
[2] See above, p. 47.   [3] Liudprand, *Legatio*, 200–1.
[4] Radulfus Glaber, in *M.G.H.Ss.*, vol. 7, 96 ; Hugh of Flavigny, *M.G.H.Ss.*, vol. 8, 392 ; Gay, *L'Italie Méridionale*, 427.

The final breach came during the Papacy of the French reformer Leo IX and the Patriarchate of Michael Cerularius. The Norman invasions of Southern Italy complicated and eventually strained political relations between Rome and Constantinople. Meanwhile Cerularius, irritated by the Pope's treatment of him as a subordinate and determined to give spiritual precedence to no one, reverted to Photius's taunt of heresy. Letters and embassies became more acrimonious, till in May 1054 once again, as in the days of Photius and Nicholas, the two great pontiffs of Christendom placed each other under the ban. And again the Churches of the East followed Cerularius, as the champion of the attitude that they shared. This time the schism was lasting. But so little did the Byzantines now concern themselves about Rome that none of the contemporary chroniclers troubled to mention the event.[1]

The Crusades brought East and West into closer contact, with unhappy results. The Comnenian Emperors were glad to be able to hold out the hope of reunion as a move in the diplomatic game, but each year the reunion grew more unlikely. Political mistrust made the Latins hate and suspect the Greek schismatics while the Greeks despised and loathed the rough Latin heretics. The Latin persecution of the Syrian Christians, who looked to the Emperor as their protector, embittered the situation. The enmity was intensified by the massacre of the Italians in Constantinople in 1183, and reached its terrible climax in the Fourth Crusade.

The Fourth Crusade destroyed the last chance of a genuine reunion. Pope Innocent III had been genuinely horrified by the news of the sack of Constantinople, but he determined to make full use of the advantages that it provided for Rome. All over the newly-won Latin dominions the Church was put into Latin hands and the schismatic

[1] See Bréhier, *Le Schisme Oriental, passim.*

Greeks must tread the path of persecution. A few Greeks bowed to the Papal authority and retained their positions ; but they were regarded as traitors and excommunicated by the majority, who proudly went into exile, believing now, with Nicetas Acominatus,[1] that it must have been the Pope who, for all his protests, had really been the wire-puller in the Fourth Crusade. Michael Acominatus still, indeed, kept up relations with the waverers, much though he disapproved of their weakness ; but such forbearance was very rare.[2] Innocent III then adopted a milder tone, reproving the new Latin bishop of Athens for over-great persecuting zeal, and promising negotiations. However, his emissaries, the tactful Cardinal Benedict and the tactless Cardinal Pelagius, were each instructed to make no concessions.[3] The Greeks on their side were equally uncompromising. In 1207 the leading Greeks of Constantinople wrote to Innocent a letter which contains a summary of the whole Greek point of view. They would accept the rule of Sireris (Sir Henry, the ablest of the Latin Emperors), they said, and would give honorary distinction to the ' Lord Pope of Elder Rome,' but they disapproved of the *Filioque* clause and of the sort of supremacy claimed by the Pope Innocent should call a Council, they maintained.[4]

The two attitudes remained irreconcilable. And, so long as the Latin Empire endured, political considerations prevented any likelihood of a serious attempt at reunion. The Nicæan Emperors stood for autonomy, and found their strongest support in the Western Emperor Frederick II. John Vatatzes took the question of reunion so lightly as to suggest that if the Pope gave up the *Filioque* clause then

---

[1] Nicetas Choniates, 715.

[2] He still wrote friendly letters to the clergy that remained in Attica.

[3] See Norden, *op. cit.*, 182 *sqq.*, 212 *sqq.*

[4] Given in *M.P.G.*, vol. 140, 293 *sqq.*

the Greeks would condone the Latin usage of unleavened bread.[1]

The recovery of Constantinople altered the situation. It had alarmed Rome at first, and the Pope hastened in 1262 to offer the same indulgences to those that fought against the Emperor Michael Palæologus as to those that crusaded against the Moslems.[2] But Michael, on bad terms with his own Church and terrified of attacks from the West, genuinely believed in the wisdom of a union, whatever it might cost. At the Council of Lyons in 1274 his envoys agreed in his name to acknowledge the suzerainty of Rome. But Constantinople would not follow him. There was a general outcry. The Patriarch Joseph and even his own sister Eulogia, his most intimate counsellor, broke with him and led the opposition.[3] He could not carry the reunion through. Rome grew angry and adopted a bullying tone. He must force it on the Empire by May 1, 1282, or he would be excommunicated and his enemy Charles of Anjou be encouraged and supported against him. Michael was in despair, but in March the Sicilian Vespers broke Charles's power and saved him. The episode had not endeared the Papacy to Constantinople. Michael considered himself personally bound by the Union of Lyons all his life ; but his successors reverted to independence.[4] Talk of reunion still persisted through the Fourteenth Century. John Cantacuzenus suggested that a Council, as œcumenical as possible, in some maritime town between Rome and Constantinople, might solve the problem, but nothing was done.[5] Meanwhile, the Exile at Avignon and the Great Schism weakened the influence of the Papacy.

When in the early Fifteenth Century the Empire was

---

[1] Negotiations given in Mansi, *Concilia*, vol. 23, 47 *sqq.*
[2] *Registres d'Urbain V*, ed. Guiraud, no. cxxxi.
[3] Pachymer, I, 379 *sqq.*   [4] Chapman, *op. cit.*, 113 *sqq.*
[5] Cantacuzenus, III, 60.

clearly dying and the Papacy had recovered some of her prestige, desperate Imperial politicians revived the movement. Manuel II freely held out hopes of reunion as a bait to the West, and advised his son to promise negotiations but to protract them indefinitely. The pride of the Latins and the obstinacy of the Greeks would never agree, he said ; and attempted union would only make the schism the wider.[1] But John VIII would not take the advice. For the promise of a crusade against the Turks, he committed the Empire to the Council of Florence, where under his pressure the majority of a delegation of the Greek clergy agreed, after interminable discussions, that *ex Filio* meant the same as *per Filium*, and that they would recognise the universal supremacy of the Roman bishopric, saving the rights and privileges of the Eastern Churches—whatever that might mean.

Had the Union of Florence been followed by the promised Crusade, Constantinople might possibly have accepted it in gratitude. But the Pope was promising what he could not fulfil. No one now crusaded at the Pope's will. The only expedition to the East was that of the King of Hungary and his allies who had their own interests there to safeguard ; and it met disaster at Varna in 1446. As it was, John VIII gained nothing from the Union except the hatred of his subjects. The settlement reached at Florence lasted till the fall of the Empire ; but it was never accepted by the vast majority of the citizens of Constantinople. Though in the Empire's death-throe the differences were forgotten and Unionists and Nationalists alike took part in that last solemn Mass in Saint Sophia, yet the Grand Duke Lucas Notaras was not alone in his declaration that the Sultan's turban was better than the Cardinal's hat. Nor was he unreasonable, for the Sultan left the Greeks their autonomous Church to keep their spirit alive through the centuries

[1] Phrantzes, 178.

of political darkness, but Rome would have robbed them of their spirit.

The story of the relations of the two great Churches is one that does little credit to Christendom. But to attempt to assign right and wrong, morally or historically, is useless, and apologists that write long works to justify either cause waste their time. The difficulty was that each Church had its own conception of Christian organisation and authority. While Rome went further and further down the path towards Papal Infallibility, Constantinople remained doggedly faithful to the democratic ideas of the early Christians. ' How can we accept decrees as to which we have not been consulted ? ' asked Nicetas of Nicomedia of Anselm of Havelberg when they discussed the question of Union in the Twelfth Century ; [1] and Rome's demand of absolute submission was no answer.

The autonomy that Rome would deny her was given by Constantinople to the national Churches within her sphere. The Cypriot Church had claimed autonomy since the Council of Ephesus (431) ; [2] and Constantinople never sought to control though she sought to influence the Patriarchates of the East. The foreign Churches created by her own missionary zeal, the various Caucasian and Slavonic Churches, were encouraged to have their own language and were permitted in due course to govern themselves. The Byzantine ideal was a series of autocephalous State Churches, linked by inter-communion and the faith of the Seven Councils. Even a subject-country might retain her Church. When Basil II conquered Bulgaria, he left the Bulgarian Church with its native priests and its Slavonic ritual ; he only insisted that its primate should be a Greek, to ensure that the organisation was not used for nationalist propaganda. [3]

---

[1] Norden, *op. cit.*, 97–9.   [2] Mansi, *Concilia*, vol. 4, 1469.
[3] Gelzer in *B.Z.*, vol. 1, 245 *sqq.* ; vol. 2, 2 *sqq.*

There were many of these autocephalous daughter-churches ; for the Byzantine Church was a great mission-ising force. The Caucasus, the Balkan peninsula, the Russian plains, all owed their Christianity to Constantinople ; and Cyril and Methodius, the apostles to Central Europe, were sent out originally from the Imperial Court. Under Photius it seems that there was a definite school at Constantinople for educating missionaries to the Slavs.[1] The secular Government naturally liked to encourage work that tended to increase its sphere of influence ; but there is no reason to doubt the genuine altruistic intentions of the Church, nor to minimise the gifts of civilisation that it brought to the converted nations.

The Byzantine Church has not been kindly treated by historians. Its piety was not the piety of the West. Its monasticism tended more and more to develop into quietism ; it set an almost hysterical store on the value of repentance. Its passions were quickly roused, and many of its synods and councils were enlivened by scenes of most unseemly violence. Whereas in the West it was the eschatological problem that mainly occupied the Christian's mind, the Eastern Christian was eager to enter into the state of grace, the right relationship to God, here and now. To that end the nature of the Incarnation of Christ, his Mediator, was of paramount importance. To that end if he could achieve a mystic union with God all other forms of religion seemed worthless in comparison. But too often the Orthodox Church has been denounced as being unintellectual and unprogressive. Neither of these charges is fair. Neither Quietism nor the doctrine of Grace, it is true, invites intellectual support, but the long series of writers from Saint Paul to Gennadius, whose services she used, is a sufficient refutation. The Church did not indeed produce an

[1] Photius, *Epistolae*, *M.P.G.*, vol. 103, 904–5 ; *Vita S. Nahum*, ed. Lavrov (in Slavonic), 4–5.

I

Aquinas ; she never advanced her doctrine much beyond the Seven Councils. But the reason was a certain tolerance, a feeling that the Christian must work out his own salvation, within the bare limits of the Orthodox faith of the Councils. There was to be no rigid Scholasticism to tell him what and how to think. Many points of doctrine were left unsolved, particularly eschatological points, such as the existence of Purgatory. The study of Greek philosophy was encouraged, so long as it did not lead to heterodoxy like the neo-paganism of John Italus. The man in the street indeed felt that this was sometimes carried too far, and that these philosophical students were a menace to the State ;[1] but John Mauropus, the pious Bishop of Euchaïta, wrote a poem in the Eleventh Century, asking Christ to count Plato and the neo-Platonist Plutarch as Christians, because their doctrines were so noble.[2] Psellus, indeed, when he was dabbling deeply in thaumaturgy and astrology, found it advisable to assure the ecclesiastical authorities that he was doing nothing contrary to Christian doctrine, but his word was enough.[3] Gemistus Plethon, who hoped that in a few years Christianity would disappear, when it came to a question between the Greek and Latin Churches, violently opposed the latter as being far the greater menace to thought. After the fall of the Empire, Plethon's last book was, it is true, banned by the Greek Church ; but as it was openly anti-Christian, no one can be surprised ; and Gennadius was very sad at the necessity of destroying so fine an intellectual work.[4]

Nor was the Church intolerantly rigid about its usages. The Orthodox might rail at the Latins for using unleavened

---

[1] The argument of the pseudo-Lucianic *Philopatris* (probably Tenth Century).   [2] Quoted in Soyter, *Byzantinische Dichtung*, 26.

[3] Psellus, *Chronographia*, II, 77.   But see Bandinius, *Catalogus Codicum Graecorum Bibliothecae Laurentianae* (Florence), Vol. II, 547–8, for a record of an MS. of Psellus's admission of faith.

[4] Gennadius, letter in *M.P.G.*, vol. 160, 663 *sqq.*

bread and fasting on Saturdays ; but good Churchmen
were taught that allowances had often to be made, and
under some circumstances rules can be broken. Saint
Symeon the New Theologian severely reproved his disciple
Arsenius for being shocked when the Saint gave a dyspeptic
visitor the pigeon's flesh that he required although it was a
fast day.[1]

For non-Christians the authorities were less kindly. The
Jews in particular were subjected to periodical persecution.
Heraclius was particularly severe against them, owing to
a prophecy that the Empire would be destroyed by a
circumcised race ;[2] and later Emperors reverted to the
task of suppressing them. It was a mark of Romanus I's
admirable piety that he gave orders for their banishment.[3]
But it is noticeable that the persecutors were the lay powers,
not the Church. With the Moslems the Church was often
on friendly terms. Certain Califs and Emperors would
encourage amicable debates between exponents of the two
religions. The Emperor Manuel Comnenus even managed
to induce the Church to remove the anathema on the God
of Islam, but that was considered heresy.[4] But the Patriarch
Arsenius was broad-minded enough, in the Thirteenth
Century, to allow the Seljuk Sultan to bathe in a bath
belonging to the Church, and to order a monk to administer
the Sacrament to his children without having made sure
that they were properly baptised.[5] In times of war there
might be high feelings and persecution on either side, but
on the whole the relations between Byzantium and Islam
compare favourably with those between Byzantium and
Rome.

Like most religious bodies of the Middle Ages the Byzan-

---

[1] *Vita S. Symeonis Novi Theologii*, 66.
[2] Fredegarius in *M.P.L.*, vol. 71, 646.
[3] Maçoudi, *Prairies d'Or*, trans. Barbier de Meynard, II, 8–9.
[4] Nicetas Choniates, 278–284.   [5] Pachymer, I, 258.

tine Church was surrounded with superstition. The passion
with which it fought for its images has made history inclined
to exaggerate this quality. Actually to the East the West
seemed far more superstitious. In the East statues in three
dimensions had been debarred as idols in the days before
Iconoclasm, and pictures in the flat were allowed because
of their direct spiritual reaction. The Puritan Asiatic strain
in the Byzantines never disappeared. The Burgundian
La Brocquière thought, in the Fourteenth Century, that
they did not pay as much regard to their relics as his
countrymen would have done.[1] Nevertheless there was in
the heart of the people a great love for their images and
for the stupendous collection of relics that the piety of
generations of Emperors had built up. Belief in the miraculous powers of the portraits, the emblems and the very
bones and belongings of God and His Saints, was widespread. Even the most highly educated intellectuals, like
Anna Comnena, felt that there was something in it. The
thaumaturgy that had characterised the last centuries of
pagan Rome survived in a Christian form in Byzantium.
The sick went now to be healed to the Churches of Saint
Cosmas and Saint Damian or the Archangel Michael, as
once they had gone to the temples of Asclepius ; and
miracles still saved holy fortresses, though the Palladium
was now the Virgin's Cloak or the bones of some saint.
This vivid piety was one of the most striking characteristics
of Byzantine life.[2] The Church made full use of it, but
whether it was to the benefit of the Church is somewhat
doubtful.

Taken in all, the Byzantine Church was, like the civil
administration, well suited to its circumstances and times.
It had its dark periods. Under Justinian and under the

[1] La Brocquière, *Voyage d'Outremer* in Schefer, *Recueil de Voyages*,
vol. 12, 163.
[2] See below, p. 212.

Comneni, it was an almost lifeless department of State, while at the other extreme, anarchy often tended to a slackening of its discipline. The monasteries in particular were in need of constant supervision. After the attacks on them by the Iconoclasts, Saint Plato had great difficulty in restoring the needful laws of celibacy, refusing to permit even female animals within the monastery walls.[1] At the chaotic close of the Eleventh Century things were even worse. Saint Christodulus could not induce his monks to stay quietly by themselves at Patmos, and Alexius I had to advise him to allow a few lay families to settle there to lessen the severity of life.[2] Even monks from Athos appeared at the Imperial Court to complain that the presence of Vlach shepherd-boys on the Holy Mountain was leading to unnatural vice, and Alexius discovered that they had invented the scandal to give them an excuse to visit Constantinople. The Patriarch eagerly tried to stop such laxities, but the Metropolitans would not back him up sufficiently.[3]

Such episodes were, however, exceptional. On the whole the personnel of the higher clergy was a guarantee against them. The Church was a democratic institution. It was possible for any orthodox Christian, however humble his origin, to attain to the Patriarchal throne ; merit was in theory the sole criterion, and in practice, except when an Emperor deliberately appointed a nonentity—an action that was always unpopular—the Patriarchs were of a very high level of ability ; often even when a nonentity was appointed, as when John Vatatzes elevated the colourless Arsenius rather than Blemmydas, he somehow rose to the occasion and in no way disgraced his position. Almost all took seriously their rôle of Keeper of the Empire's conscience, fearlessly denouncing vice in high places, like Chrysostom

---

[1] Theodore Studites, *M.P.G.*, vol. 99, 824–5.
[2] Miklosich and Müller, *Acta et Diplomata Graeca Med. Aevi*, vol. 6, 45 *sqq.*
[3] Meyer, *Athosklöster*, 163 *sqq.*

or Polyeuct, or seeking to save the victims of the people's rage, as Joseph, who attempted to rescue the hated Catalans from the massacre of 1307.[1] The metropolitans and the bishops appear less often in the limelight, and so it is less easy to generalise about them. Throughout Byzantine history they included men like Saint Gregory Nazianzene, George of Pisidia, John Mauropus of Euchaïta and Michael Acominatus of Athens ; and, despite occasional simony, there is no reason to suppose that the general average was either ill-educated or incompetent. Indeed, the worldly possessions that they had to administer called for a certain competence, which was tested at the time of foreign invasions ; for when the military and civil powers retreated before the enemy, it was left for the bishop to look after the interests of his flock ; Demetrian, Bishop of Chytri in Cyprus, even journeyed to Baghdad in the interests of the Cypriot Christians under the Saracen yoke.[2] Even the local saints and hermits, though their mode of life seems to us painfully and unnecessarily squalid, often exercised a beneficent moral and political influence. The Phocian Luke the Less, the Argive Nicon Metanoeite or the Calabrian Saint Nilus— whose career belongs more to the Italy of the Saxon Em-perors—all were important and valuable servants to both the Church and the State. Of the quality of the village priests we know practically nothing. Probably, then as now, they were humble in their habits and seldom well educated, but performed their duties as best they could.

The Byzantine Church was indeed an admirable State Church. Its rich ritual enhanced the majesty of the Empire, its saints and its icons brought it down to the level of the people, its obstinate refusal to submit to foreign dictation built up the sentiment of nationality, and there was enough freedom in its theology not to stifle the intel-lectual activity on which the Empire prided itself. Centuries

[1] Pachymer, II, 531.   [2] Pargoire in *B.Z.*, vol. 16, 204 *sqq.*

of Turkish oppression were to force the Orthodox to learn the lowering art of living in the dark ; but so long as Constantinople endured as a free Christian city, its Church remained the most civilised religious organisation that the world had so far known.

CHAPTER VI

The Army: The Navy: The Diplomatic Service

I. The Army [1]

The administration of Byzantium was closely bound up with her military forces. The Empire was beset with enemies; never for a moment could the Government feel free from the danger of foreign invasion, of some irruption that might threaten the Capital itself. Its very existence depended upon the proper control of the nations around —upon an efficient and ever-ready army and navy and on a ceaseless diplomacy.

The Byzantines were not inherently a militaristic people. Martial prowess was indeed admirable in their eyes, but not the one desirable quality, as in the chivalrous West; the triumphant general remained a valued servant of the State. It was necessity that forced them in time to mould themselves on military lines and to give military affairs their scientific attention. It was all to their advantage. Byzantium was the one place throughout the Middle Ages where the means of war, army organisation and strategy, were carefully and calmly studied. Byzantium produced a series of able military writers and many of her historians took an interest in military affairs. From them we can trace, with certain gaps, the development of the history of Byzantine arms. In the early centuries we have the Fourth-

[1] See Oman, *History of the Art of War*, 3–37, 169–226; Diehl, *Justinian*, 145–245 (with bibliography); Aussaresses, *l'Armée Byzantine*; and works cited above, page 88, note 2.

Century Italian Vegetius [1] and the pedantic late Fifth-
Century theorist Urbicius.[2] Procopius, in the Sixth Century, is above all a military historian ; and the Emperor
Maurice a few decades later wrote his *Strategicon*, an invaluable treatise on the army of the time.[3] About the
year 900 the Emperor Leo VI, one of the few Emperors
who never soldiered himself, compiled a full treatise on all
military matters known as the *Tactica* ; [4] about 960 one
of Nicephorus Phocas's generals dedicated to his sovereign
a handbook dealing with war on the eastern front,[5] and a
little later another such handbook was written by an author
unknown to us.[6] In the Eleventh Century the old soldier
Cecaumenus wrote down discursively some of the fruits
of his experience : [7] while in the early Twelfth all Anna
Comnena's verbosity cannot altogether conceal her interest
and grasp of military affairs. But by then the Byzantine
army was already in decadence.

When Constantine founded his City on the Bosphorus,
the Roman army was undergoing a period of change.[8]
The Third Century had been disastrous. The army
organisation had shown its dangers. The Prætorian Guard
made and unmade Emperors ; and the great provincial
governors with whole legions at their beck were in almost
perpetual rebellion. Diocletian, and Constantine after him,
attempted reform. They set up a regular frontier-force
of hereditary soldiers paid in land—the *limitanei*—and
then founded a mobile central army—the *Comitatenses*—

---

[1] *Epitoma Rei Militaris*, ed. Lang.
[2] Usually printed along with Onosander's *Strategicon*.
[3] Maurice, *Strategicon*, ed. Scheffer.
[4] Leo VI, *Tactica*, M.P.G., vol. 107.
[5] Nicephorus Phocas, *De Velitatione Belli*, printed with Leo Diaconus
in the Bonn *Corpus*.
[6] *Liber de Re Militari*, ed. Vari (in Teubner series).
[7] Cecaumenus, *Strategicon*.
[8] See Grosse, *Römische Militärgeschichte*, *passim*, and bibliography.

under the Emperor, which could be rushed to any point desired.

But this was not enough. In equipment and tactics the army was growing out of date. The heavy legionary was no longer a match for the cavalryman of the Barbarians. Julian's victory over the Germans at Strasburg in 357 was the last triumph of Roman infantry. Twenty-one years later, in the colossal disaster of Adrianople, it showed its helplessness before the Gothic horsemen. Already the desirability of cavalry had been realised and the cavalry corps increased. Now the need was greater than the supply. Theodosius I, called up to rebuild the Empire as quickly as possible, decided to call in barbarian cavalry to defeat barbarian cavalry. He instituted the *fœderati*, barbarian regiments or whole tribes who took service with the Romans under the leadership of their prince. It was a desperate remedy ; and it ruined the West. The *fœderati* might check Attila, but their leaders, become great Roman generals, were too powerful. Barbarians like Ricimer and Odoacer disposed of the Imperial crown at their pleasure, till they decided that it would be simpler to have no Emperor at all in Italy. In the East, after the failure of the Goth Gainas, the Imperial family were just able to keep the *fœderati* in check, till Leo I and his son-in-law Zeno were able to reduce their power to a manageable level by calling in troops from the wilder tribes of the Empire to balance them, Isaurians and Armenians from the Asian hills.

By the Sixth Century [1] the *fœderati* were reduced to reasonable and useful limits. They were balanced now by the heavy cavalry from Asia Minor, the Cataphracti that Procopius admired so much ; and it was these cavalry troops, cuirassiers armed with bows, who won the victories

---

[1] See Diehl, *op. cit.* ; Bury, *Later Roman Empire*, II, 76 *sqq.* ; Oman, *op. cit.*, 3–37.

of Justinian's reign. But the *fœderati* had left behind a bad system of recruiting which spread over the whole army. It was the general who collected and supported his men, not the central Government. Regiments or legions with regular names were unknown now ; each corps was called after its commander. Collectively they were known as the Bucellarii. The system was made worse by Justinian's habit of never entrusting any of his generals with much power or much money. As a result his wars were continually hampered by mutinies and discontent, and his victories due to the genius of his two great commanders, Belisarius and the eunuch Narses.

The financial difficulties of Justinian's later years and of Justin II's reign resulted in the diminution of the foreign mercenaries. The Empire could not afford the *fœderati*. This might weaken the numbers of the Imperial army ; but it enabled the next Emperors, Tiberius and Maurice, to abolish the system of the Bucellarii—the name however lasted to describe a regiment—and reorganise the whole army, making it dependent on the Emperor. The *Strategicon* gives a picture of the new army. The unit is the band, *numerus*, *arithmos* or *tagma*—the transition from Latin to Greek was not yet complete, and the drill words were particularly mixed. The band consisted of 300 or 400 men, commanded by a *comes* or tribune. Six, seven or eight bands form a *moira* under a moerarch or dux. The numbers were kept purposely vague so that the enemy could never calculate the army's size. The grouping together of the bands was the commander-in-chief's business when war broke out. There were no permanent regiments, except for the Bucellarii, the Fœderati and the Optimati, the remnants of the foreign mercenaries forming now some sort of Imperial guard. Maurice, further, had a scheme for introducing a territorial force. He wished all free-born men to learn archery and possess a bow and javelin, so that they could defend their districts in time of invasion.[1] How far this was carried out, we cannot tell. Certainly in the frontier fortresses citizens were called upon to help in the defence.

It was the army reorganised by Tiberius and Maurice that Heraclius led to victory in the long Persian Wars and that, exhausted, was overwhelmed by the onrush of the Arabs. The Saracen conquests robbed the Empire of Egypt, Africa and Syria, and only with difficulty, after years of chaos, was the frontier of Asia Minor held against them. During these years the reorganisation of the army was further developed, through stages that we cannot trace : till at last, in the Eighth Century, the Isaurian Emperors perfected the system of themes.[2]

The origin of the theme system lay in the stationing of certain regiments or themes, certain regular combinations of bands, to defend certain fixed districts, and then the appointment of the regimental commander or strategus to the head of the civil government also. The districts thereupon were known as themes ; and at first each was called after the particular regiment that occupied, as the Optimatian or the Bucellarian. But as the Empire grew more orderly and civil life recovered, new themes were added in reclaimed districts and on the frontier. These themes were given geographical names, as Charsianian or Seleucian, after their chief towns, or Cappadocian or Peloponnesian, after the old name of the province. The themes were subdivided into two or perhaps three turmarchies or *merê*, the district occupied by each turma or main division of the regiment, under a turmarch or merarch. The turma was in its turn divided for military purposes into three *moirai*, each under a drungarius, and the moira into 10 bands or *tagmata* under a comes. As the frontier was pushed forward turmarchies would be detached from their original themes and with the

[1] Maurice, *Strategicon, passim.*   [2] See above, p. 88 *sqq.*

addition of the new territory be raised to be themes themselves. Thus Leo VI created the theme of Seleucia.
Certain frontier districts, particularly the passes, were
kept outside of the thematic organisation and were
under permanent military occupation. These were called
Kleisourai or Clissuræ, and their commander a Clissurarch.
They too might be raised to be themes.

The thematic army was primarily a defensive weapon ;
and in the days when the Empire was perpetually on the
defensive it was the most important arm. The Strategus
of the Anatolic theme, the senior Strategus, up to the Ninth
Century was the Commander-in-Chief in Asia, and even in
the Tenth Century he ranked extraordinarily high in the
official hierarchy. Attached to the troops of the Clissuræ—
possibly at times in control of them—were the border barons,
the Akritæ, such as the epic hero Digenis, who carried on a
permanent free-booting warfare against the Saracen, but
probably joined the Imperial armies for any organised
expedition.

During the Ninth Century a new branch of the army rose
in importance, the *Tagmata* or four regiments of Imperial
guards, the Scholæ, the Excubitors, the Arithmos or Vigla
(or Watch) and the Hicanati.[1] The last was apparently
the foundation of Nicephorus I, the others descended from
the Palace guards of the Earlier Empire. These were
cavalry regiments, probably not of great strength—the
Schools in the Tenth Century numbered only 1,500 men—
each under a Domestic, except the Vigla, which was under
a Drungarius. Attached to them were the Numeri, foot-
soldiers numbering about 4,000, and the Hetæria, the
present Imperial Guard, recruited from foreigners—the last
successors of the *fœderati*. These troops were usually
stationed in Thrace or Bithynia, and accompanied the
Emperor when he went campaigning, and gradually, if the

[1] Bury, *Imperial Administrative System*, 47–68.

Emperor did not campaign in person, the Domestic of the Scholæ acted as commander-in-chief. During the long period, almost a century, from Basil I to Nicephorus II, when none of the Emperors was a soldier, he was by far the most important military official in the Empire, though in precedence he still ranked below the Strategus of the Anatolics ; and the transition to offensive warfare in the course of this period only enhanced his position : till in 963 the Domestic of the Schools Nicephorus Phocas was the obvious candidate for the Empire during the minority of the purple-born Emperors.

The duties of the various troops were carefully laid down. The thematic army guarded against foreign raids. When for instance the Saracens crossed the frontier the local commander at once told the Strategus of the theme. He sent at once to warn the neighbouring themes, while his cavalry set out to pursue and hang on to the skirts of the raiders, and the infantry occupied the passes through which they would have to return. The neighbouring themes meanwhile collected their main troops and prepared to converge on some point for which the enemy were expected to be making.[1] If the concentration were well timed the invaders might be caught and surrounded, as when in 863 the Saracen general Omar was trapped by the thematic army of Asia on the Halys.[2] Counter-raids ought also to be made, and the fleet should be told to ravage the Saracen coasts.[3]

When the Byzantine army made a counter-attack, the Emperor or the Domestic of the Scholæ led the Tagmata out from Constantinople and was joined at fixed points on the great Military Road through Asia by detachments of troops from the various themes.[4] These consisted mainly of

[1] Leo, *Tactica*, 977 *sqq.* ; *De Velitatione Belli, passim,* esp. 215–17.
[2] Bury, *Eastern Roman Empire*, 281–4.   [3] Leo, *Tactica*, 980.
[4] Ramsay, *Historical Geography of Asia Minor,* 197 *sqq.*

infantry, though each theme sent some of its cavalry, as we know that the Emperor was expected to be accompanied by at least 8,200 horsemen, and the Tagmata probably did not number much more than 6,000.[1] Very little information has survived about the procedure actually adopted during an offensive in the enemy's country. When Leo VI wrote they were rare and he barely mentioned them. Even Nicephorus Phocas's soldier described the old defensive warfare, though he said that his experiences were out of date nowadays.[2] It is only in the little anonymous handbook (the *Liber de Re Militari*) that the invasion of foreign lands is contemplated ; and even so, though at the time John Tzimisces was leading his armies to Palestine and the suburbs of Baghdad, the rules laid down are cautious and somewhat indefinite, and chiefly deal with the siege of enemy cities.

Caution, indeed, was the keynote of Byzantine strategy. The attacks of Barbarian and Infidel were so frequent and often so unexpected, that a bold aggressive policy was scarcely ever practicable. The Byzantine army was not vast, like the army of the Saracens, and it was expensive. It had therefore to be used to the best advantage, without waste of life or equipment. Every Byzantine textbook insists on the folly of rashness ; generals must beware of ambushes and surprise attacks, and never leave their flanks unguarded. They must have reliable scouts and use stratagems and tricks wherever possible. Indeed, the morality preached was of a low level. A word that is pledged must be kept ; captives' lives must be spared, and women unharmed ; peace terms must not be harsh if the enemy fought gallantly. But insincere parleys were recommended, to gain time and to spy on the enemy ; enemy

[1] Bury, *Imperial Administrative System*, 53 sqq. ; *Eastern Roman Empire*, 227–8.
[2] *De Velitatione Belli*, 183–5.

generals should be sent incriminating letters so as to embroil them with their commanders ; morale might be maintained by telling the soldiers news of imaginary victories.[1]

Such devices may have had their uses ; but the real strength of the Byzantines lay in the intelligence with which they faced their various enemies. They made it their business to learn each opponent's particular methods of warfare and the best way to counter them. Thus the Franks were victims to their own rashness ; they could be led on into ambushes. Their commissariat was bad and hunger tempted them to desert. They were insubordinate to their commanders, and they were corrupt. If a pitched battle, where their valour and their personal strength helped them, were avoided, they could easily be worn out.[2] The Turks, who included Magyars and Petchenegs, were on the other hand cunning themselves, and consisted of hordes of light horsemen. The Byzantine general should, after having guarded against ambushes, close in to battle as quickly as possible. His heavy horsemen could ride them down, and they could not break his infantry lines.[3] The Slavs, light foot-soldiers, were dangerous only in difficult hill country. In the plains they were too badly armed and too undisciplined to stand up against the Imperial troops.[4] The Saracens remained the most important enemies. They could amass enormous armies, they moved with great speed and they had made a certain study of the art of war. But they remained somewhat disorganised, and their morale was not good in defeat. A night attack when they were laden with booty and so moving unusually slowly might make them panic, and they were affected by the weather, being dispirited in cold or rain. As man to man, their cavalrymen were no match for the Byzantine ; and so a pitched battle need not be feared unless the numbers were disproportionate.[5] Similarly the

---

[1] Leo, *Tactica*, 1048 *sqq.*   [2] *Ibid.*, 964 *sqq.*
[3] *Ibid.*, 956 *sqq.*   [4] *Ibid.*, 968 *sqq.*   [5] *Ibid.*, 972 *sqq.*

art of siege-warfare had its special rules according to the nature of the town besieged and the surrounding country.[1] These rules were carefully laid down, but they were not rigid. A new device was always welcome. Cecaumenus urged generals to think out fresh methods ; [2] and Anna Comnena praised her father Alexius I for the novelties that he introduced.[3] Also, the besieged should examine and find out their enemy's strength and temperament. Cecaumenus recommended sorties and a certain amount of trickery ; [4] while fortification had long been a careful study.

The strength of the Byzantine army was its heavy cavalry-men, the Caballarii. These wore steel caps and mail shirts, with steel frontlets for the officers and front-rank men ; they had linen and woollen cloaks to put on over their armour according to the weather. Their arms were a sword, a dagger, a bow and quiver, and a lance. The tuft in the cap, the lance-pennon and the cloak, all were coloured according to the regiment. The foot-soldiers were mostly light archers —certain provinces supplied javelin-men instead—but there were also heavy infantry men who wore mail and carried axes, lances, swords and shields. It was they that would hold difficult mountain-passes where cavalry could scarcely be employed. Greek fire, the main feature of Byzantine naval warfare, was only used by the military to drive off besiegers.[5]

Various data are given as to the pay of the troops. The salaries of the Strategi of the military themes in Asia ranged from 20 lb. of gold to 40 lb. a year (21,600 to 43,200 gold francs). Turmarchs apparently received at least 3 lb (3,240 gold francs) and lesser officers 2 lb. or 1 lb. Among the men, recruits apparently were given 1 nomisma for the

---

[1] Leo, *Tactica*, Cecaumenus, *Strategicon*, 26-35, dealing with the defence of fortresses.

[2] Cecaumenus, *op. cit.*, 14. [3] Anna Comnena, 408.

[4] Cecaumenus, *op. cit.*, 17.

[5] Leo, *Tactica*, 717 *sqq.* ; Oman, *op. cit.*, 184 *sqq.*

first year, 2 for the second, and so on till twelve or in some cases eighteen were reached. Cecaumenus recommended very strongly that soldiers' pay should never be cut. It has been calculated that the armies in the Eastern themes, including Thrace and Macedonia, cost the Treasury at least £500,000 or 22,500,000 gold francs a year. The pay was given out by the Chartularius of each theme, an official controlled by the central Government.[1] The soldiers were, however, often paid in land. The cavalrymen were drawn largely from small-holdings whose owners had an hereditary obligation to serve, and in return escaped all taxes except the land-tax.[2] The obligation might however be avoided ; the widowed mother of Saint Euthymius the Young (born about the year 820) married him off early, in order that having two women to support and a holding to keep up he might be excused his military service.[3] The Hetaerii were so well remunerated that foreigners would pay to be allowed to enter their ranks.[4]

At its height the Byzantine army probably numbered only about 120,000, some 70,000 for the armies of the Eastern themes, and the rest made up from the Western themes and the regiments of central army.[5] But we must add to this the vast number of camp-followers who accompanied the army. Soldiers were allowed to take slaves and servants with them, in order that they might not be fatigued by having to pitch their tents or dig trenches. The commissariat was done by non-combatants. A corps of non-combatant engineers was always present to lay out the camp for the night.[6] Moreover, there was a highly efficient medical corps with an ambulance

[1] Bury, *Eastern Roman Empire*, 225–7.
[2] See Rambaud, *L'Empire Grec*, 287–96, and references on page 96, note 4.
[3] See Bréhier, *Les Populations Ruraux*, in *Byzantion*, vol. 1, 183.
[4] Constantine Porphyrogennetus, *De Ceremoniis*, 1, 692–3.
[5] Bury, *op. cit.*, 226.
[6] Leo, *Tactica*, 792 *sqq.*

organisation of which any army might be proud : [1] while
huge baths were built for the soldiers' benefit at the great
military stations such as Dorylæum.[2]

In 1071 the Emperor Romanus Diogenes, violating as he
went every canon of Byzantine strategy, led his troops to
disaster at Manzikert. The Byzantine army never recovered, not so much owing to that one great cataclysm
itself, but because in consequence of it Asia Minor was
mainly lost and the whole thematic organisation was upset.
The eunuch Nicephorus the Logothete and after him
Alexius I managed to patch together an army which beat off
the Normans and the Petchenegs and did good service under
his son John—to be wasted in Armenia and Hungary by
his grandson Manuel and lost at last at Myriocephalum.
But this was a haphazard army gathered from day to day as
best it could be managed with no organisation to maintain
it ; for economy it had to be disbanded every winter.
The Emperors had to rely more and more on foreign
mercenaries. Foreigners had always been employed to be
the bodyguard of the Imperial Court : while the rebel
Bardas Phocas had a guard of picked Georgians, all equally
tall and clad in white armour.[3] The famous Varangian
Guard was founded at some date during the first half of the
Eleventh Century.[4] By the reign of Alexius it contained
foreigners of every description—Russians, ' Colbingians,'
Turks, Alans, English, Franks, Germans and Bulgars [5]—
and formed with the Hicanati, the Vestiantes, the Immortals
(the remnants of the old Tagmata, collected after Manzikert by the eunuch Nicephorus in 1078) and the Archonto-
puli (founded by Alexius for the sons of dead noblemen),

[1] Leo, *Tactica*, 820 *sqq.*   [2] Ibn-Khurdadhbah, ed. de Goeje, 81.
[3] Psellus, *Chronographia*, I, 10.
[4] See Vasilievsky, *The Varangian-Russian Guard* (in Russian), in
Journal of Ministry of Public Instruction of S. Petersburg, 1874–5.
[5] *Jus Graeco-Romanum*, III, 373.

the nucleus of the whole army. It was the Varangian
Guard, consisting largely of Englishmen, that the Normans
defeated at Dyrrhachium in 1081. There was no thematic
army. The themes were disordered and the Comneni
preferred to centralise. There were two chief commands
now, the Domestic in the East and the Domestic in the West,
instead of the various Strategi. Additional troops were
provided by foreign mercenaries.[1]

In the earlier Eleventh Century it had been a fixed rule
never to give foreigners high commands. Peter, ' the
nephew of the King of Germany,' who took service under
Basil II was for all his merits never given rank higher than
that of a provincial domestic.[2] Under the Comneni
foreigners were employed even in the most responsible
positions. Alexius's Grand Hetæriarch was a Scythian :
though Bohemond was considered grossly impertinent when
he asked to be made Domestic of the East.[3] But Manuel I
and Maria of Antioch gave many of the most important posts
to Latins.

The mercenary system depended on large sums of ready
money in the Treasury. Under the Angeli the money began
to fail. Finally, in the crisis of 1204 when the foreign
soldiers demanded their pay, none could be provided.
And so the foreigners, their only loyalty being financial,
refused to fight and Constantinople was left defenceless.

The Nicæan Emperors with their rigid economies managed to build up a small army and to settle militia on the
frontiers, paying them with the old system of small-holdings.
But the Palæologi could not afford to maintain indigenous
troops. The story of the Catalan Company warned them of
the dangers of hiring mercenaries, but they had no alternative. The post of the Grand Domestic, their commander-
in-chief, was often almost a sinecure. The man-power of

---

[1] Buckler, *Anna Comnena*, 353 *sqq.*
[2] Cecaumenus, *Noutheticos*, 95–6.   [3] Anna Comnena, 208, 267.

the Empire was rapidly declining ; and to keep up an
army in peace-time was an unthinkable extravagance.
Long before Constantinople fell to the Turks the Byzantine
army was a thing of the past. All the legacy that the great
soldiers had left to their impoverished descendants was the
long line of walls that for so many centuries were the bulwark
of the Christian East.

II. *The Navy* [1]

The army was very much the Senior Service in Byzantium.
The navy was never given the same importance and attention. Till Leo VI wrote his *Tactica* there had been no book
written on naval warfare in Byzantium, and he only devoted
a few short chapters to it ; [2] and only one other writer
returned to the subject, the Paracoemomenus Basil, whose
Naumachia has never, however, been published. Constantine
VII provides some incidental information ; but historians
such as Anna Comnena obviously regard naval affairs as of
little interest compared to military. Consequently we know
less of the naval history of Byzantium ; and it is tempting to
minimise its significance.

In the great days of the Roman Empire, when the Mediterranean was a Roman lake, a large fleet had been unnecessary. The fortress of Byzantium should keep the pirates of
the Black Sea coasts from invading civilised waters, where
only a small police-force was required. Even during the
first Gothic invasions very few ships had been enough to

---

[1] See Neumann, *Die Byzantinische Marine, H.Z.*, vol. 45, 1 *sqq.* ; Bury,
Appendix 5 to Gibbon, *Decline and Fall*, vol. 6, and *Naval Policy* in
Centenario di M. Amari, II, 21–34 ; Baynes, *Byzantine Empire*, 143–9,
217–20 ; Buckler, *Anna Comnena*, 381–6.

[2] Leo, *Tactica*, 989 *sqq.*

blockade the coast and make the barbarians move on.   It
was only when the Vandals came to Africa and built a fleet
that the inadequacy of Rome's naval policy was displayed.
But the Fifth-Century Emperors neither in the East nor in
the West made more than half-hearted attempts to overcome
the lack, and even Justinian was aided more by the decline
of the Vandal sea-power than by any sea-power of his own.

The Byzantine navy really began under the Heraclian
Emperors.   The growing sea-power of the Arabs demanded
a counter-blast ; and the many invaders of the Empire made
land-travel so difficult that properly guarded sea-routes were
advisable..   When the themes were being founded, two naval
themes were included, where the governor was an admiral,
not a general.   These were the Cibyrrhæot theme, covering
the southern coast of Asia Minor, and the Ægean, made up
of the islands and parts of the western coast of Asia Minor.
Each was under a drungarius, and the two drungarii were
under the supreme command of the Strategus of the Cara-
bisiani.   It was this fleet that twice drove off the Arabs
from Constantinople and preserved Sicily for the Empire.
But it grew too powerful.   In 698 it dethroned Leontius,
placing an admiral Apsimar on the throne.   In 711 it
dethroned Justinian II.[1]   The soldier Emperors of the
Isaurian dynasty were frightened.   Moreover, while the
Asiatic soldiery supported their Iconoclastic schemes, the
navy was largely recruited from provinces devoted to image-
worship, a devotion consonant with the superstitious soul of a
sailor.   The Arab sea-power was on the decline, so they
considered it safe to abolish the supreme command, degrade
the maritime themes, and greatly reduce the number of
ships.[2]

It was a mistaken policy.   By the Ninth Century Arab
fleets again appeared, and robbed the Empire of Sicily and,
worse, of Crete, turning Crete into a pirate-base that

[1] Theophanes, 370, 380.   [2] *Ibid.*, 410.

endangered all the Ægean coasts. The fleet had to be revived. Its rebirth coincided, possibly with reason, with the final death of Iconoclasm. Theodora and Michael III and after them Basil I reorganised the whole navy. The organisation of the maritime themes was restored ; a little later the theme of Samos, including Smyrna, was added to their number. The European themes of Hellas, the Peloponnese, Cephallonia and the Italian themes were given naval establishments. There was to be a large Imperial fleet stationed at Constantinople, under the Grand Drungarius, one of the high officials in the hierarchy. The Strategi of the Naval themes still, however, drew a salary smaller than that of any of their military compeers—only 10 lb. of gold a year.[1]

The new navy was efficient and successful. It could not save Sicily, but it won back Southern Italy for the Empire, and expeditions up the Adriatic under Basil I's great admiral Ooryphas made the Dalmatian coast declare a long-forgotten allegiance.[2] The Saracen pirate Leo of Tripoli managed, despite it, to sack Thessalonica in 904, but it hounded him down to his death a few years later.[3] Under Zoe Carbopsina it destroyed a Saracen robbers' nest on the River Garigliano and under Romanus I it performed a similar task as far off as Fréjus.[4] In 961 Crete was at last restored after two failures, in 902 and 949. Thereafter the Arab sea-power was over ; and Nicephorus Phocas could say with truth to the Italian ambassador Liudprand, ' I alone command the sea.'[5] Already Constantine VII had claimed the supremacy right to the Straits of Gibraltar.[6]

[1] Bury, *Eastern Roman Empire*, 229–31.
[2] Constantine Porphyrogennetus, *De Administrando Imperio*, 130.
[3] Theophanes Continuatus, 405.
[4] Liudprand, *Antapodosis*, 61–2 ; Leo Ostiensis, I, 50 *sqq.* ; Flodoard, *M.P.L.*, vol. 145, 431 ; Liudprand, *op. cit.*, 135, 139.
[5] Idem, *Legatio*, 182.
[6] Constantine Porphyrogennetus, *De Thematibus*, 58.

But in its turn Byzantine sea-power declined. Partly again it was due to the over-great power to which an admiral might attain—Romanus Lecapenus found his naval command the best stepping-stone to the throne—and the civilian Emperors of the Eleventh Century deliberately reduced armaments. The absence of any strong rival sea-power made a fleet seem an unnecessary extravagance. Already in 992 Basil II gave the Venetians the duty of policing the Adriatic and arranged for them to carry Imperial troops when it was required. In the East the Seljuk conquests disorganised the Maritime themes. By the time of Alexius Comnenus, when again the Empire needed ships to defend her, Italian mercenaries had to be hired. Alexius tried to rebuild the Imperial navy and eventually his fleet was able to oppose the Pisans and Genoese. But the later Comneni could afford neither the men nor the money. Manuel I spent all that was available on military campaigns, and the fleet disappeared. The outcome was the disaster of 1204.

The Nicæan Emperors seem to have turned their energies to their navy. Certainly by the reign of Michael Palæologus and the recovery of Constantinople there was a small but serviceable Imperial fleet. Indeed, throughout the period of the Palæologi the fleet was probably in a better condition than the army ; and the chief admiral, now called the Grand Duke, ranked almost as high as the Grand Domestic—relatively higher than ever the Grand Drungarius had ranked.[1] But the fleet was too weak to stand up to the great Italian navies, and in the chaos of the last decades it, too, almost disappeared. But there were still a few Greek ships to fight against the Turks in the final Siege, notably the Imperial transport carrying corn to the beleaguered City, that fought her way against such incredible odds into the harbour.[2]

[1] Codinus, *De Officiis*, 28.   [2] Phrantzes, 247.

The usual Byzantine man-of-war was a dromond or 'runner,' a bireme containing anything from just over a hundred to three hundred men. In addition there were biremes of a different design, apparently swifter, known as Pamphylians. The admiral's flagship was in the Tenth Century a large Pamphylian. There were also galleys with single banks of oars.[1] In addition merchant ships might be commandeered for service. The fleet that Justinian II sent against Cherson was fitted out by all the guilds of Constantinople and included merchant ships ; [2] and it was an impromptu fleet of old ships and merchant ships that beat off the Russian raid of 941, when the Imperial fleet was away in the Ægean.[3]

We are given certain figures as to the size of the fleet in its great days. Three hundred ships are said to have been sent against Egypt in 853 ; but many of these may have been small skiffs.[4] In the Cretan expedition of 902, the Imperial navy provided 60 dromonds and 40 Pamphylians and the thematic navy from the Cibyrrhæot, Ægean and Samian themes 35 dromonds and 35 Pamphylians, while Hellas sent 10 dromonds.[5] The Calabrian theme seems to have maintained seven ships in 929.[6]

The ships might be armed with battering-rams, but their great weapon was Greek or maritime fire.[7] This chemical substance was apparently of various kinds and used in various ways. Chiefly it was either thrown in hand grenades which exploded and caught fire when they hit the enemy ship ; or else whole pots were sent through the air by cata-

[1] Leo, *Tactica*, 992 *sqq.* ; Bury, Appendix 5 to *Decline and Fall*, vol. 6, 539.
[2] Theophanes, 377.   [3] Liudprand, *Antapodosis*, 137 *sqq.*
[4] Tabari, trans. in Vasiliev, *Byzantium and the Arabs* (in Russian), I, Addenda, 51–2.
[5] Constantine Porphyrogennetus, *De Ceremoniis*, 151 *sqq.*
[6] Ibn-Adari in Vasiliev, *op. cit.*, II, Addenda, 149.
[7] Bury, *loc. cit.* ; Schlumberger, *Récits de Byzance*, 2ᵐᵉ série, 37–48.

pults ; and it also seems that the force of gunpowder may somehow have been used to propel combustibles through tubes to objects at some distance. The recipe of Greek fire was kept a closely guarded secret, which ought never to be given away.[1] There were stores of it in the great seaside towns. The capture of Mesembria by Krum in 812 was a great disaster in that it placed a supply in the Bulgar Khan's hands.[2] The invention was said to have been made by a certain Callinicus of Heliopolis in the Seventh Century and some form was used to beat off the Arabs in the great sieges of Constantinople. But probably the various forms were not perfected till the Ninth Century. Leo VI speaks of it as a new discovery.[3] In the Tenth Century Mark the Greek gives the recipe, a little vaguely ; [4] and it seems that the Arabs learnt how to manufacture it before the Crusades. It only went entirely out of use when in the Fourteenth Century it was superseded by gunpowder and cannon.

The tactics that Leo VI recommends for the navy are almost more cautious than those suggested to the military. Pitched battles should be avoided except when the opposing fleet is at a disadvantage ; detached skirmishing is much wiser. If a pitched battle is unavoidable the crescent-formation, loved of the ancient Greeks, is advised. Signalling was done by flags or by lights at night. Navigation was carefully studied—winds and currents should be known and precautions taken against them ; difficult coasts should be avoided. If however the weather could be used to destroy an enemy squadron, that was the cheapest and therefore the best form of victory.[5]

But Leo VI obviously did not take much interest in naval

[1] Constantine Porphyrogennetus, *De Administrando Imperio*, 84.

[2] Theophanes, 499.   [3] Leo, *Tactica*.

[4] *Liber Ignium ad Comburendos Hostes* in Hofer, *Histoire de la Chimie*, vol. I.

[5] Leo, *Tactica, loc. cit.*

warfare, nor did he much understand it. The amateurish-ness of his knowledge is far more apparent in his naval chapter than in any of his military chapters. There is no professional record of the functions and ideals of naval war-fare in Byzantium. The navy did many great services there ; and Cecaumenus was justified in calling it ' the glory of Romania.' [1] But the latter-day Romans viewed their glory without enthusiasm. Storms and rocks filled the sea with danger ; many an armada had been destroyed by the hand of God. They preferred a science where their intelli-gence would give them a more certain advantage, and instead they studied warfare by land.

III. *The Diplomatic Service*

Well though the Byzantines organised their army and navy, they preferred nevertheless to economise in their use. An active diplomacy was kept up, to embroil foreign nations with each other and so maintain an equilibrium that would prevent any potential enemy from invading Imperial territory.

Very little information has survived as to the organisation of Byzantine diplomacy. The Foreign Secretary of the Empire was the Logothete of the Course, the minister who was, it seems, in closest touch with the Emperor and inter-viewed him daily.[2] Foreign business was therefore largely directed by the Emperor himself. It was the Logothete's busi-ness to see to the reception of foreign embassies, and probably he too fitted out the Imperial embassies to foreign courts and selected the personnel. But certain diplomatic affairs were conducted by the local authorities. Thus it was usually the Strategus of Cherson (in the Crimea) who arranged the

---

[1] Cecaumenus, *Noutheticos*, 101.   [2] See above, pp. 91–2.

missions to the nations of the Steppes. In the story of
Justinian II's adventures it was from Cherson that the
embassies to the Chazars set out.[1]   Under Zoe Carbopsina
it was the Strategus John Bogas who visited the Petchenegs
to incite them against Bulgaria ; [2] and Constantine VII
regarded Cherson as the proper base for Steppe diplomacy.[3]
Possibly the Toparch of Gothia, an official who apparently
existed in the early Tenth Century, was the head of the
diplomatic bureau of Cherson.[4]   In Italy it seems that the
local Strategus or Catepan dealt with the Arabs,[5] though big
embassies to the Italian courts were equipped at Constantinople.[6]   In the mid-Tenth Century it was not the
Strategus but the Archbishop of Otranto, Vlattus, who
journeyed to El-Mahdia to buy back Christian prisoners ;
but then he had influence there, his sister being in the
Calif's harem, and when he returned unofficially to con-
tinue his good work, he was put to death.[7]

There was no Diplomatic Service in the modern sense.
Diplomatic establishments were not kept up permanently
in any foreign country : though the Strategus of Cherson
kept a large bureau which gathered information about the
politics of the Steppes. There were probably certain
officials who were always sent out as ambassadors when
they were required. In Leo VI's reign the Magister Leo
Choerosphacta was sent on embassies first to Baghdad and
later to the court of Bulgaria.[8]   It was usually the same
ministers who would go, whenever a truce was arranged
with the Arabs, to conduct the exchange of prisoners on the

[1] Theophanes, 378.   [2] Theophanes Continuatus, 387.
[3] Constantine Porphyrogennetus, *op. cit.*, 72, 244 *sqq.*
[4] Uspenski, *Russia and Byzantium* (in Russian), *passim.*
[5] E.g. Cedrenus, VI, 355.
[6] E.g. Constantine Porphyrogennetus, *De Ceremoniis*, 661.
[7] *Vita S. Nili*, M.P.G., vol. 120, 117–20.
[8] His very interesting correspondence is published—ed. Sakkelion in
Deltion, vol. 1, 377–410.

frontier—presumably they were Arabic linguists. Under Romanus I the Patrician Constans undertook the various embassies to the Caucasus, but afterwards rose to be Grand Admiral.[1]

The external characteristic of Byzantine diplomacy was a stiff formality, designed to enhance Imperial dignity. The foreign ambassador arriving at Constantinople was at once hedged round with etiquette—largely to ensure that he should see no unauthorised person. When he was ushered into the Presence he was greeted after a set formula, and received in precedence according to his country's importance. By the treaty of 927 the Bulgarian ambassadors, representing a monarch related to the Imperial house, were given a special precedence over all other ambassadors ; this lasted till the suppression of the Bulgarian dynasty by John Tzimisces.[2] Throughout the first interview the Emperor remained impassive, a deity. The ambassador was expected to prostrate himself before the Emperor. Later he would enter into personal relations with the Emperor at a State banquet, or possibly he might be granted a personal interview. If he were from a barbarian nation, the mechanical toys of the Palace would be turned on to impress him. The golden lions would roar and the golden birds would sing, and while the ambassador was prostrate the throne would be lifted to the sky and Majesty would appear clad in a different and richer robe. The more sophisticated ambassador would be entertained with displays of the Palace treasures or relics—exhibitions that would make him gasp to see so many priceless objects—or occasionally he might be taken to the Games.[3] But he was subject all the while to a strict supervision ; he was to return to his home having

---

[1] Constantine Porphyrogennetus, *De Administrando Imperio*, 208.
[2] Liudprand, *Legatio*, 186.
[3] Constantine Porphyrogennetus, *De Ceremoniis*, 566 *sqq.*, 680 *sqq.* ; Liudprand, *Legatio, passim.*

learnt and seen nothing except what had been intended by
the Imperial Government. If he behaved disrespectfully,
or if his credentials were addressed only to the Emperor ' of
the Greeks,' like those of the Papal legates in 968, he would
be thrown at once into prison.[1] There was no diplomatic
immunity for persons who slighted Imperial dignity and the
usages prescribed by the Imperial Court.

Imperial embassies abroad travelled with a sumptuous
train laden with rich presents, jewels, gold, silks and
brocades. These were mainly destined for the monarch for
whose court the ambassadors were bound ; but influential
ministers were also to be wooed with gifts.[2] The Imperial
intelligence department was supposed to know whose support it was worth while to obtain in Pavia or in Baghdad.
When Nicephorus Uranus was sent to Baghdad in 980 he
was told to be particularly amiable to Adhoud ed-Dauleh,
the most important of all the Calif's counsellors.[3]

Beneath the veneer of pomp Byzantine diplomacy was
subtle, far-sighted and somewhat unscrupulous. Treaty
obligations were always carefully observed ; but the
Byzantines saw nothing wrong in inciting some foreign tribe
against a neighbour with whom they were at peace. Leo VI,
who was too pious to fight himself against his fellow-
Christians the Bulgarians, did not hesitate to subsidise the
heathen Hungarians to attack them in the rear ;[4] and
similarly Nicephorus Phocas incited the Russians against the
Bulgarians, though he was at peace with the latter.[5] It was
a basic rule in Byzantine foreign politics to induce some other
nation to oppose the enemy, and so to cut down the expenses
and risks of a war. Thus it was the Frankish troops of the

[1] Liudprand, *op. cit.*, 201.

[2] Constantine Porphyrogennetus, *op. cit.*, 661.

[3] Yachya of Antioch, ed. Rosen, 20.

[4] Leo, *Tactica*, 957 ; Constantine Porphyrogennetus, *De Administrando
Imperio*, 168 *sqq.*

[5] Cedrenus, II, 372.

Western Emperor Louis II rather than Byzantine troops that drove the Saracens from Southern Italy and recaptured Bari in 871.[1] The Byzantines merely managed to be there in time to take the fruits of victory and to manœuvre the Franks out of the reconquered province. Thus, again in Southern Italy a century later, when the Western Otto II embarked on schemes of conquest there, at a time when Basil II was in the throes of a great rebellion, the small Byzantine garrison withdrew after encouraging and probably paying the Saracens to check the German advance. Then when the German cause was lost at Stilo and the Saracens retired laden with booty, the Byzantine garrisons returned.[2] And thus Alexius I, though he had not invited nor altogether desired their help, manipulated the early victories of the Crusaders against the Seljuks to his sole advantage.

With the nations of the Steppes such tactics were habitual. Too often in the past convulsions there had resulted in barbarian tribes forcing their way into the Empire ; but after the Seventh Century none managed to settle south of the Danube. Potential invaders were crushed on the Steppes or, like the Hungarians, were side-tracked into Central Europe. Constantine VII gives the recipe according to which such results were achieved in the Tenth Century. Against the Chazars, for instance, one could call in the Petchenegs or the Black Bulgarians ; against the Petchenegs the Russians and the Hungarians, and so on.[3] Every nation had its potential enemies that could be used as a counter-balance. To the last the Byzantines were adept in the art of playing nations against each other.

Marriage occupied a large part in Byzantine diplomacy. Even the Emperors were not above wedding foreign brides. Two Chazar princesses sat on the Imperial throne, wives of Justinian II and Constantine V. Romanus I married his

---

[1] Gay, *Italie Méridionale*, 79 *sqq.*   [2] *Ibid.*, 324 *sqq.*
[3] Constantine Porphyrogennetus, *op. cit.*, 67–72, 80–1.

grandson, the future Romanus II, to a bastard princess from
Italy.   Michael VII's wife was the lovely Maria of Alania.
Under the Comneni and the Palæologi wives from the West
became the general rule ;   there was a long series of ill-
fitting Western-born Empresses, whom Byzantine pride
would never allow to be popular in Constantinople.   But
diplomatically these marriages were failures ;   they brought
no advantage, nothing but odium to the Emperor.   The last
of the Emperors, Constantine XI, saw its folly and, on the
eve of the City's fall, was seeking a bride from the East.[1]
On the other hand, the marriage of Byzantine ladies to
foreign potentates was often well worth while.   Constantine VII maintained that there were three things that no
Emperor should ever grant to a foreigner—a crown, the
secret of Greek Fire, and the hand of a purple-born princess ; [2] and the precept was seldom disobeyed.   Romanus
I, to Constantine's disgust, gave his granddaughter Maria to
the Tsar of Bulgaria ;   and Constantine's own grand-
daughters, Theophano and Anna, became respectively
Western Empress and Grand Duchess of Russia.   The latter
case was particularly humiliating, as the Grand Duke
Vladimir was an incorrigible barbarian ;   Basil II only con-
sented to sacrifice his sister to secure urgent diplomatic ends
—to convert the Russians and turn them into allies and to
save Cherson.   It was only under the Nicæans and the
Palæologi that Emperors' daughters were frequently married
abroad, chiefly to the monarchs of the Slavs.   In the last
centuries the Emperors of Trebizond found that the far-
famed beauty of their daughters was an invaluable asset ;
but in using it they were acting in a way of which traditional
Imperial diplomacy disapproved.   But ladies of less exalted
birth were frequently and usefully sent out from Constantinople to civilise a princely husband in a distant land.   As the

---

[1] Diehl, *Figures Byzantines*, II, 164–290.
[2] Constantine Porphyrogennetus, *op. cit.*, 84.

Armenian and Caucasian dynasties gradually came within the Imperial sphere of influence, their members were encouraged to seek their brides from the great City. Some handsome young woman of a good family, preferably connected to the Imperial House, would set out for Taron or for Ani itself, with a sumptuous dowry and probably a minor relic as a wedding-present from the Emperor—Romanus III gave his niece a nail of the True Cross when she married King Bagrat of Abasgia,[1] and similarly Theophano had gone to the West with the whole body of Saint Pantaleon of Nicomedia [2]—and the grateful husband would look with renewed respect on the court at Constantinople. Lombard princes of Southern Italy had already in the late Eighth Century been given wives from Byzantium—such as Grimoald of Benevento who married Constantine VI's sister-in-law.[3] Two doges of Venice in the Eleventh Century married Byzantine brides, John Orseolo and Domenico Selvio ; Byzantine ladies sat on thrones in Russia in the Eleventh Century.[4] In the Twelfth, under the Comneni, their sphere was enlarged. Maria Comnena and Theodora Comnena, each the niece of an Emperor, were Queens of Jerusalem ; another niece of Manuel I married the Duke of Austria—sacrificed, her mother's court-poet declared, to the wild beast of the West.[5] But by then the old exclusiveness of the Porphyrogennetæ was discarded, with the result that the honour of an Imperial bride was less and so their diplomatic value declined.

At the same time, Byzantium loved to collect pretenders to foreign thrones. Claimants to the Bulgarian and Serbian crowns were invariably to be found at the Imperial Court,

[1] Brosset, *Histoire de la Georgie*, i, 316–17.
[2] Hugo, *Chronicon*, in *M.G.H.Ss.*, vol. 8, 374.
[3] *Vita Philaretis*, ed. Vasiliev, *Izvestiya* of *Russian Institute at Constantinople*, vol. 5, 78.
[4] E.g. Theophano Muzalon (Loparev in *V.V.*, vol. i, 159).
[5] Miller, *Recueil des Historiens des Croisades (Grecs)*, ii, 768.

usually married to ladies of Constantinople. Romanus I, even though Peter of Bulgaria had married his own grand-daughter, took steps to secure the person of Peter's elder brother Michael whom he kept in an honourable position at Constantinople.[1] When Charlemagne put an end to the Lombard Kingdom, the former Crown Prince Adelchis fled to Constantinople, where he was given support in all his schemes.[2] Even only half a century before the final fall of the Empire, a Turkish pretender was kept at Constantinople and launched against the Sultan Murad II.[3]

Byzantine diplomacy was very expensive. Dowries, gifts, subsidies to whole nations, all involved the treasury in enormous sums. Even economic blockades, sometimes effectively employed towards the Saracens,[4] were costly for the Empire also. The Government was moreover perfectly willing to pay its enemies direct not to invade its territory. Lawless princes across the frontier thus became clients, almost wage-earners, much preferring a regular income of Byzantine gold to the uncertain takings of a raid. At times even, if Byzantium was for some reason unwilling to undertake a war, a yearly sum of money would go to Baghdad or to Preslav. The Calif or the Tsar might call it tribute, if he chose. To the Emperor it was merely a wise investment ; when he was ready to fight the payment would cease. But it all depended on a full treasury. So long as the money was there Byzantine diplomacy flourished. But when Constantinople was no longer the financial centre of the world, then there came the decline.

[1] Theophanes Continuatus, 419.
[2] Einhard, *ad annum* 788.   [3] Ducas, 117 *sqq.*
[4] Schlumberger, *Epopée Byzantine*, II, 452 *sqq.*

CHAPTER VII

Commerce

If Byzantium owed her strength and security to the efficiency of her Services, it was her trade that enabled her to pay for them. Her history is fundamentally the history of her financial policy and of the commerce of the Middle Ages.

Few cities have enjoyed so magnificent a commercial site as Constantinople, placed on the sea-channel between North and South and the land-bridge between East and West. And few races have been commercially as adept as the Greeks and the Armenians who formed her citizens. It was hardly a matter for wonder that Constantinople was for centuries a synonym for riches, a city of whose treasure 'there was neither end nor measure.' But the treasure had not been won all by accident. Care as well as circumstances were needed to enrich the City.

Till Columbus and Vasco da Gama opened out a new era the main trade of the world was from the Farther East to the Mediterranean. The Mediterranean sphere could feed itself and supply its own necessities ; but whenever it grew prosperous it longed for the luxuries that only the East could provide. In the early centuries A.D. the Eastern trade was highly flourishing. Rome busily imported spices and herbs and sandalwood from the Indies, and above all silk, especially raw silk, from China. This all had to be paid for, and the Mediterranean exports of glass and enamel and made-up stuffs was not nearly enough. An

enormous sum of bullion went annually to the East ; and
the drain led to the depression that gradually enveloped
the Roman world.   But the demand for silk still continued ;
and it became the preoccupation of the authorities to find
the cheapest route for it to take.

There were various routes for the Eastern trade to
follow.[1]   It might go across Turkestan to the Caspian and
then either take a northern route to the Volga and to the
Black Sea at Cherson, or a southern route through Northern
Persia to Nisibin on the Imperial frontier or through
Armenia to Trebizond.   It might cross India and Afghan-
istan and the centre of Persia to Nisibin or to Syria.   It
might go by sea up the Persian Gulf and then cross to
Syria ; or it might go by sea all the way, up the Red Sea
to Egypt.   Only two routes avoided Persia, the northern-
most which depended on a rare stability amongst the nations
of the Steppes, or the southernmost, the sea-route, which
needed a mercantile marine east of Suez.   Persia was a
menace to trade.   She put on high tariffs, and at times of
war she cut off the entire supply.   Actually a periodical
enforced restriction was not bad for the Empire's balance
of trade, but it caused unemployment in the silk-factories
all over the Empire.   Imperial diplomacy throughout the
Fifth and particularly the Sixth Century sought to safeguard the two free routes, negotiating with the Hunnish
and Turkish Kingdoms on the Steppes or with the Abyssinians, whose Kingdom of Axum commanded the Red
Sea.

The Sixth Century was the great age of the Eastern trade.
The Empire under Anastasius and the early years of the
House of Justin was in a state of revived prosperity, and
the way from the East ran through orderly peoples.   Silk
still travelled mainly overland through Persia to the Imperial
customs-stations at Nisibin and Dara.   Thence it would

[1] Heyd, *Histoire du Commerce du Levant*, 1, 1–24.

go to be made up at Constantinople or in the factories at
Tyre and Berytus. But some travelled with all the spices
of the Indies by the sea-route. A retired sailor, Cosmas,
surnamed Indicopleustes, the Sailor of the Indies, wrote a
book to prove from his wide experience that the earth was
flat ; and in it he describes the Indian trade.[1] The clearing-
house of the whole East was Ceylon. There the Eastern
goods, silk from China, silk, aloes, cloves and sandalwood
from Indo-China, pepper from Malabar, copper from
Calliana (near Bombay) and musk and castor from Sindu
were all collected along with the jewels of Ceylon. The
silk was usually captured by the Persian merchants who
took it up the Persian Gulf. The other goods were carried
chiefly by Abyssinian ships to Adulis on the Red Sea, the
capital of Axum, and thence, more exclusively by Imperial
ships, to the customs-station at Jotabe, at the end of the
Sinai peninsula and on to Clysma, near Suez, where there
resided an Imperial official, the Logothete, who yearly
visited India. Imperial ships did not often actually visit
Ceylon, though there were Christian Nestorian colonies
there and at Calliana and Malabar, and Socotra had many
Greek-speaking inhabitants. But the currency preferred
by the Eastern merchants of all races was the Imperial
coinage, which greatly assisted the Imperial trade. The
Abyssinians also conducted a trade with Central Africa, often
accompanied by Imperial merchants. Every other year
they would sail far to the south, then march inland, and in
return for various made-up articles they would come back
laden with ingots of gold. Cosmas himself on a southerly
voyage had once seen albatrosses.[2] Throughout the Mediterranean world the Eastern merchandise was disseminated
by Syrian merchants, who had their stations in every port,

[1] Cosmas Indicopleustes, *Cosmography* (trans. McCrindle, *Hakluyt
Soc.*).

[2] Cosmas, *passim*, esp. 40.

and acted incidentally as news-carriers. A Syrian trader told Saint Symeon Stylites the story of Saint Genevieve.[1]

In the course of Justinian's reign the position began to alter. His Persian wars interfered with the silk-supply and his attempt to keep the price of silk down merely ruined the private manufacturers : whose factories he then bought up, thus, half-accidentally, turning silk into an Imperial monopoly. Justin II, finding the Empire still starved of silk by the Persian wars, attempted to open out properly the route across the Steppes, but the task was beyond Imperial diplomacy. But meanwhile two Nestorian monks had arrived in Constantinople with the secret of the silk-worm and its eggs in their hollow staves.[2] It was some time before the cultivation of the worm became at all wide-spread in the Empire ; but henceforward the import from the East began to decline.[3]

Then came the Arab conquest of Syria and Egypt. Though the Empire as a whole might suffer, Constantinople gained. The Syrian mercantile marine was destroyed, and the Greeks were left with the Eastern Mediterranean trade. At first the direct traffic between Syria and the Empire was interrupted. Even in the Eighth Century trade went round by Egypt, Africa, Sicily and so by Monemvasia to the Ægean—such was the route chosen by the plague that ravaged Constantinople under Constantine V.[4] But gradually Oriental goods rediscovered the road by land across Asia Minor or went still more often to the Black Sea at Trebizond, whence Greek ships took them to be cleared at Constantinople. The silk industry was growing all the while, and the Imperial factory at Constantinople soon had a world-monopoly of made-up precious stuffs. The Arabs

---

[1] *Vita S. Genofevae*, in *Bibliotheca Hagiographica Latina*, 3335, § 27.
[2] Procopius (Loeb Series), vol. 5, 226 *sqq.*
[3] For silk, see Bury, *Later Roman Empire*, II, 330 *sqq.*
[4] Theophanes, 422–3.

to the east and the Chazars to the north as well as the
Western nations all clamoured to buy the brocades of
Byzantium.

In the Ninth and Tenth Centuries Byzantine trade was
at its height. Greek ships indulged mainly in a coastal
trade, particularly in the Black Sea. The Eastern Mediterranean trade was small. The import of corn from
Egypt and Africa stopped with the Arab conquest and the
perpetual development of agriculture in Asia Minor ; and
the Arab pirates of the Ægean discouraged maritime enterprise. But Far Eastern merchandise and Indian herbs were
still imported, travelling either across Persia and Armenia
to Trebizond or up the Persian Gulf to Baghdad and then
northward to the same port. The Arabs had captured the
whole Indian Ocean trade—the Axumite Kingdom had
fallen—but they would not reopen the Suez route. Harun
Al-Raschid had thought of constructing a canal there but
was frightened lest Greek ships should then capture the
Red Sea trade.[1] But this merely added to the importance
of Trebizond, which became the great port of the East.
After the reconquest of Antioch a certain amount of the
Eastern trade was diverted by Aleppo to Antioch and to
the sea at Seleucia. Meanwhile the Northern trade was
developing. The furs and slaves and dried fish of the
Steppes were brought by the Chazars and their neighbours
to Cherson in the Crimea or were taken by Russian ships
from the Dnieper to Constantinople :[2] while Baltic amber
and Central European furs and metals found their way to
Thessalonica, to be disseminated thence by the ships of the
Greeks.[3] Greek ships also carried some of the trade
between Constantinople and the West. Bari, the capital

[1] Maçoudi, *Prairies d'Or*, trans. Barbier de Meynard, 1, 98.
[2] See Vasiliev, *Economic Relations between Byzantium and Old Russia* in
Journal of Economic and Business History, vol. 4, 314 *sqq.*
[3] Constantine Porphyrogennetus, *De Administrando Imperio*, 177 *sqq.*

of Byzantine Italy, was a flourishing port ; but it was served chiefly by its local marine. And gradually the local Italian merchant-fleets ousted the Greeks from Italian waters.[1] The growth of the wealth of the West meant new activity in all the Italian ports. By the Tenth Century Amalfi and to a lesser extent Naples and Gæta had developed wide overseas connections ; and a little later Pisan and Genoese traders appeared. By the Tenth Century there was a permanent Amalfitan Resident in Constantinople, and a growing colony ; and by 1060 the Amalfitan patrician Pantaleon had a magnificent palace there. But the chief port of the West was Venice, admirably situated to carry the German as well as the Lombard trade. By the end of the Tenth Century, the Adriatic was in the hands of the Venetians. They were still nominal vassals of the Empire, and the Imperial authorities would continually, with varying success, issue edicts forbidding them to trade with the Arabs. Basil II gave them special privileges ; they were allowed to pay a reduced export-tax when leaving Constantinople, on condition that they policed the Adriatic and guaranteed to carry Imperial troops, if required. The goods imported into the Empire by the Venetians were mainly arms, slaves, wood and rough cloth. The slave market at Venice was particularly well known. Basil I's ambassador bought some Slavonic missionaries there, and there were continual protests against the selling of Christians to the infidel.[2] Ambassadors from the West, such as Liudprand, usually travelled by Venetian ships ; they also carried the mails.[3]

The Eleventh Century began the decline of Byzantine commerce. In the last quarter of the century misfortunes crowded on the Empire. Its economic life was upset by the loss of the bulk of Asia Minor to the Seljuks, which

[1] See Heyd, *op. cit.*, I, 100–3.
[2] *Vita S. Naum*, 4.   [3] Liudprand, *Legatio*, 183.

destroyed the organisation of the Imperial army and fleet
and the food supply. Norman invaders troubled the West
and in 1147 Roger II captured Thebes and Corinth and
carried off silk-worms and weavers to Italy, breaking the
old Imperial monopoly.[1] Finally the Crusades altered
the trade-routes of the world, to the detriment of Constantinople. Goods no longer travelled to Trebizond or across
Asia Minor—the Seljuks stood in the way—but were
embarked at the ports of Latin Syria and carried by Italian
boats directly to the West, avoiding the customs-dues of
Byzantium. Constantinople only had the Northern trade
left. This might have been enough ; for the Far Eastern
trade was taking more and more a northerly route, travelling
by land through Turkestan to the Black Sea. But political
circumstances placed this too in the hands of the Italians.
In return for the necessary help of their navies or as a
precaution against their piratical raids, the Emperors of
the Comnenian dynasty yielded more and more privileges,
first to Venice and next to Pisa and Genoa. Their merchants were allowed to pay customs-duties of only 4 per
cent., instead of the 10 per cent. that even Imperial citizens
had to pay. Meanwhile they were given districts in the
City itself and in other ports where they set up self-governing
communes. By 1180 there were 60,000 Westerners in
Constantinople. Under Andronicus I there was a reaction ;
great massacres of the Italians occurred throughout the
Empire, and the privileges were withdrawn. But it was
too late. The embittered situation led to the Fourth
Crusade and the ruin of the Empire.[2]

The Latin Empire died in its infancy. The Latin
principalities were not to endure for long. But Venice
laid the foundations of a commercial dominion that would
command all the trade of the East. Her colonies were

[1] See Chalandon, *Domination Normande en Sicile*, II, 145–7.
[2] Heyd, *op. cit.*, I, 190 *sqq.*

placed all over the Eastern Mediterranean, the Ægean and the Black Sea.

The Palæologi recovered the Empire with the help of the Genoese ; and the Genoese had to be paid. Their reward was the rest of the Black Sea trade and the town of Pera across the Golden Horn. With only two towns in the Black Sea were they forbidden to trade ; Matracha (probably on the Taman peninsula) and Rosia (Kertch) were reserved to the Greeks. But the Greek marine was killed in the competition. The great boom of the Black Sea trade caused by the prosperity of the Mongol Empire enriched the coffers of the Genoese alone. Under the Empire of the Palæologi, while Pera flourished and developed, Constantinople gradually dwindled. Her factories still made world-famous luxuries, but her markets stood empty and her quays deserted, save for the boats that carried the goods across to the Genoese wharves at Pera. Thessalonica retained prosperity longer. Greek merchants there still controlled the exports of the Balkans ; but the shipping was mainly in Italian hands. The same was true of Trebizond, where the Persian and Caucasian trade still brought money to the Treasury of the Grand Comnenus, but the Genoese carried it to the West.[1]

It was her position on the world trade-routes that gave Constantinople her great days of prosperity. A flat rate of 10 per cent. was placed on all exports and imports. The import duties were collected at Abydos on the Hellespont or Hieron on the Bosphorus, the export duties at Constantinople. Till the Italians won their special privileges no goods could pass through the Straits without paying their dues.[2] This provided the Imperial Treasury with a constant stream of wealth, so long as the Empire's neighbours were prosperous enough to afford merchandise with these

[1] Heyd, *op. cit.*, II, 93 *sqq.*, 257 *sqq.*, 379 *sqq.*
[2] Bury, *Eastern Roman Empire*, 217–19.

surcharges added to its price. When the whole world, as in the Seventh Century, or even only the East, as in the Eleventh, was in a state of disorder and poverty, the Empire at once suffered. Her customs made the through-traffic too expensive.

She also suffered because her own local manufactures were of a luxury nature. The factories were mainly in Constantinople. The biggest was probably the Imperial gynæceum, where vast numbers of workmen and women were employed in making up the silks and brocades and cloths of gold that were the delight of all the world. The gold-smiths' and jewellers' works were nearly as important. Byzantine gold cups, enamelled reliquaries, carvings in ivory or semi-precious stones were equally renowned; and occasionally they would produce a masterpiece like the roaring golden lions of the Palace. Various parts of the Empire also produced wines, which were sold to the tribes of the North. These exports were very strictly controlled. It did not suit the authorities to allow the luxury goods to become too common outside of the Empire. Their price and their rarity had to be kept up. Certain cloths were indeed not put on the market at all and only went abroad as occasional presents to foreign courts. Liud-prand, the Italian ambassador, who attempted to smuggle some silks out of Constantinople in 968, had them all confiscated by the customs officials. Merchandise, before it could be exported, had to be marked with the State seal.[1]

Certain other towns had their factories. Before the Arab conquest Tyre, Berytus and Alexandria all made up silk,[2] and by the Eleventh Century Thebes and Corinth were centres of the silk industry. Carpets were made in

---

[1] *Le Livre du Préfet*, ed. Nicole, 27-8, 35-8; Liudprand, *Legatio*, 204-5.

[2] Antoninus Martyr, 92; Falke, *Kunstgeschichte der Seidenweberei*, 1, 48.

the Peloponnese. By the Tenth Century Sparta exported them to Italy.[1]

The chief imports were raw silk, especially up to the Seventh Century, though what were called ' Indian goods ' were popular even in the Tenth ; timber and furs from the North : arms—Arab lances were much liked, and the Venetians brought a lot of arms from the West : a few made-up luxury goods, such as Persian carpets, and precious spices from the East : and, above all, slaves, from both Venice and the Steppes. All these imports were subject to the 10 per cent. duty, levied at Abydos or Hieron. The Empress Irene allowed free imports for a time ; but her successor Nicephorus I reimposed the duty, and even made arrangements by which goods, particularly slaves, sold by Western merchants in markets west of Abydos, should not, as they had hitherto done, escape the imposition.[2] During the Nicæan Empire John Vatatzes put an entire embargo on foreign goods.[3] The customs-officers were known as the Commerciarii, and were part of the bureau of the Sacellarius.[4]

Foreign traders were carefully supervised by the Prefect of the City. They had to report themselves on arrival at his bureau, and they might only stay three months in the City. Any goods that they had left to sell after this period would be sold for them by the Prefect, who would hold the money over till the next year. Their purchases were carefully supervised by the authorities, to see that they did not contravene the customs-regulations. Certain nations, such as the Russians and later the Italians, won special privileges and freedom from tolls, in return for political services. In the Tenth Century the Russians were allowed

---

[1] *Vita S. Niconis Armenii*, in Martène and Durande, *Collectio Veterum Scriptorum*, vol. 6, 884.

[2] Bury, *loc. cit.*   [3] Gregoras, 43.

[4] Bury, *Imperial Administrative System*, 88.

free lodgings and baths at Saint Mamas just outside the
City, which however they could only enter under escort,
during their visit : while special grants were given to the
commissioners of the Grand Duke of Russia, who conducted
them.[1]

Trade within the Empire chiefly dealt with the necessities
of life. Corn had come from Egypt and Africa before the
Arab conquest. Afterwards it was grown in Asia Minor
and later in Thrace and was carried to Constantinople
chiefly by sea from the local ports. Meat came also from
the same districts. The Seljuk conquest restricted the
agriculture of Asia Minor ; and in the later years of the
Empire the decline in the population of Constantinople
was undoubtedly accelerated by the increasing difficulty
of finding food for a great city, particularly when the
State could not afford many imports.[2]

The business life of the Empire was hemmed round with
innumerable regulations. Byzantium has been accused of
being the paradise of monopoly privilege and protection.
The charge is not altogether fair. Protection was undoubtedly a Byzantine ideal. State intervention to help industry
was frequent : though the tariffs were also for purposes of
revenue. Privileges were granted to foreign traders, especially, and fatally, from the Twelfth Century onward ; and
there were State monopolies, such as the silk trade and,
for obvious reasons, the manufacture of armaments. But
there was not much legalised corruption, as far as we can
judge. When Leo VI's favourites were given special
privileges with regard to the trade of Thessalonica, the
transaction was considered so scandalous that such occur-
rences cannot have been usual.[3] The restrictions and rules

[1] *Chronique dite de Nestor*, ed. Léger, 35 *sqq.* ; Vasiliev, *op. cit.*, 323–6.
[2] Bratianu, *L'Approvisionnement de Constantinople* in *Byzantion*, vol. 5,
83 *sqq.* ; vol. 6, 641 *sqq.*
[3] Theophanes Continuatus, 357.

ordained by the Government and the vast bodies employed
to enforce them prevented much private enterprise even of
a corrupt nature.

Everything was circumscribed. Money could only be
lent at a fixed rate of interest. Before Justinian's day the
maximum rate had been 12 per cent. Justinian allowed
12 per cent. only for money used on transmarine enterprise; professional money-lenders (usually the goldsmiths)
might charge 8 per cent., ordinary persons 6 per cent. and
the wealthy magnates only 4 per cent. But these calcula-
tions had been made originally when there were 100
nomismata to 1 lb. of gold. Constantine had reduced the
number of nomismata to 72; and throughout Byzantine
history the fixed rate of interest tended to adjust itself to
the new figure, to the lender's advantage: till by the
Tenth Century 6 per cent. had changed to be 6 nomismata
per 1 lb. of gold, that is to say 8·33 per cent.; and maritime
speculation would bring in 16·66 per cent.[1] But this was
not really enough; storms and pirates and faulty charts
placed too many dangers in the way. Investors, particularly as the legal process for the recovery of debts was
clumsy and slow and there was a prejudice against usurers,
naturally preferred to invest in land, to the ultimate detriment of the Empire. The risks of maritime trade are
further illustrated by the ' Rhodian Code,' the commercial
law of the Isaurians. There the assumption is that the
merchant and the shipowner, usually the captain, work
in partnership and share the burden of any loss to the
cargo, though the passengers might also be members of the
joint-stock company. These conditions probably continued
even after the Isaurian legislation was withdrawn.[2]

The control exercised by the State over trade and industry
was effected through a system of guilds. A handbook

---

[1] See Bury in Gibbon, *Decline and Fall*, vol. 5, Appendix 13, 533–4.
[2] Ashburner, *Rhodian Sea Law, passim.*

written about the year 900, known as the *Eparchikon Biblion*
or Book of the Prefect, survives to give some idea of the
system.[1] The Prefect was the official in charge of it all,
though the Quæstor dealt with public works, and one or
two guilds were under him. Every industry had its guild,
and no man might belong to two ; and each guild appointed
its president, whose nomination had probably to be endorsed
by the Prefect. The guild as a whole bought the raw
material needed by the industry, and divided it up amongst
its members, who sold the finished goods in a definite
public place at a profit fixed in the Prefect's bureau. The
hours of labour and the workmen's wages were equally
ordained. Middlemen were thus rendered unnecessary ;
and any attempt to buy up large quantities of goods and
retail them at suitable moments was strictly forbidden.
The bakers and butchers, on whose efficiency the victualling
of the City depended, were subject to particularly minute
supervision, and the price of foodstuffs was kept forcibly
low even in times of famine. The bakeries had been a
State monopoly, controlled by the Quæstor, till Heraclius
abolished the doles of free bread ; and the tradition of
State interference lingered. Nicephorus Phocas was accused
of making a handsome profit when Emperor by buying up
the corn supply of the Empire during a famine and selling
it at an enhanced price to the Guild.[2] Any infringement
of the guild regulations was punished by expulsion from
the guild, that is to say an enforced retirement from business.
Various degrees of mutilation might be added if the offence
was particularly outrageous. The guilds might also, it
seems, be called upon to perform certain unpaid public
services. The shipowners had to help in a naval emergency ;
and probably the duties of the demes with regard to fines
passed, when the demes became more or less nominal, to
the guilds. There was no unemployment. Workmen could

[1] *Le Livre du Préfet*, ed. Nicole, *passim*.   [2] Cedrenus, II, 369–70.

not be dismissed without the greatest difficulty, and if any able-bodied man were out of work he was at once made to take on some job of public utility or charity under the Quæstor.[1] ' Idleness,' said Leo the Isaurian in the *Ecloga,* ' leads to crime, and any superfluity resulting from the labour of others should be given to the weak, not the strong.' [2] The silk guild was in a position apart, as the silk industry was a State monopoly. Its director was a Government official of considerable importance.[3] The conspirator Leo Phocas in 972 tried to win the support of the director of the time because of his great influence over the workmen.[4]

The system lasted throughout the existence of the Empire. Constantinople, it seems, kept it to the last, and it can be seen in Thessalonica in the Fourteenth Century. It guaranteed the interests of the consumer and it allowed a certain profit to the merchant, though he could never make a fortune and enterprise was thus discouraged. But it could prove very expensive to the State and it was only workable when Constantinople enjoyed a monopoly of the commerce of her world. Foreign competition broke it down. From the Eleventh Century onwards Italian intervention in the Eastern Mediterranean trade, intensified a little later by the Crusades, hastened on the steady debasement of the coinage, which would be the main cause of the decline and fall of Byzantium.

Cosmas, the Sailor of the Indies, attributed the prosperity of Imperial commerce to two causes, Christianity and the coinage. While the commercial advantages of Christianity may be questioned, the Imperial coinage was certainly an indisputable asset. From Constantine I to Nicephorus Botaniates, for over six centuries, it retained its value unimpaired. Byzantium was monometallic ; the coinage was

---

[1] Bury, *Imperial Administrative System,* 74.
[2] *Ecloga,* in Leunclavius, *Juris Graeco-Romani,* 1, 87–8.
[3] *Le Livre du Préfet,* 30 -45.   [4] Leo Diaconus, 146–7.

based on the pound of gold. The standard coin, the
nomisma, was, since Constantine's day, worth one seventy-
second of 1 lb. of gold—the equivalent of 14·40 gold francs.[1]
The nomisma was subdivided into 12 *miliaressia*, each
further divided into 12 *pholles*. Nicephorus Phocas was
accused of introducing a debased nomisma—probably
falsely, as it left no mark. Botaniates reduced the amount
of gold in the coin. Alexius I attempted to restore it, but
found himself forced to pay out his expenses in a coinage
that he invented—nomismata mainly of brass, two-thirds of
the value of the gold nomisma.[2] The system would not
work. Under the Comneni the nomisma began to fall,
very slowly at first; the ' Bezant ' was still acceptable
abroad. After 1204 and under the Palæologi the fall grew
more and more rapid, till it was only a sixth of its previous
value and too unreliable to have any circulation outside of
the Empire.

Of the cost of living in Byzantium we have little definite
evidence. Corn was the same price in 960 as it was in
1914 (1·85 gold francs per modium), but all other goods
were probably from five to six times less expensive.
Nicephorus I attempted to keep prices down by restricting
the amount of coinage in circulation ; but there was
probably a gradual rise throughout the Empire's life, with
an increase in the monetary stock beginning under the
Isaurians. Corn certainly rose to be about twice the price
under the Palæologi that it had been under the Macedonians ; but this was largely because the Seljuks had
destroyed the agriculture of Asia Minor, and wars and the
difficulties of transport reduced the corn that was available.
Moreover, the unceasing collapse of the currency was
bringing increasing financial chaos.[3]

[1] Andreades, *De la Monnaie dans l'Empire Byzantin*, in *Byzantion*, vol. 1,
75 *sqq.*
[2] Chalandon, *Alexius 1er Comnène*, 301 *sqq.*   [3] *Ibid., passim.*

M

Indeed, the days of the Palæologi are a sad last chapter to the Empire. The coinage that the King of Ceylon liked above all others was now dishonoured even in Pera. The merchandise that paid rich tolls at the wharves of Constantinople was carried past her walls now by the Genoese without calling or travelled by a far-away route by Syria and ships of Venice. Her situation was valueless now, and her monetary pride humbled and discarded. The tragedy of the long death of Byzantium is above all a financial tragedy.

CHAPTER VIII

Town and Country Life

Of the daily life of the inhabitants of the Empire it would be rash to generalise. Our sources are very scanty. The lives of the great, of the Imperial Court and the higher nobility, are illustrated, in varying detail, by the historians and chroniclers ; but of the merchant classes, of the farmers, of the poor in town and country, we only know scraps of information, given mostly in the lives of the popular saints or in the legal handbooks of the rules that governed their lives. Moreover, in the eleven centuries that elapsed between the first and last Constantine, all the outward circumstances of life were altered many times over. The citizen of the Empire remained to the end consciously the most civilised product of the human race, consciously Roman, consciously orthodox and consciously the heir to Greek refinement ; but the smooth-faced noble of the Fourth Century, clad in the loose folds of a toga and speaking a sonorous Latin, would never have recognised his successor of the Fifteenth Century, bearded and turbaned, in a stiff coat of brocade, speaking a Greek whose vowel sounds had lost their variety.

Even the racial basis of the Empire was continually changing. The Empire was at the outset cosmopolitan, what the Greeks called œcumenical, embracing the civilised world. Nationality was a conception alien to it. When the old Roman Empire began to disintegrate, the new Empire based itself not on nationality but on orthodoxy, after the

Fifth Century, and on the Greek language, in the Seventh. Its ethnology remained complex. The proportion of pure Greeks was probably small. New strains, Illyrian, Scythian and Asiatic, had mixed with Greek blood already in the Hellenistic age. Under the Romans the races of the whole Mediterranean world intermarried and amalgamated. Hamites from Egypt, Semites from Syria united with the tribes of Europe. The Emperor Philip was an Arabian, Heliogabalus a Roman-Syrian half-breed. This catholicity lasted into the Byzantine era. Arcadius, a Spaniard by descent, married a Goth, Eudoxia, and their son Theodosius II married a pure Hellene. Late in the Seventh Century a Syrian was Bishop of Rome. The inhabitants of Constantinople were drawn from every tribe, though the nobility liked to claim Roman descent.

The loss of Egypt and Syria in the Seventh Century restricted the admixture of blood. Henceforward the backbone of the Empire was the people of Asia Minor, a mixture of Phrygian, Hittite, Gallic, Iranian and Semitic and many other stocks, in proportions that no one can tell. But there were still new strains coming in. Chief of these were Slav and Armenian.

The Slav invasions, starting in the Sixth Century, at first only disturbed the ethnology of the Balkan provinces and a little later the Greek peninsula. When things became more settled there was an increasing amount of intermarriage, and by the outset of the Ninth Century men of mixed or even pure Slav descent were occupying high positions in the Empire. The Pretender Thomas was a Slav, as were many of the great people of the Tenth and Eleventh Centuries, the Empress Sophia, wife of Christopher Lecapenus, or the Patriarch Nicetas. After the conquest of Bulgaria the aristocracy was further leavened by intermarriage with the Bulgarian royal and noble families. By the end of the Eleventh Century the Slavs were either completely absorbed within the Empire, or were entirely attracted away to the independent Slav states of the Balkans.

The case of the Armenians was slightly different. They immigrated not in whole tribes, except when there were forced transportations, but rather as individual adventurers, fulfilling very much the rôle that the Scots play in English history. Too prolific for its restricted valleys, the race sent its more enterprising sons to seek power and fortune in the greater scope that the Empire afforded. Already in the Sixth Century Justinian's great general Narses had been an Armenian ; but it was in the Ninth and Tenth Centuries that the movement reached its height. The Emperor Leo V was an Armenian adventurer ; Basil I the son of Armenian deportees ; John I Tzimisces was an Armenian noble. When Romanus I ruled the State and his son Theophylact the Church and John Curcuas was General-in-Chief, the whole Empire was in Armenian hands. Continually we hear of princesses or high officials of Armenian blood, and Armenian artisans and merchants could be found in every city. The only sphere to which they did not penetrate (with the exception of Theophylact, a cynical Erastian appointment) was the Church. The Armenian immigrant had, on entering the Imperial service, to renounce his heresy and accept the doctrine of Chalcedon ; but the ecclesiastical authorities never liked the converts and distrusted their conversion. The Seljuk invasions and subsequent upheavals in Asia cut Armenia off from the Empire ; and the stream gradually ceased. The stoppage was a loss to the Empire. The Armenians had provided not only many of its most vigorous rulers, but also a large proportion of its best business brains ; and they had a large, but still disputed, influence on Byzantine art and craftsmanship.

No other race immigrated on so influential a scale as the Armenians ; but throughout Byzantine history a flow of

adventurers came to seek their fortune under the Emperor
from innumerable countries.   There was continual passage
to and fro across the Saracen frontier.   Byzantines went
over to Islam and Arabs to Christianity according as the
Emperor or the Calif offered the better opportunity.   The
father of the epic hero Digenis Akritas was a Saracen convert ; the Emperor Nicephorus I was of Arab blood.[1]   The
immigrants from the North and the West, particularly in the
later centuries of the Empire, tended to return home when
their fortunes were made—the Varangian to the mists of
Scandinavia or England, the Frank to Flanders or to
Catalonia.   But they might stay ; they might marry ; their
cross-bred children might govern the Empire in the next
generation.   There was extraordinarily little racial prejudice amongst the Byzantines ; their blood was too much
mixed.   Anyone who was orthodox and spoke Greek was
acceptable to them as a fellow-citizen.   Their deep contempt for foreigners was directed against them as heretics
and as boors unacquainted with the refinements of the
Imperial civilisation.   An alien who was converted and
naturalised could marry any Byzantine, whatever his or her
origin.   Byzantine gentlewomen freely were wedded to
Frankish or Eastern adventurers ; among the brides of
Emperors were two Chazars of pure Turkish origin and
numberless princesses from the West.   It is true that when
Justinian II forced a senatorial lady to marry his own negro
cook, decent feeling was outraged, but almost more, probably, from snobbery than from colour-prejudice.[2]   The
increasing contact with the West and the slow martyrdom of
the Empire at the hands of the Italian republics made
foreigners more hated in Constantinople ; but it was the
alien civilisation rather than the alien blood that was
anathema.   The Slav nations who owed their culture to
Byzantium met with no such racial dislike except in times of

[1] Michael Syrus, 15.   [2] Theophanes, 379.

war ; and even the Turks, who borrowed Byzantine trappings, seemed preferable to the fellow-Christian Franks.

The only race settled in the Empire that could never
amalgamate because of its religion was the Jews. The Jews
were, however, never very numerous. There were Greek-
speaking settlements in Asia Minor,[1] and by the Twelfth
Century, at least, small colonies could be found in every
Byzantine town ;[2] but in business they were no more
astute than the Greeks and the Armenians, and they were,
it seems, subjected to additional taxation and periodical
persecution. If however they became converts they might
even join the ranks of the aristocracy. The Empress Irene's
sister married a descendant of a certain Sarantapechys, a
renegade Jew from Tiberias.[3]

Both the admixture of races and the intensity of national
feeling were to be seen at the most extreme in the capital
itself, Constantinople. From the moment of its foundation
Constantinople dominated the Empire. The bureaucracy
and the finances were more and more centralised there ; its
position made it the economic and strategic key to two
continents. To rule the Empire the first essential was to
hold Constantinople. Rome was already declining when the
new capital was founded, and there was no other great city
in the West ; Carthage and Milan were both some way
behind. The Patriarchal cities of the East, Alexandria and
Antioch, were more formidable rivals ; Alexandria till the
Arab conquest was little less important than Constantinople,
but in her hatred of the Imperial Government she increasingly took up an attitude of championing local rights and
aspirations, which lessened her œcumenical importance.
Antioch, on the other hand, gradually declined from
geographical reasons. As the West grew poorer and more
disorderly, merchandise from the East that had been carried

[1] See Reinach, *Contrat du Mariage* in *Mélanges Schlumberger*, 1, 118 *sqq.*
[2] Benjamin of Tudela, 10.   [3] Theophanes, 474.

to the Mediterranean by way of Antioch took now a more
northerly route and went through Asia Minor to the new
metropolis. By the Seventh Century Constantinople was
left without a peer.

Already by the Fifth Century the population of Constantinople, excluding its suburbs, must have numbered about a
million persons, and it remained roughly at that level till the
Latin conquest, after which it declined rapidly, to be well
under a hundred thousand in 1453.[1] The area of the City
was even greater than such a population would justify.
The base of the triangle on which it stood was some five
miles across, where the land-walls built by Theodosius II
stretched across in a double line from the Marmora to the
Golden Horn, pierced by eleven gates, the military alternat-
ing with the civil. From either end the sea-walls ran for
some seven miles each before they met at the blunted apex
on the Bosphorus. Within the walls were various crowded
towns and villages separated by orchards and parks. Like
Old Rome, Constantinople could boast of seven hills.
These rose steep over the Bosphorus and the Golden Horn,
but from the Sea of Marmora the slopes were gentler and the
lay-out more spacious.

The traveller arriving by sea from the south or the west
would have seen, as he approached the City, on his right
hand the domes and tiled porticoes of the Great Palace, with
Saint Sophia rising behind, and gardens stretching down to
the Bosphorus, then the huge curving wall which still holds
up the southern end of the Hippodrome, rising above the
ornate Palace harbour and Church of Saint Sergius and
Saint Bacchus and a low-lying district full of smaller palaces.
At intervals to the left the sea-wall with its occasional towers
would be broken to admit of a small artificial harbour for
ships that did not wish to pass round to the Golden Horn.

[1] See Andreades, *De la Population de Constantinople*, in *Metroon*, vol. 1 ;
Pears' *Destruction of the Greek Empire*, 192 *sqq.*

Round these harbours the houses would cluster close ; behind, especially in the valley of the little River Lycus, there were orchards and even corn-fields, but the summit of the ridge was dominated by the Church of the Holy Apostles and other great buildings. Further still to the left the landscape flattened out. On the shore there was the populous district of Studium with its famous monastery. Behind, the tops of land-walls could be seen coming down to the sea, but even beyond the walls' end the houses of the suburbs were thick along the coast for another two miles or so. From across the great harbour of the Golden Horn the appearance of the City was very different. There, in front of the walls, you saw a foreshore, increasing gradually with the centuries, covered with wharves and warehouses and quays at which the merchant-ships were moored, and farther up even houses were built out on piles over the water. Numerous gates opened into the busy districts behind. Here there was little greenery to see. The steeper slopes that led up to the central ridge were covered with houses, except only for the citadel quarter at the eastern end and the more spacious district of Blachernæ at the extreme west where an Imperial palace and a very holy church gave an air of dignity to the quarter. Between was the centre of the City's commercial energies, the offices of the shipowners and the exporters, the establishments of the foreign traders. It was here that the Italian merchants were first allowed to settle.[1]

The smartest shopping district lay inland. Along the central ridge from the entrance of the Palace and the Hippodrome for two miles there ran westward the street called Mesê, the Central Street, a wide street with arcades on either

---

[1] Gyllius, *De Topographia Constantinopoleos* ; Du Cange, *Constantinopolis Christiana* ; Mortmann, *Esquisse Topographique de Constantinople* ; van Millingen, *Byzantine Constantinople* ; Ebersolt, *Constantinople Byzantine et les Voyageurs du Levant.*

side, passing through two forums—open spaces decorated with statues—the Forum of Constantine, close to the Palace, and the larger Forum of Theodosius, and finally branching into two main roads, the one going through the Forums of the Bull and of Arcadius to Studium and the Golden Gate and the Gate of Pegæ, the other past the Church of the Holy Apostles to Blachernæ and the Charisian Gate. Along the arcades of the Mesê Street were the more important shops, arranged in groups according to their wares—the goldsmiths and next them the silversmiths, the clothiers, the furniture-makers and so on. ·The richest of all were near the Palace, at the Baths of Zeuxippus. There were the silk emporia in the great bazaar known as the House of Lights because its windows were illuminated by night.[1]

There was no particular fashionable residential district. Palaces, hovels and tenements all jostled together. The houses of the rich were built in the old Roman manner, two stories high, presenting a blank exterior and facing inward round a courtyard, sometimes covered in, and usually adorned with a fountain and any exotic ornament that fancy might suggest. Poorer houses were constructed with balconies or windows overhanging the street, from which the idler ladies of the household could watch their neighbours' daily life.[2] The residential streets had mostly been built by private contractors, but a law of Zeno's attempted to introduce some order. Streets had to be 12 feet wide, and balconies might not extend to within 10 feet of the opposite wall and must be 15 feet above the ground. Outside staircases were forbidden, and where the streets had already been built less than 22 feet wide windows for prospect were not allowed, only gratings for ventilation. This law remained the basic charter of Byzantine town-planning.[3] There were strict regulations about drainage. All the drains led care-

[1] Cedrenus, 1, 648.   [2] See de Beylié, L'Habitation Byzantine.
[3] Codex Justiniani, viii, x, 12.

fully to the sea, and no one, except an Imperial personage, could be buried within the City. Medical officers in each parish gave further attention to the public health.

In contrast to the narrow streets there were wide public gardens, kept up at the municipal expense. The Great Palace and its grounds occupied the south-eastern corner of the City, its buildings extending for almost a mile. Adjoining it was the Patriarchal Palace with all its dependencies, and there were other Imperial palaces throughout the City. At almost every corner you would see a church ; there were the vast Churches of Saint Sophia, of the Holy Apostles, the New Basilica of Basil I, and a hundred smaller sanctuaries. Many of them had monasteries attached, in huge austere enclosures, and hospitals and orphanages and hostels. There were university buildings, libraries, aqueducts, cisterns, public baths, and above all the great Hippodrome. A statue of Aphrodite marked the only brothel in the City, in the quarter called Zeugma on the Golden Horn.[1] The main streets, especially the forums and the Hippodrome, were museums where the choicest pieces of antique sculpture were displayed. In the earlier centuries there had been a definite Museum, the House of Lausus, but it was burnt down with all its treasures in the year 476.[2] The statuary in the streets, however, survived till it was destroyed or stolen by the Latin crusaders.

Round the City were the suburbs, some, like Chalcedon or the later Italian Galata, busy commercial towns, others, like Hieron, where Theodora had her favourite palace, or the villages up the Bosphorus, mainly residential resorts, to which the wealthy would retire in the summer. At Pegæ, just outside the walls, was a famous shrine of the Virgin. At Hebdomon, seven miles from the milestone at the Great Palace Gate, was a famous parade-ground where many vital scenes in Byzantine history took place.

[1] Codinus, 50, 119 ; Cedrenus, II, 107–8.   [2] Cedrenus, I, 616.

The outward appearance of the City in its hey-day must remain a matter of conjecture. The fantastic domes and pediments and coloured arcades that form the background in the illuminated manuscripts give too gay an impression, for the Byzantine architect kept his richest effects for within. But even under the Palæologi when huge tracts of the City lay in ruin and the Great Palace itself was uninhabitable, travellers were impressed by the splendour that Constantinople still presented.

The appearance of the wealthier citizens was equally impressive. The Roman toga was discarded in the Fifth Century for long coats of stiff brocade. The scaramangium, the robe that every noble wore on ceremonious occasions— they were mainly stored in the Palace—was a garment copied from the Huns and inspired long ago, probably, by the mandarins' robes of China.[1] As the centuries advanced clothes grew more elaborate ; strange head-dresses were carried by both sexes, peaked hats rimmed with fur or high bulging turbans. From the Seventh Century onward beards became habitual ; to shave the chin was Western and vulgar. Cosmetics were fashionable especially under the Palæologi. Even young and lovely women covered their faces in paint. The Burgundian La Brocquière was horrified by the amount used by the Empress Maria, who was one of those far-famed beauties, the Princesses of Trebizond.[2]

The daily life had a background of regulation and ceremony as stiff as the daily apparel. The authorities interfered everywhere. Prices, profits, hours of labour, all were controlled from the bureau of the Prefect of the City. The Church had its own instructions for fasts and for festivals. The Emperor, supreme ruler of the Empire, had a life even more circumscribed than any of his subjects. Quite apart

[1] Kondakov, *Les Costumes Orientaux à la Cour Byzantine*, in *Byzantion*, vol. 1, 7 *sqq.*

[2] La Brocquière, *Voyage d'Outremer*, 157.

from the business of government which, were he conscientious, took up most of his time, he had almost daily ceremonies to attend, where he was paid the adoration due to Divinity ; and whatever were his views about sport he must show himself to his people at the performances in the Hippodrome. Continually he must change his robes, he must walk in long processions with a diadem weighing down on his head, he must receive ambassadors and be prepared to be raised on his throne suddenly high into the air to impress the simple foreigners. In the summer he might retire for a holiday to a cool suburban palace, but more probably he would have to lead his armies over the highlands of Asia Minor. Leo VI and his son Constantine VII found time to write books, but they were neither of them soldiers, nor was Theodosius II, who like Constantine VII was skilled as a painter.[1] Emperors who meant to live a life of pleasure on the throne either had to have capable but loyal ministers or else remained on the throne for a very short time.

Till the Twelfth Century the Emperor lived almost entirely in the Great Palace, though he might occasionally visit his other palaces in or around the City. The Great Palace,[2] called by Western travellers the Bucoleon, from the Palace harbour of that name, where a huge statue of a bull fighting a lion used to stand, was an unmethodical conglomeration of buildings, halls, oratories, baths, residential wings, built by various Emperors in their turn. Of the Palace in the days of Justinian we know little. After the Seventh Century parts apparently needed repairing. Theophilus built the famous reception hall, the Triconchus. Basil I made many additions, while Nicephorus Phocas constructed a wing down by the sea, where he liked to reside and where he was murdered. The Comneni, though both Alexius I and John I remained faithful on the whole to the Great Palace, preferred the Palace of Blachernæ on the

[1] Cedrenus, I, 587.   [2] See Ebersolt, *Le Grand Palais*.

Golden Horn at the north-west corner of the City ; and
Manuel I resided there almost exclusively. He was a great
huntsman and it suited him better to live close to the walls,
instead of having to ride some five miles through the streets
before he could reach the country. The first Latin Emperors
settled in the Great Palace ; but Baldwin II could not afford
to keep it up. During his reign even the Blachernæ Palace
fell into disrepair. When Michael Palæologus entered the
City the Great Palace was in too bad a condition to be
worth rebuilding, considering the general poverty ; and even
Blachernæ took several weeks to clean before it was fit for
use.[1] The Palæologi all lived at Blachernæ, and the Great
Palace, by the time of the Turkish Conquest, had only a few
of its buildings still standing.[2]

The whole wealth of Constantinople astounded the
Crusaders of 1204. Villehardouin could not believe it to be
true.[3] But while the Palace of Blachernæ with its marbles
and mosaics and frescoes and brocades impressed them
beyond all measure, the Great Palace was even more
stupendous. There were kept the main stores of treasures,
bullion, jewellery and precious stuffs. There were the
Imperial reception-rooms, with the golden lions that roared
and the golden birds that sang, made for the Emperor
Theophilus. There too, to sanctify the place above all
others, was the finest collection of relics in all Christendom.
A lighthouse stood on a hill in the Palace precincts, to guide
boats into the Bosphorus, and by it was a chapel of the
Mother of God, the museum where these priceless treasures
were stored, till the Crusaders divided them up between them
and Baldwin II pawned the best that were left.[4]

---

[1] Pachymeres, I, 161.

[2] Pero Tafur, *Travels and Adventures*, trans. Letts, 145–6.

[3] Villehardouin, *La Conquête de Constantinople*, ed. Bouchet, I, 171.

[4] See Ebersolt, *Les Sanctuaires de Byzance* ; de Riant, *Exuviae Sacrae Con-
stantinopolitanae*. See below, p. 215.

The Palace was the centre of Constantinople. From with-in its walls the whole Empire was governed. Control of the Palace meant control of the Empire. It was the Empire's richest merchant house. The silk trade was an Imperial monopoly, and in the Gynæceum, the women's quarters, were the looms on which the costliest stuffs were woven. In addition to the public offices and the vast quarters of the Emperor there were the buildings where the Empress and her court resided, rooms under her sole control where the Emperor never penetrated without her permission. Indeed, when the Empress Theodora died in 548 and her widower Justinian went through her belongings he found hidden away in an inner room the heretic ex-Patriarch Anthimus whom she had concealed for twelve years.[1] But though the Gynæceum was tended by eunuchs and men never came there, the Empress left it as she pleased. She would visit the Emperor in his own quarters and dine with him in his halls ; as regent she would interview her ministers wherever she chose. Within the Palace she was almost more powerful than the Emperor.

The Empress was traditionally chosen by the Bride-show. Envoys would go all over the Empire to collect beautiful and well-educated maidens from whom the Emperor had to make his choice. Often political considerations or an in-calculable passion provided the Emperor with a bride and the expedient was unnecessary ; but it was used when Irene wished to marry her son Constantine VI [2]—when Irene rather than the Emperor seems to have made the selection ; the bride was morally admirable but not attractive, though the agents had carefully measured her height and her feet,—when Stauracius was married [3] and, more famously, when Theophilus chose Theodora, passing by the poetess Casia because of the pertness of her repartee.[4]

[1] John of Ephesus, 247–8.   [2] *Vita Philaretis*, 74–6.
[3] Theophanes, 483.   [4] Georgius Monachus Continuatus, 790.

Adjoining the Palace were the two other great centres of the life of the City, the Church of the Holy Wisdom, Saint Sophia, and the Circus or Hippodrome.[1] The Hippodrome was a vast erection, capable of seating some 40,000 persons. In the buildings that clustered round were the stables of all the gladiatorial animals and the hovels of the innumerable Circus servants. Circus entertainments were free, sub-sidised by the State. To watch the games in the Hippo-drome, the combats with beasts and the chariot-races, was the great recreation of the populace ; and in the contests between the Circus-factions, the Blues and the Greens, feeling ran so high as to cause political complications and riots. The Emperor and the Empress had to attend the performances ; the Imperial box, the Cathisma, could be reached directly from the Palace. An elaborate ritual ordered their move-ments and prescribed the whole method of the racing and the prize-giving. In the earlier centuries the Hippodrome became the place where the Emperor could interview and make announcements to his people. He would be acclaimed there as Emperor. It was there that Ariadne announced to her subjects whom she had chosen to be her husband and Emperor ; [2] it was there that Justinian argued with the angry rioters in the Nika sedition.[3] In later years, however, by the Tenth Century, such scenes usually took place in the great square in front of the Palace. It was there that the populace demanded Constantine VII for their Emperor in 944 [4] and Zoe for their Empress in 1032.[5] The Hippodrome was grow-ing less popular. The charioteers of the Fifth and Sixth Centuries, such as Porphyrius in the reign of Anastasius, had been the idols of the City,[6] and Hippodrome intrigues

---

[1] Bury, *Later Roman Empire*, I, 81 *sqq.* (with references).
[2] Constantine Porphyrogennetus, *De Ceremoniis*, I, 417–8.
[3] Bury, *Nika Riot*, 98 *sqq.*   [4] Liudprand, *Antapodosis*, 142–3.
[5] Psellus, *Chronographia*, I, 102 *seq.*
[6] See Bury, *Later Roman Empire*, I, 84.

such as those that surrounded the youth of Theodora could affect the politics of the Empire. By the Ninth Century this was altered. The professional charioteer sank into the background. It was more the amateur rider like Basil the Macedonian who attracted attention or like Philoræus, a stable-boy of the Tenth Century who was the cynosure of all Byzantium for having galloped round the Circus standing on his horse and playing with both hands with his sword.[1] The introduction of Western Chivalry by Manuel Comnenus made the Hippodrome for a while the scene of knightly tourneys. Under the Palæologi it was left almost deserted : though young princes and nobles would go there from time to time to practise feats of horsemanship and play polo.[2]

The nobles that could afford them all had their town houses, though they might visit their country seats in the summer ; but to be forced to reside there permanently was the equivalent of exile and disgrace. The men usually held some Government appointment, and would spend their time doing their work. Otherwise with their wives they would wait about the Imperial Court—on feast days the men would file ceremoniously past the Emperor and the ladies past the Empress—and would indulge in intrigue. They would, as far as possible, turn their own palaces into little courts, building up a circle of client saints and poets. The nobility of the earlier Empire had lost its wealth and power during the invasions of the Seventh Century and under the tyranny of Emperors such as Phocas and Justinian II. Till the Ninth Century land was an uncertain investment. The one great family that emerges is that of the Melisseni,[3] who seem to have been a Constantinopolitan family, deriving their wealth probably from town-property : though later they established themselves in the Greek peninsula and were flourishing still at the very eve of the

---

[1] Cedrenus, II, 343.   [2] La Brocquière, 158.
[3] See Du Cange, *Familiae Byzantinae*, 145.

N

Empire—the last Duchess of Athens was a Melissena.   But
from the latter half of the Ninth Century onward families
appear owning vast estates in Asia Minor, for example the
Phocæ, the Ducæ, the Scleri, the Argyri and the Comneni.
A little later, after the conquest of Bulgaria had settled
the European provinces, the great European families come
on to the scene, the Cantacuzeni, the Bryennii, or the Tornicæ,
an Armenian princely house settled near Adrianople, while
the Ducæ acquired European estates.   Tracing the descent
of the great Byzantine families is, however, difficult, in that
either from snobbishness or a love of variety children would
often take the mother's rather than the father's surname.
Thus Anna Dalassena's father's name was Charon, her
mother being a Dalassena ; [1] the later Ducæ were, according to Psellus, Ducæ only in the female line ; [2] Anna
Comnena's sons were surnamed Comnenus and Ducas,
though their father was a Bryennius. [3]

The great families led clannish lives, working and often
living together.   In the early pages of Anna Comnena's
history we find the Comneni brothers acting as a unit under
the rule of their mother, Anna Dalassena, and furthering
the interests of the ablest but not the eldest of them, Alexius.
These same pages show us how exciting and how agitated
the lives of the aristocracy could be in any crisis, the men
continually riding out of the City by night for refuge or to
woo the support of the army, the women, who were usually
the more dangerous intriguers, hurrying, often in vain, to
the sanctuary of some altar. [4]   Even in more peaceful
times the wealth of the nobles made their positions insecure.
Under Nicephorus Phocas, Romanus Saronites found the
suspicion and surveillance to which he was subjected, just
because he was very rich—he owned the circus-rider

---

[1] Bryennius, 17.   [2] Psellus, *Chronographia*, II, 140.
[3] Prodromus, *Epithalamium, M.P.G.*, vol. 133, 1397-406.
[4] Anna Comnena, 52 *sqq.*

Philoræus—and the son-in-law of a former Emperor, Romanus I, such a strain that in despair he thought of rebelling, but on the advice of Saint Basil the Less he retired to a monastery.[1]

Of what great riches in Byzantium consisted we cannot conjecture. There is no information about wealth in the earlier Empire. When Justinian abolished the Consulship, it was costing its holders about £90,000 yearly, and no private individual could possibly afford it.[2] Riches decreased in the Seventh and Eighth Centuries. Theoctiste, the mother of Theodore of Studium, who was wealthy and very generous, only gave her servants bread and lard and wine, with meat or chicken on saints'-days and Sundays, and was considered rather extravagant ; but we do not know how many servants she had.[3] The Sixty Martyrs of Jerusalem travelled, we are told, with a princely train, in about 730. Danielis, the widow that befriended Basil I, owned the better part of the Peloponnese and left the Emperor 3,000 slaves.[4] The Paracœmomenus Basil, a self-made man, though he was the bastard son of an Emperor, even in his worst days of disgrace took about with him a following of 3,000 attendants.[5] The sums mentioned in the epic of Digenis Akritas have unfortunately been touched up with a poet's licence. It is hard to believe that his wife's dowry was really worth nearly 9,000,000 gold francs, and would have been far larger had the hero wished : while the hero's palace, entirely panelled with gold and with mosaics, represents the ideal country-house, rather than one that was ever actually erected.[6] But even the humble-born agriculturalist Philaretes in his richest days

[1] *Vita S. Basilii Minoris, A.S. Boll., March 26, 761.*

[2] Procopius, *Historia Arcana*, 23.

[3] Theodore Studites, *M.P.G.*, vol. 99, 884 *sqq.*

[4] Theophanes Continuatus, 321.   [5] Leo Diaconus, 47.

[6] Digenis Akritas, ed. Sathas and Legrand (*Monuments de la Langue Néo-Hellenique*, vol. 6), 108–16, 224 *sqq.*

gave dinner parties to thirty-six guests round a table of ivory and gold, and owned 12,000 head of sheep, 600 oxen and 800 horses at pasture, 200 oxen and 80 horses and mules for work and a large number of serfs. His wealth was derived from property round the market towns of Asia Minor ; he had no house in Constantinople to keep up.[1] Private wealth subsisted even under the Palæologi. Metochites's description of his palace destroyed in the riots shows it to have been full of marble and precious metals and sumptuous to an extent unknown in the contemporary West ;[2] and, according to his enemies, Lucas Notaras was concealing in 1453 bullion enough to have bought a whole new army for the rescue of the City.[3] To the last the aristocracy remained an aristocracy of wealth.

In consequence there was nothing closed about the ranks of the aristocracy. Anyone with enough money invested in land, the one safe permanent investment, might found a noble family, buying a title, so that his sons became members of the senatorial classes. The most reputable way was to be a public servant, probably a soldier, and to be rewarded by the gifts of large estates. Thus it was that the prosperity of the Phocæ was begun by the great soldier the elder Nicephorus. Or else the Emperor might be interested in the children of some statesman or some friend of his. Thus Theophanes, the sainted chronicler, was as a boy the protégé of the Emperor Leo IV, because his dead father had been distinguished as a Strategus of the Ægean islands ; and had Theophanes wished he might have enjoyed every worldly blessing.[4] Thus too the Comneni, two young Thracian brothers, were patronised by Basil II, whom their

---

[1] *Vita Philaretis, passim.*

[2] Guilland, *Le Palais de Métochite, Revue des Études Grecques,* vol. 35, 82–95.

[3] Phrantzes, 291.

[4] *Vita Theophanis,* ed. Loparev, in *V.V.,* vol. 17, 92.

father had served, and given lands in Paphlagonia : [1] or,
in a humbler way, Romanus Lecapenus was helped on in
the navy by Imperial influence, because his father, a
peasant called Theophylact the Unbearable, had once
saved the life of Basil I.[2] To acquire one's estates purely
by financial adroitness, as for instance the Patrician Nicetas
in the early Tenth Century, was, it seems, somewhat less
respectable.[3] It was also more unsafe. The Emperors
were terrified of such tendencies, and the ambitious landowner might find himself, like the Protovestiary Philocales,
forced to return to poverty on the grounds that he had
contravened the Statutes of Pre-emption.[4] The Emperors
also sought to prevent the increase of estates whose
nucleus had been respectably acquired ; but that was more
difficult.

We know very little about the amenities of Byzantine
society life. Court ceremonies probably provided all the
formal entertainment in Constantinople itself, but intimate
parties seem to have been frequent. Pulcheria would dine
every Sunday after Service with the Patriarch to discuss
Church politics with him.[5] It was at a small dinner which
Basil the Macedonian and his wife were giving to Michael
III that Basil was provoked to plot the murder of the
Emperor.[6] In the lives of the Saints we hear of friends
dining with monks at their monasteries or saints refusing
to come to the feasts of their richer patrons. Photius gave
intellectual parties where books were discussed [7] and so,
centuries later, did Metochites.[8] Country-house parties did
not exist, for the country-house was the place of exile or

[1] Bryennius, 19.   [2] Georgius Monachus, 841.
[3] Constantine Porphyrogennetus, *De Thematibus*, 54.
[4] *Jus Graeco-Romanum*, III, 307–16.
[5] *Lettre à Cosme*, trans. Nau, *Patrologia Orientalis*, vol. 13, 278.
[6] Georgius Monachus Continuatus, 835.
[7] Photius, *Bibliotheca*, M.P.G., vol. 103, 41–4.
[8] See Sathas, *B.G.M.*, vol. 1, 19 *sqq.*

discreet retirement : save only when distinguished travellers were passing by, ambassadors, Imperial ministers or the Emperor himself. Philaretes had to entertain the mission that was searching for possible brides for Constantine VI.[1] Alexius I stayed with relatives of his wife's when travelling through Thrace.[2] When Eustathius Maleïnus entertained Basil II, the munificence of the hospitality proved, as in the English instance of Lord Oxford and Henry VII, the host's undoing. Basil had not realised that his subjects were so powerful.[3] Cecaumenus was emphatically of the opinion that house-parties are a mistake. Guests, he says, merely criticise one's housekeeping and attempt to seduce one's wife.[4]

Like the Imperial Palace, the palaces of the nobility had their Gynæcea, their women's quarters. But the women shared fully in the men's lives. Unmarried girls lived in a certain seclusion, and might never see their husbands till the marriage was fixed ; but, once married, they moved with complete freedom, often, like Theoctiste, dominating the whole family circle. The mother was particularly respected. The power of Anna Dalassena was notorious, but her sons' deference to her was thought not unreasonable. When Digenis Akritas dined at home—he dined simply, waited on by only one footman, whom he would summon with a bell—he and his wife would go to the dining-room as soon as the meal was ready and lie on couches, but his mother was expected to arrive a little late and was given a chair.[5] Even in the twilight of the Empire it was only the influence of the last of the Empresses, the dowager Helena Dragases, that kept the peace between her sons, Constantine XI and his brothers.[6]

In the frequent conspiracies that enlivened the lives of

---

[1] *Vita Philaretis*, 74.   [2] Anna Comnena, 223.
[3] *Jus Graeco-Romanum, loc. cit.*   [4] Cecaumenus, *Strategicon*, 42–3.
[5] Digenis Akritas, 244.   [6] Phrantzes, 206.

the aristocrats women invariably played a part and usually shared in their men's punishments, being however spared the worst physical indignities and sufferings. Anna Dalassena was once relegated to a convent ; [1] the wife of Constantine Ducas, after his revolt failed in 913 and he was blinded, was forced to retire to her country estates.[2] On the other hand, the wife of Bardas Phocas, who had even defended the fortress of Tyriæum for him against the Imperial troops, was never as far as we know punished at all after her husband's cause was lost at Abydos.

The lives of the poor are much the same in any time or country, passed in an anxious search for the means of livelihood. The poor of Constantinople lived in great squalor, their slums jostling against the palaces of the rich, but they were perhaps better off than the poor of most nations. The Circus, their one recreation, was open to them free. The distribution of free bread had been stopped by Heraclius,[3] but free food was still provided for men that undertook work for the State, such as keeping parks and aqueducts in repair or helping in the State bakeries. It was the Quæstor's business to see that the destitute were thus given useful work and that there was no unemployment.[4] To further this, no one was allowed to enter the City except on authorised business. There were, moreover, almshouses and hospitals for the old and infirm, founded usually by the Emperor or some noble and attached to and managed by a monastery or convent. We possess the title-deeds of several of the foundations of the Comneni.[5] For the children of the poor there were the State orphanages. The Orphanotrophus, the official in charge of the orphanages, had early become an important member of the State hierarchy, with enormous sums under his control. Under

[1] N. Bryennius, 35, 40.   [2] Theophanes Continuatus, 385.
[3] Chronicon Paschale, 711.   [4] See above, p. 91.
                    [5] See below, p. 238.

the Iconoclasts the Church for a while captured the manage-
ment of the orphanages, but the Macedonian Emperors
restored it to the civil powers and enhanced the position
of the Orphanotrophus.[1] The biggest orphanage was in
the precincts of the Great Palace. An earthquake destroyed
it in Romanus III's reign, but Alexius I refounded it,
forgetting the cares of State as he watched over the
children.[2]

With all these charitable institutions there was probably
very little actual starvation. It is noticeable that when
the populace rose up in riot, it was never prompted by
anarchical or communistic desires. The rabble might wish
to depose an oppressive minister or destroy hated foreigners,
but it never sought to alter the structure of society. Indeed,
it was to rescue the purple Imperial blood from the over-
boldness of some usurper that the People most often gave
expression to its basic sovereignty.

There was however, besides the free poor, a considerable
slave population. How large this was it is impossible to
say. For Christians to be slaves was felt soon to be wrong :
though the serfs in the country districts were little better
than slaves. But at any rate till the Twelfth Century
infidel and heathen-born slaves were employed in private
service and in the State mines and other State works.
These were either unredeemed Saracen captives, or more
often merchandise brought by traders from the Steppes.
The Russians in particular usually sold the victims of their
raids in the markets of Constantinople. But there was all
the while a growing sentiment against slavery. Theodore
of Studium forbade monasteries to employ slaves ; and
there was a special tax on them. Alexius I in particular
legislated to allow them to marry freely.[3] Yet even in the

---

[1] Bury, *Imperial Administrative System*, 103 *sqq.*
[2] Anna Comnena, 409 *sqq.*
[3] *Jus Graeco-Romanum*, III, 407 *sqq.*

late Twelfth Century the Archbishop Eustathius of Thessalonica owned large numbers which he ordered to be freed
after his death, because slavery is unnatural.[1] Gradually
the spread of civilisation raised the price of human goods
to an impossible height ; but domestic slaves were probably
still to be found in Constantinople in the Fourteenth Century.
The slaves in private hands probably led fairly comfortable
and not intolerable lives, though their State-owned comrades
might be treated like cattle.[2]

Between the poor and the nobility fluctuated the middle
classes. Diocletian had intended that everyone should
follow the father's profession—the soldier's son should be
a soldier, the baker's a baker. To a certain extent this
endured ; but society had not remained as static as Diocletian had wished. If there were one son to carry on the
family business his brothers might enter the Church, the
Army or the Civil Service, and if they succeeded there
the whole family might share in the new fortune. There
would be grants of money, land would be bought, and so
a new branch of the nobility would appear. John the
Orphanotrophus, Zoe's minister, was of middle-class birth,
and his sister married a ship's chandler. But he succeeded
in raising one of his brothers and after him his nephew,
the chandler's son, right to the Imperial throne.[3] Or a
sister might make a splendid marriage, for beauty would often
raise a girl high above her station. Theodora, the circus-
born actress, and Theophano, the inn-keeper's daughter,
both became Empresses, and there were other instances
almost as spectacular. Regularly the Emperor's new
relations-in-law would flock to the Palace and would start,

[1] Eustathius, *M.P.G.*, vol. 136, 1289–90.
[2] For the question of slavery see Chalandon, *Jean 1ᵉʳ Comnène*, 612 ;
Constantinescu, in *Bulletin of the Roumanian Academy*, vol. 11, 100 ;
Boissonnade, *Le Travail dans l'Europe Chrétienne au Moyen Age*, 55, 76, 413
(minimizing the extent of slavery).
[3] Psellus, *Chronographia*, 1, 44, 69.

whatever their origin, on a new career of aristocracy. Ambition was a common characteristic in Byzantium, and middle-class parents would do everything to encourage their clever children. Psellus's mother took great trouble to give her boy the education that she had never received, though all her relatives would gather together and say that it was not worth while.[1] The mother of Saint Theodore the Siceote dreamed of a great career for him in the army and was deeply disappointed when he chose the unprofitable path of saintliness.[2] Saint Mary the Younger's sister, herself the wife of an officer, married her to a promising colleague of her husband's, who rose in a short time from a drungarius to Turmarch of Bizya, and might have reached greater heights but for the unnerving tragedy of his wife's death as the martyr to his roughness. Their twin sons had been destined one for the Army, one for the Church.[3]

Psellus's account of his home life in the funeral oration of his mother shows a very united family, which she entirely dominated. The one person that Psellus really loved was his sister, who died at the age of eighteen. They were not well off, but they kept one or two servants, and Theodote found time after her marriage to teach herself to read and write properly, for her own education had been unusually neglected. The father was a merchant, but Psellus with his unusual abilities was brought up to be a scholar and was even sent to travel, to study under the best masters. They were a very pious family, particularly Theodote, who half-hoped that Psellus would have ecclesiastical ambitions.[4]

The household of the Turmarch of Bizya was somewhat richer. It contained several servants and a gynæceum ; but the Turmarch's attempts to keep his wife inside the

[1] Psellus, *Funeral Oration* in *B.G.M.*, vol. 5, 12–13.
[2] *Vita S. Theodori Siceotis*, *A.S. Boll.*, April 22, 33 *sqq.*
[3] *Vita S. Mariae Junioris*, *A.S. Boll.*, November 9, 692–3.
[4] Psellus, *op. cit.*, *passim.*

gynæceum were considered wrong, and it was unchristian of him not to let her come to the party that he was giving on the Sunday before Lent.[1]

For a boy to be really successful, it might be wise to castrate him ; for Byzantium was the eunuch's paradise. Even the noblest parents were not above mutilating their sons to help their advancement, nor was there any disgrace in it. A eunuch could not wear the Imperial crown nor could he, from his nature, transfer hereditary rights ; and therein lay his power. A boy born too close to the throne could thus be side-tracked and then be safely allowed to go forward as he pleased. Thus Nicetas, the young son of Michael I, was castrated when his father fell, and later, despite his dangerous birth, rose to be the Patriarch Ignatius.[2] Thus Romanus I castrated not only his bastard Basil, who as Paracœmomenus, the Great Chamberlain, ruled the Empire for several decades, but also his youngest legitimate son, Theophylact, whom he intended to be Patriarch.[3] A large proportion of the Patriarchs of Constantinople were eunuchs ; and eunuchs were particularly encouraged in the Civil Service, where the castrated bearer of a title took precedence of his unmutilated compeer and where many high ranks were reserved for eunuchs alone. Even over the army and the navy a eunuch was often in command. Narses in the Sixth Century and Nicephorus Uranus in the Tenth were perhaps the most brilliant examples. Alexius I had a eunuch admiral, Eustathius Cymineanus : [4] while after the disasters of the Manzikert campaign it was a eunuch, Nicephorus the Logothete, who managed to reform the army.[5] A few posts such as the Prefecture of the City were traditionally closed to them ;

[1] *Vita S. Mariae Junioris*, 695–6.
[2] Theophanes Continuatus, 20, 193.
[3] Maçoudi, *Le Livre de l'Avertissement*, trans. Carra de Vaux, 235.
[4] Anna Comnena, 244.   [5] N. Bryennius, 81.

but it was only when Western notions of sex and chivalry began to infect Byzantium that any stigma was attached to castration. In reality it was the employ of eunuchs, of a strong bureaucracy controlled by eunuchs, that was Byzantium's great weapon against the feudal tendency for power to be concentrated in the hands of an hereditary nobility, which provided so much trouble for the West. The significance of eunuchs in Byzantine life was that they gave the Emperor a governing class that he could trust. Nor is there any evidence that their physical limitations warped their characters. Throughout Byzantine history eunuchs appear no more corrupt nor intriguing, no less vigorous or patriotic than their completer fellows.

In the lower classes eunuchs were rarer, though it might help a doctor's practice if he were castrated, as in that case he could attend convents and women's hospitals. Some female institutions were, however, so strict as to insist on women doctors only.[1]

The general fluidity of society was helped by the interest that everyone took in trade. The conception that it was degrading to make money was another Western notion alien to Byzantium. The Imperial Court was the biggest business-house in Constantinople, with its monopoly of the silk trade. Individual Emperors were not above commercial enterprise. Nicephorus Phocas speculated in the corn-trade, with greater profit than honesty,[2] while John Vatatses made enough money out of his poultry-keeping to buy his Empress a new crown.[3] The nobility often had their commercial activities ; the widow Danielis was a carpet-manufacturer,[4] and Leo VI's favourite Musicus was interested in Thessalonica harbour.[5] Even the Church appeared on occasion as a banking concern, financing

---

[1] See below, p. 238.   [2] Cedrenus, ii, 369–70.
[3] Gregoras, i, 43.   [4] Theophanes Continuatus, 318.
                    [5] Ibid., 357.

Heraclius's wars against the Persians.[1] It was not, however, possible to make a great fortune out of commerce. With the strict regulations imposed by the State for the welfare of the citizens, profits were forcibly kept low. Millionaires usually owed their wealth to real estate only. But probably the control of the State was exercised with a certain elasticity. The parents of Saint Thomaïs of Lesbos, when trade was bad in the island, were freely allowed to move to Chalcedon and set up a business there, despite the official disapproval of movement within the Empire ; [2] and the ban on immigration into Constantinople did not prevent large numbers of Armenians from coming to the capital and opening shops and factories.

To come to Constantinople was the natural aim of every ambitious man, for Constantinople was the undoubted centre of the Empire. In Europe, Thessalonica alone could in any way compare with it. Thessalonica stood at the end of one of the great trade-routes of Europe, coming down from the Hungarian plain to Belgrade and running due south up the Morava and down the Vardar. It had been a great city from the earliest days of the Empire. At the close of the Ninth Century it took over the bulk of the Bulgarian trade,[3] and thenceforward, despite its sack by Arab pirates in 908, it steadily grew. At the great annual fair of Saint Demetrius the town was crammed full for a week of traders and adventurers from all over the world. The Satirist Timarion has left a vivid picture of the bustle and the gaiety of it all.[4] Under the Palæologi Thessalonica became more prosperous than the capital itself. Its nobles and merchants were probably richer than those of Constantinople, and it was an intellectual

[1] See Bury, *Roman Empire from Arcadius to Irene*, II, 224.
[2] *Vita S. Thomaïdos, A.S. Boll., November* 9, 233.
[3] Constantine Porphyrogennetus, *De Administrando Imperio*, 79, 177.
[4] See Tozer, *Byzantine Satire, J.H.S.*, vol. 2, 235 *sqq.*

centre. The other European towns of the Empire, with the exception of a few ports, Mesembria, Dyrrhachium, Patras and Bari, were sleepy market-towns or else important as fortresses ; though by the Twelfth Century Thebes had an important local silk industry.

In the earlier days Alexandria and Antioch had been worthy rivals to Constantinople, but the loss of the great south-eastern provinces to the Arabs had inaugurated their decline. In Asia Minor there were several large fortress-towns and provincial capitals, but the ports alone had any active life. Smyrna lost some of its importance when the trade-route went north to the Bosphorus. Trebizond, however, to the last was the great port for Armenia and Persia and the East, and as the capital of an independent Empire for two and a half centuries its prestige was greatly enhanced ; like Thessalonica it became an intellectual centre, being particularly famed for its astronomers and mathematicians. Nicæa had its hallowed past to distinguish it, and enjoyed a new prosperity as the capital of the Empire in exile. Brusa was famed for its waters. It was the chief spa of the Byzantines and was patronised in particular by the Empress Irene.[1] Antioch was still a great city when the troops of Nicephorus Phocas reconquered it for Byzantium, but it was declining, and declined still further during the Crusades, for all that it was the capital of a Latin principality—the Arab trade reached the Mediterranean farther to the south.

Life in the country districts was by no means uniform In the European districts you would find Slavs, Albanians or Vlachs leading a pastoral existence according to their old tribal customs in and out of the estates of the Greco-Roman nobility. Even in Asia Minor there were little colonies of alien races, Syrians, possibly, or Bulgarians, scattered throughout the land. On the whole, the country-

[1] Procopius, *De Aedificiis*, 315 ; Theophanes, 471.

side was occupied by village communities of two sorts, the servile and the free.[1] The servile villager or serf was bound to the soil. His master, the landowner, paid the taxes but took the produce of the land. The serf's children were serfs like himself, though by the master's favour they might leave the soil and enter other professions, such as the Church. There were also tenant farmers on many of the estates of the rich. These paid their rent in money or in kind and counted as free men, but in fact found it impossible to change their lot for the better. They were fixed where they were. The free villager was almost equally bound to the soil, for the central authorities disliked any desertion of the land. Their great preoccupation was the feeding of Constantinople, and for that the provincial corn-fields, of Thrace and of Asia Minor, were increasingly necessary. The free villager was liable for certain taxes on his holding and his heirs were liable after him ; and it was made difficult for him to get rid of his land. Consequently he could not afford to leave the village. A further system made his bonds tighter. The village community was taxed as a community. Thus if any member defaulted, an extra payment fell upon the whole of his neighbours. It was to their interest to keep him at work in their midst.

Servile villages had been more common in the days of the great landowners of the earlier Empire ; but in the chaos of the late Sixth and the Seventh Centuries rustic society was reorganised and free communities became the rule. The State used particularly to pay soldiers with gifts of land, held on the condition of military service, thus creating a class of hereditary military small-holders. Gradu-

---

[1] For the agrarian question, see Panchenko, *Rural Property in Byzantium, Izvestiya of Russian Institute at Constantinople*, vol. 9 ; Sokolov, *Law of Property in the Greco-Roman Empire* (both in Russian) ; Ashburner, *The Farmer's Law, J.H.S.*, vol. 30, 97 *sqq.*, vol. 32, 875 *sqq.* ; Testaud, *Des Rapports des Puissants et des Petits Proprietaires Ruraux dans l'Empire Byzantin*.

ally as order was restored the great landowner reappeared. The rich would take over the poor man's obligations, paying his taxes in return for his produce and thus turning him into a tenant or into a serf. The harvest sometimes failed, and then the small-holder could not afford to exist as a free man. Or a pious villager might die, leaving his holding to the Church ; and the Church, like the nobility, sought to invest its money in land. Thus new territorial magnates appeared, lay and ecclesiastic, who were dangerously rich and whose intervention upset the system of taxation. Against this the Emperors legislated in vain. Romanus I in his Pre-emption statutes ordained that only the poor could buy up the lands of the poor and the buyer must belong to the village community, a relative having the first offer.[1] But though subsequent Emperors repeated his injunctions,[2] it was obviously hopeless, for in hard times it was only the rich that had the ready money to pay the taxes which the State relentlessly demanded. It was a vicious circle, inevitably leading to the free small-holder becoming more and more infrequent as the centuries advanced. The Isaurians had attempted to abolish serfdom ; the Macedonians were obliged to restore its legal rights.

The Farmer's Law of the Eighth Century gives a picture of the community life.[3] Round the village were the orchards and vineyards, fenced in, and outside them the arable fields, unfenced but equally in private ownership. On the outside ring was the rough pasturage, held in common ; but were it cleared and cultivated it passed into the hands of the reclaimer. Heavy penalties were laid upon anyone who voluntarily or from carelessness did damage to the villagers' property. The thief of a cattle-bell was held responsible for the animal, the thief of a sheep-dog for the whole flock. The man who let his beasts into his stubble before all his

---

[1] *Jus Graeco-Romanum*, III, 234 *sqq*, 242 *sqq*.
[2] *Ibid.*, 252 *sqq.*, 306 *sqq.*   [3] Text in Ashburner, *op. cit.*

neighbours' crops were in was liable to a fine, for the beasts might stray. Provisions were made against all contingencies, and the criterion was the harm done to the farming of the community as a whole. The lives of the Saints supplement the picture. The sense of neighbourly obligation was always very strong. When Philaretes, in the late Eighth Century, fell on hard times, his neighbours all assisted him, and when he had to entertain the Imperial mission they supplied him with food.[1] Military service was a burden, particularly in frontier districts where a special militia would be convened in case of invasions—with justification, for the invaders would often sweep through the district destroying the crops for the year and carrying off the cattle and the sheep. But it was possible to evade military service even on a military holding. There were always complaints at the heavy taxation, but the tax-collector acted as the friend of the people in times of famine, providing food for the district. Order was well kept. There were police to keep down the robbers. Passports were needed for travel in frontier districts.[2] Except among the nobility and the Church there was little wealth. Saint Theodora of Thessalonica, the daughter of the village priest of Ægina, was considered to have made an extremely good match when she married a man who died soon after, leaving her 300 *nomismata* (4,320 gold francs) and 9 slaves.[3] The fear of invasions had depopulated and impoverished the countryside. The State used drastic measures to attract new settlers. In the Ninth Century, Saint Athanasia of Ægina, a comely but pious widow, found herself one day, to her horror, obliged to marry a barbarian immigrant.[4] Yet many districts, particularly the Ægean islands, long remained deserted. The Tenth-Century story of Saint

---

[1] *Vita Philaretis, passim.*   [2] *Op. cit., passim.*
[3] *Vita S. Theodorae Thessalonicensis*, ed. Kurtz, 1 *sqq.*
[4] *Vita S. Athanasiae Aegineticae, A.S. Boll.*, August 14, vol. 3, 170 *sqq.*

o

Theoctiste of Lesbos, for all its suspicious resemblance to
that of Saint Mary of Egypt, was perfectly possible. She
lived naked and undisturbed for many years on an Ægean
island, having escaped from Saracen pirates, and was
eventually found by some Eubœans who had come there
for sport. They told about her to a monk of Paros who
repeated the story to Nicetas the Magister one evening
when he was storm-bound there on his way to an embassy
to Crete.[1]

Travel in the Empire was not much encouraged ; settled
communities were easier to tax and control, and the only
migrations approved of by the authorities were the forced
migrations of Armenians to Europe or Slavs to Asia to isolate
unruly elements. But enterprising men like Basil the Macedonian managed to find their way to Constantinople ;
promising youths were willingly allowed to tour the Empire
in search of the best teachers ; and pilgrimages either to
the Holy Land or still more to see the relic collections of
Constantinople were always permissible.[2] Lawsuits continually brought visitors to the capital, and charitable
Emperors, such as Romanus I, would build hostels in which
they could stay.[3] From coastal districts, from Trebizond,
or Thessalonica, the journey would usually be made by
sea. There were however good roads, well kept up largely
because of their military value and probably cleared of
civilian traffic when an army was passing by.[4] The upkeep
was paid for partly by toll-gates ; only Government servants,
foreign ambassadors and certain high nobles were exempted
from paying the tolls. Two main roads led from Constantinople to the East, the one, the Military Road, running

---

[1] *Vita S. Theoctistae Lesbiae, A.S. Boll., November* 9, 221 *seq.*

[2] Cecaumenus, *Strategicon,* 78.

[3] Theophanes Continuatus, 430.

[4] See Ramsay, *Historical Geography of Asia Minor, passim,* esp. 197–
221.

through Dorylæum, branching east of the Halys, one arm
going on past Sebastea to Armenia, one turning south and
leading to Cæsarea and Commagene or through Tyana to
the Cilician Gates and Syria ; the other, the Pilgrims' Road,
was a little shorter but less easy. It began its course
further to the north, through Ancyra, then turned south
to Tyana. In Europe the chief road, if conditions permitted
its use, was the old Via Ignatia, going from Dyrrhachium
to Thessalonica and carried on to Constantinople. The
Belgrade-Sofia-Adrianople road was seldom wholly in
Byzantine hands.

Considering their diversity of blood, of the means of life
and the long changing centuries of their Empire's existence,
it might seem rash to credit the Byzantines with national
characteristics. Yet throughout Byzantine history certain
traits appear so persistently as to deserve the description
of the Byzantine temperament. The most striking is the
religious sense. The whole of Christendom in the Middle
Ages was deeply religious, deeply concerned with the future
of the soul. But the Byzantine was religious with a savage
intensity that was rare in the West. He demanded theological accuracy, but still more he longed for personal
contact and experience. His Empire was theocratic. The
pomp and glory of the Court was to elevate God's Viceroy ;
it was as much part of the worship of God as were the
services in the churches. The festivals and carnivals that
enlivened the Byzantine year, though they might afford
worldly delights, were all incidents in the perpetual liturgy.
The simple pagan attitude of the Ancient Greeks towards
pleasure was entirely lost ; a transcendental sense of religion
obscured the joys of life. Byzantine poets found their
natural expression in hymns, pæans in celebration of God's
majesty or descriptions of mystic communion. Even the
worldliest writers, men like Psellus, take religion for granted
and assume the relative unimportance of life on earth,

apologising for an interest in the pagan sciences : while
the opponents of religion, rationalists like Constantine V,
who would not allow even the apostles the title of Saint,[1]
and debauchees like Michael III and Alexander, all expressed their emancipation in mock-ritual and the Black
Mass.[2] They could not free themselves entirely from the
atmosphere.

But though the splendour of their life was designed as
homage to God, the Byzantines most admired those who
gave up the pleasures of the world and prepared themselves
for eternity by contemplation and the subjection of the
flesh. The monasteries and convents were crowded. After
the worries of house-keeping, the ardours of a business life
or the strain of high politics, it was pleasant to retire to
monastic peace, and to fortify the soul in calm and beautiful surroundings. But monastery life was hardly rigorous
enough. Monks were a deeply respected class, and to like
their company was a sign of grace—such a taste added
greatly to Romanus I's popularity,[3] and Alexius I, to
please his mother, always kept a monk in his tent when
campaigning ; [4] but far more reverend and far more influential were the hermits who lived in solitary squalor in
caves or on pillars. Many Lives exist of these self-denying
saints illustrating the prodigious influence that they wielded.
The holy Luke the Less was almost the chief authority in
Greece in the Tenth Century ; the Strategus would continually visit his cave to ask and follow his advice.[5] Saint
Nicon, surnamed Metanoeite or ' Repent Ye,' ruled in the
Peloponnese a little earlier,[6] and a little later Saint Nilus
dominated Calabria and later even exercised power over

---

[1] *Vita S. Stephani*, *M.P.G.*, vol. 100, 1148.
[2] Theophanes Continuatus, 244–5, 379.
[3] *Ibid.*, 433–4.   [4] Anna Comnena, 23.
[5] *Vita S. Lucae Minoris*, *M.P.G.*, vol. 111, 465 *sqq.*
[6] *Vita S. Niconis Metanoeite*, in *Neos Hellenomnemon*, vol. 3, 74–5.

the Rome of the Ottos.[1] Saint Nicephorus of Miletus was
powerful enough to make Nicephorus II remit the tax on
Church oil.[2] Particularly admired were the Stylite saints
who passed their lives on the tops of columns. There was
a long reverend sequence of them from the first Symeon
in the Fourth Century onward.[3] Saint Daniel the Stylite
had a column at Constantinople in the Fifth Century and
was particularly fashionable at Court. Whenever there had
been a storm the Emperor Theodosius II would send out
at once to inquire how he was, and at last after great
persuasion induced him to allow a little roof to be built
over his head. When it was discovered that the column
was of faulty construction, the architect was threatened
with death.[4] He was a great healer, as was Saint Symeon
the Young, who, after precociously saying, at the age of
two, ' I have a father but I have none, I have a mother
but I have none,' went to live on a pinnacle rock near
Antioch.[5] Saint Alypius the Paphlagonian and Saint
Lazarus the Galisiote governed monasteries from their
columns ; the former was paralysed after standing up for
fifty-three years and had to lie down.[6] The Seventh-
Century Saint Theodore the Siceote spent one Lent in a
cage, but his disciple Arsinus lived forty years on a column
near Damascus.[7] Saint Theodulus, a correspondent of
Theodore of Studium, painted daring pictures on his
column-top.[8] There were even one or two female Stylites.[9]
The last eminent Stylite, Saint Luke, lived under Romanus
I, whose reign was a golden age of Saints. Saint Luke's

[1] *Vita S. Nili*, M.P.G., vol. 79.
[2] *Vita S. Nicephori Milesii*, ed. Delehaye, 144.
[3] See Delehaye, *Les Saints Stylites*.
[4] *Vita S. Danielis Stylitae*, in Delehaye, *op. cit.*, 44–6, 53.
[5] Delehaye, *op. cit.*, lxiv.
[6] *Ibid.*, lxxxii, *sqq.*, cviii *sqq.*   [7] *Ibid.*, cxxiii–iv.
[8] Theodore Studites, *Epistolae*, M.P.G., vol. 99, 957.
[9] See Delehaye's note in *Analecta Bollandiana*, vol. 27, 391–2.

column was at Chalcedon, and his proximity to the capital made him a most useful healer. He cured two servants of the Empress Sophia, a steward and the man that stoked the furnace that heated her bath, and even healed an early illness of the Prince-Patriarch-designate, Theophylact.[1] His contemporary Saint Basil the Less was also patronised by the Lecapeni Court. He advised the Empress Helena how to have a son.[2]

After the Tenth Century saints become rarer, though there were still Stylites in the Eleventh and Twelfth Centuries, and it was possible even later to win martyrdom and a halo by going, like Saint Nicetas the Young in the Fourteenth Century, amongst the Moslem Turks and making a disturbance during Ramadan.[3] The call of the monasteries never faltered. The princesses of the Comnenian dynasty frequently declared their longing to retire, though few followed it up ; and the many dowagers who found their way to convents usually did so not of their own volition. But the last Empress, Helena, ended her days at her own desire as the nun Hypomene.[4]

It was possible also for men of action who did not wish to absent themselves altogether from the world to take partial vows of asceticism. Nicephorus Phocas was much admired for his abstention from meat, and when, tempted by ambition for the Empire and love for the Empress, he broke it on his marriage night with Theophano, it was a serious blow to his prestige ;[5] and though he maintained a venerable dirtiness in his person and his linen, to the disgust of the Italian Ambassador Liudprand,[6] his broken vow had lost him for ever the affections of Constantinople.

---

[1] *Vita S. Lucae Stylitae*, ed. Nau, *Patrologia Orientalis*, vol. 11, 235, 239–10.

[2] *Vita S. Basilii Minoris*, 762–3.

[3] Delehaye, *Le Martyre de S. Nicetas le Jeune*, in *Mélanges Schlumberger* 205 *sqq.*

[4] Phrantzes, 210.   [5] Cedrenus, ii, 351.

[6] Liudprand, *Legatio*, 177.

The liking of almost all the Emperors for monastic company was helped by their interest in theology. Religious discussions were the main substance of conversation at many of the Emperors' tables ; and it was a terrible surprise and shock to Cinnamus and the Bishop of Neopatras when Andronicus I asked them to talk about something else, as religion was so boring.[1] Andronicus deserved the dreadful fate that overtook him soon afterwards.

The religiosity was freely accompanied with superstition. The love of the Byzantines for their relics was fully shown by their pride in the great collections at Constantinople. Every century new relics would be added. Saint Helena laid the foundation of the Palace collection in the days of Constantine. Heraclius added many of the holy objects of the Passion kept at Jerusalem to save them from the Persians and the Arabs—the Wood of the Cross, the Holy Blood, the Crown of Thorns, the Lance, the Seamless Coat and the Nails. Holy corpses were already pouring in. Helena brought Daniel ; Saint Timothy, Saint Andrew and Saint Luke arrived under Constantius, Samuel under Arcadius and Isaiah under Theodosius II, the Three Children under Leo I, Saint Anne under Justinian, and Mary Magdalene and Lazarus under Leo VI. Romanus I added the Image of Edessa, Nicephorus Phocas the hair of John the Baptist and John Tzimisces the sandals of Christ. The mantle of Elijah was kept in the New Basilica, the loaves of the miracle under the Column of Constantine, while the relics of the Virgin could mostly be seen at her churches at Blachernæ and Chalcopratia.[2] The relic-museums had no rivals in the world ; and despite the State's dislike for unauthorised strangers, pilgrims who desired to pay worship there were always encouraged and

[1] Nicetas, 430–1.
[2] See Ebersolt, *Les Sanctuaires de Byzance*, and Riant, *Exuviae Sacrae*, *passim*.

assisted. The story of the Iconoclastic controversy showed how much holy pictures meant to the Byzantine. But religious objects were also of highly practical value. Not only were many of the monks and hermits efficient healers, but the Christian shrines took over the beneficent qualities that their pagan predecessors had possessed. Men and women went no more to the temples of Asclepius or of Lucina to cure their ills. Instead they crowded the Church of Saint Damian and Saint Cosmas the Anargyri, the Free Doctors. The shrines of the Archangel Michael were very medicinal, particularly his cathedral at Chonæ, while Saint Diomede was almost as efficient.[1] For sexual complaints men had recourse to Saint Artemius and women to his partner Saint Febronia.[2] Saints could even protect a city. Twice Saint Demetrius in person saved Thessalonica,[3] while Constantinople was under the care of the Virgin ; and Edessa was long able to rest in peace relying on Christ's promise that it would never be captured.[4] The promise however wore out.

The superstition had its darker side. Devils and demons were everywhere. Satan in the form of a dog attacked Bishop Parthenius of Lampsacus.[5] Even the great Justinian sold his soul, and you could see him by night wandering through the Palace carrying his head in his hands.[6] John the Grammarian, the Iconoclast Patriarch of the Ninth Century, indulged in sorcery and held séances with nuns to act as mediums ;[7] and Photius was thought to have

---

[1] See Ebersolt, *Les Sanctuaires de Byzance*, and Riant, *Exuviae Sacrae*, *passim*.

[2] *Miracula S. Artemii, Zapiski of Historico-Philosophical Institute of S. Petersburg*, vol. 95, *passim*.

[3] *Miracula S. Demetrii, M.P.G.*, vol. 106, *passim*.

[4] *Chronicle of Joshua the Stylite*, ed. and trans. Wright, 78.

[5] *Vita S. Parthenii*, in *A.S. Boll., February* 11, 39.

[6] Procopius, *Historia Arcana*, 80–1.

[7] Michael Syrus, 114–15 ; Theophanes Continuatus, 156.

won his prodigious learning at the price of denying Christ.[1]
The Patriarch Cosmas in the Twelfth Century cursed the
Empress Bertha so that she could never bear a son.[2] His
contemporary Michael Sicidites could make things invisible,
and played practical jokes with the aid of demons.[3] Comets
and eclipses foretold disaster. There were men that could
read the future ; continually mad monks or inspired children
recognised Emperors-to-be. Astrology was a science. The
Professor Leo the Philosopher, in the Ninth Century, knew
the meaning of the stars, though people hoped that his
more successful achievements, as when he foresaw and
guarded against a famine at Thessalonica, were the results
not of magic but of prayer.[4] A fortune-teller told Leo V,
Michael II and the usurper Thomas of their exalted and
tangled futures, while Leo V learnt of his coming death
from a book of oracles and symbolic pictures.[5] The
Emperor Leo VI was surnamed the Wise for his divination.
He knew exactly how long his brother Alexander would
reign,[6] and a series of verses attributed to him peered far
into the future and foretold the disaster of 1204 and the
revived Empire of the Palæologi.[7] There were many other
prophecies of the fall of the City. Apollonius of Tyana,
that great magician, who was made a contemporary of the
foundation of Constantinople, wrote out a list of all the
Emperors that would be and buried it in the column
of Constantine.[8] Occasionally, however, prophecies went
wrong. The Athenian Catanances was very popular under
Alexius I, but when he prophesied the Emperor's death
only the Palace pet-lion died. He tried again, and this
time it was the Empress-Mother.[9] Dreams and visions

[1] Georgius Monachus Continuatus, 670 *seq.*   [2] Nicetas, 107.
[3] *Ibid.*, 193-4.   [4] Theophanes Continuatus, 191.
[5] Genesius, 8, 21.   [6] Theophanes Continuatus, 379.
[7] In *Monuments de la Langue Néo-Hellénique*, vol. 5, 1 *sqq.*
[8] *Scriptores Originum Constantinopolitani* (Teubner ed.), 191, 206.
[9] Anna Comnena, 149-50.

guided events. A dream told Leo V that Michael the
Amorian would slay him.[1] John II would not crown his
eldest son because of a dream.[2] The mother of John
Cantacuzenus, as she stood on the balcony of her country-
house one night to watch the moon rise, was warned by a
ghostly visitor that her son was in danger.[3] It was believed
that everyone had a *stoicheion*, an inanimate object with
which his life was bound up. Thus Alexander caused great
care to be taken of a bronze boar in the Circus which he
considered to be his : [4] while a wise monk told Romanus I
that a certain pillar was the *stoicheion* of Symeon of Bulgaria.
The pillar was decapitated and the old Tsar thereupon
died.[5] Other statues suffered destruction for equally surprising causes. In 1204 the furious populace destroyed a
great statue of Athene because she seemed to be beckoning
the Latins from out of the West.[6]

The Byzantines have won a bad name for corruption,
intrigue and cruelty as well as for superstition. The
paucity of Emperors that died a natural death is held up
as a proof. That personal ambition played a great part
in the life of almost every well-known Byzantine statesman
cannot be denied ; but we must remember that the less
pushful seldom have their lives recorded. There were
certainly figures like Justin I, Irene, the Cæsar Bardas,
Basil I or Cerularius in almost every generation, intriguers
devoid of scruple and honour though seldom devoid of
patriotism. But there must have been many others like
the Paracœmomenus Theophanes in the early Tenth
Century, loyal and disinterested servants of the State, of
whom we hear but little. Of the extent of the corruption
we cannot tell. At times, as under Leo VI, it was certainly
widespread ; but there is no reason to suppose that under

---

[1] Genesius, 21.   [2] Cinnamus, 15.
[3] Gregoras, II, 619.   [4] Theophanes Continuatus, 379.
[5] *Ibid.*, 411–12.   [6] Nicetas, 738–9.

Theophilus or Basil II the power of money played too large a part. The cruelty too has been exaggerated. The populace of Constantinople, like any Southern rabble, when its passions and hatred were aroused, was terrible. Fallen Emperors and ministers who had lost its favour might suffer unspeakable torment at its hands. Michael the Calfat, dragged screaming from the sanctuary of Studium, Andronicus I, his beard torn out, his teeth broken and an eye and a hand cut away, hacked to pieces in the Hippodrome, are pictures that it is not pleasant to contemplate. But no angry mob remembers to be kind.

In their calmer moments the Byzantines were less brutal. The path to the throne was often strewn with corpses, but not invariably. The punishment that the authorities most liked to inflict was immurement in a monastery, to save the offender's soul. The death penalty was seldom employed. Mutilation, the usual treatment for crime, though it horrifies modern notions, was a humane alternative to death ; and it was probably preferable to imprisonment or to fines that would leave the criminal destitute. There were many occasions where the mercy of the authorities mitigated even richly deserved punishments. The Empress Theodosia would not allow Michael the Amorian to be burnt alive, although he had been clearly convicted of high treason against her husband Leo V.[1] The punishments meted out on the Ducas conspirators in 913 were considered outrageous, because several accomplices were put to death ;[2] and everyone deplored Constantine VIII's passion for blinding, even when the victims were acknowledged offenders. He however regarded it as milder than the death penalty.[3] In his pleasures the Byzantine compares very favourably with the Roman. There was no throwing to the lions in the Hippodrome ; and chariot-racing, not

---

[1] Genesius, 20.   [2] Theophanes Continuatus, 385.
[3] Zonaras, III, 570.

gladiatorial combats, were the most-liked entertainments. The charitable organisations, almshouses and hospitals were scarcely the signs of a heartless people. The Byzantine faults seem much more to have been fickleness and a lack of personal loyalty, and a bitterness and an uncharitable cynicism that makes even the most self-revealing of their writers, Psellus, Anna Comnena or Phrantzes, somehow unattractive. It was not human life but human nature that they rated too low.

But they had many qualities. They took pride in their Empire and their civilisation. They loved learning and they loved beauty. They carried their intellectual tastes even to the extent of snobbery. Education not birth gave the *entrée* to Byzantine society. It was their ignorance of culture that made Romanus I and his friends despised in the best circles, while the Patriarch Nicetas in the Eleventh Century was laughed at for his Slavonic accent,[1] and the statesman Margarites treated with disrespect in the Thirteenth because he spoke with a rough rustic voice.[2] The Byzantines approved of a well-trained mind that could express itself delicately and quote the classics ; and many of them achieved it. And their culture was not entirely smug. They were passionately interested and inquisitive about the affairs of their neighbours, and were willing to borrow from the lore of the Arabs and the recreations of the West.

Their love of beauty went even deeper. Human beauty appealed to them. In the Seventh Century the soldiers wanted to make an Armenian Mizizius Emperor because he was so good-looking.[3] The absurd Empress Zoe was saved from contempt by her looks.[4] Even when she was sixty she looked like a girl with her golden hair and her flawless complexion, and the simple white gowns that she

---

[1] Glycas, 527–8.
[2] Acropolites, 130.
[3] Theophanes, 352.
[4] Psellus, *Chronographia*, I, 102 ; II, 49.

wore were much admired. They loved beautiful scenery.
Gardens and parks and flowers were a delight to them—
the gardens of Digenis Akritas are described with real
enthusiasm—and they would build their monasteries on
sites commanding the loveliest views that they could find.
Their buildings, their stuffs, their books, all reflected the
same yearning for beauty, but a beauty not quite of this
earth. Beauty had an inner meaning to them. It helped
their mystical contemplation ; it was part of the glory of
God. Life was drab and ugly ; but the worshipper, the
citizen in Saint Sophia or the hermit on Mount Athos
was away from it all. The human architecture of the
Cathedral and the divine architecture of the Mountain alike
raised him out of the ordinary world and made him closer
to God and True Reality. To the Byzantine beauty and
religion went hand in hand, to their mutual advantage.

The alliance is the better understood when we remember
the background to Byzantine life. The Byzantines lived
in a hard unreliable world. Beyond the frontiers roamed
the barbarians, and all too often they would burst in across
the provinces or over the sea, and their hordes would reach
the gates of the Capital itself. The watch-fires of the Huns,
the Persians, the Bulgarians, all had gleamed before the
City, the ships of the Saracens and the Russians had covered
the sea below her walls. Many a great armament had
almost succeeded before the Venetian pirates and the
Turks. In the early Eighth Century every citizen was
ordered to keep with him provisions to last three years, so
many dangers lurked around.[1]

Beset by fear and uncertainty, the Byzantine could
scarcely fail to be suspicious, to have nerves that flared
easily into fury or panic. He inevitably sought comfort
in ultra-mundane things, in union with God and the hope
of eternal life. He knew existence to be sad. The simple

[1] Theophanes, 384.

laughter and happiness of the pagans was lost. Byzantine wit was acid ; its humour found expression in mockery and sarcasm. Indeed, life seemed a mockery. This great Empire, the last home of civilisation in a dark stormy world, was continually tottering before the barbarians, and recovering only to meet a fresh attack. For centuries the great City stood inviolate, to be in foreign eyes a symbol of eternal power and riches. But the Byzantines knew that the end would come some day, that one of these on-slaughts would triumph. The prophecies written all over Constantinople on columns or in wise books told the same story, of the days when there would be no more Emperors, the last days of the City, the last days of civilisation.

CHAPTER IX

Education and Learning

A good education was the ideal of every Byzantine. *Apaideusia*, a lack of mental training, was considered a misfortune and disadvantage and almost a crime. Continual jibes were made at the ignorant—at the boorish Emperor Michael II, the victim of innumerable lampoons,[1] at the Slav Patrician Nicetas at whom Constantine VII mocked,[2] at the philosopher John Italus who never lost his Italian accent,[3] and Constantine Margarites whose speech was so common—you would have thought him brought up on barley and bran : [4] while writers such as Anna Comnena perpetually laud the possession of a well-trained and well-stocked mind.

The matter and the manner of the education did not much vary throughout Byzantine history. The first subject taught to a boy, when he was about six years old, was Grammar, or ' to hellenise his tongue.' This included, besides reading and writing and grammar and syntax in the modern sense, a knowledge of the Classics and commentaries on the Classics, particularly Homer, whose works had to be learnt by heart. Synesius in the Fifth Century talks of his young nephew's ability to repeat Homer (he learnt fifty lines a day),[5] while Psellus in the Eleventh knew the whole Iliad

[1] Theophanes Continuatus, 49.
[2] Constantine Porphyrogennetus, *De Thematibus*, 54.
[3] Anna Comnena, 133.   [4] Acropolita, 130.
[5] See Baynes, *Byzantine Empire*, 151-2.

by heart at an early age.[1] The result was that every
Byzantine could recognise a Homeric quotation. Anna
Comnena, who introduces sixty-six in her Alexiad, seldom
added ' as Homer says ' ; it was quite unnecessary. Other
poets were read and even learnt, but none had so supreme
and lasting a position. At about the age of fourteen the
pupil passed on to Rhetoric. This involved a correct pronunciation and the study of authors such as Demosthenes
and many other prose-writers. After Rhetoric, there were
the third science, Philosophy, and the four arts, Arithmetic,
Geometry, Music and Astronomy to be studied ; and Law,
Medicine and Physics might be added. Religious education
was carried on side by side with the lay teaching, but was
always separate, imparted by ecclesiastics. Children learnt
the Bible thoroughly ; next to Homer it is the chief source of
allusions and quotations in Byzantine literature.[2]

The teachers might belong to schools or universities or
be private tutors. The whole question of the educational
establishments of Constantinople is rather obscure.[3] In the
earlier days of the Empire the first instruction in reading was
probably given by a monk, but the pupil soon went to some
school, where he received all the rest of his secular education.
Constantine founded a school at the Stoa, and Constantius
moved it to the Capitol. Julian the Apostate forbade
Christians to teach in it ; and, though the ban was removed,
the chief teachers of the Fifth Century seem to have been
pagan. Theodosius II set up in the School ten Greek and
ten Latin grammarians, five Greek and three Latin sophists,
two jurists and a philosopher. Attached to the School was
a public library founded by Julian, containing 120,000

---

[1] Psellus, *Chronographia*, 1, 55.

[2] See the chapter on education in Buckler, *Anna Comnena*, 165 *sqq.*

[3] See Bréhier, *L'Enseignement Supérieur à Constantinople* in *Byzantion*,
vol. 3, 73–94 ; vol. 4, 13–28 ; Schemmel, *Die Hochschule von Konstanti-
nopel, passim.*

volumes.[1] This was burnt during Basiliscus's reign in 476. There were other universities outside of Constantinople— Antioch, where Libanius taught, and Alexandria the home of Hypatia, Berytus with its law schools, and Athens, famous for its philosophy, and Gaza for its Rhetoric.

After Justinian the School is scarcely mentioned. We know that with his passion for Christianity and uniformity he closed the School of Athens by confiscating its endowed funds, and he forbade Law to be taught except at Constantinople, Rome and Berytus : and all university teachers had to be Christian. Later in his reign he cut their salaries. Phocas is said to have finally closed the University. In the darkness of the Seventh Century education became less widely spread. During the next centuries boys were educated largely by private teachers ; Theodore of Studium and the Patriarch Nicephorus had each learnt first under his own *grammatistes*, and went later to a Church seminary.[2] Ananias of Shirak (who lived about 600–650) was taught by a fashionable teacher Tychicus of Byzantium, who had learnt Philosophy at Athens and then settled at Trebizond, where his vast library was an added attraction.[3] But meanwhile the Church was capturing education. Heraclius founded a school under Patriarchal control in the Chalcopratia, and there were schools attached to the Studium monastery and the Church of the Forty Martyrs and a large school at the Church of the Holy Apostles where in the Eleventh Century a very general lay education was given.[4] Even the youths that went to Trebizond to study under Tychicus were conducted there by a deacon of the Patriarch.

[1] Cedrenus 1, 616.
[2] *Vita Theodori Studitae*, *M.P.G.*, vol. 99, 117 ; Ignatius, *Vita Nicephori*, ed. de Boor, 170.
[3] Ananias of Shirak, trans. Conybeare, in *B.Z.*, vol. 6, 572–3.
[4] Psellus, in *B.G.M.*, vol. 5, 420.

P

Ecclesiastical control abetted the misfortunes of the Empire in working against a wide education. Lay learning with its pagan past was viewed with a certain suspicion. Pachomius in the Eighth Century contrasts the true science of Theology with profane science ' which leads many astray ' ;[1] and the Patriarch Nicephorus likens the latter to Hagar and the former to Sarah.[2] And the troubles of the Church during the Iconoclastic period enhanced the distrust. But by the Ninth Century affairs were more settled and the Church authorities were less suspicious. Better relations with the Arabs induced the study of the lore of Islam. There was a great revival of learning : though its pioneers, men like Photius and John the Grammarian, were regarded by the populace as magicians. Michael III's uncle and minister, the Cæsar Bardas, founded a new State University in the Magnaura. The Professor of Philosophy was the head—the *Oeconemicos Didaskalos*—with the Professors of Grammar, Geometry and Astronomy under him. Leo the Philosopher, who had been teaching in the Church School of the Forty Martyrs, was appointed to the post.[3] But a party in the Church—the enemies of the learned Photius—still remained hostile ; one of Leo's pupils, a monk called Constantine, wrote a venomous poem against his master, exposing the dangers of Hellenism, as the pagan culture of Greece was called.[4]

In the Tenth Century the author of the *Philopatris* might still rail against the student of Platonism,[5] and even in the Eleventh the old soldier Cecaumenus might declare that a knowledge of the Bible and of a little logic and theoretical reasoning was all that a boy needed.[6] But all the time learn-

[1] Pachomius, in *M.P.G.*, vol. 98, 1333.
[2] *Vita S. Nicephori, M.P.G.*, vol. 100, 56–7.
[3] Theophanes Continuatus, 189–92.
[4] In *M.P.G.*, vol. 107, lxi–ii.
[5] See Reinach, *Cultes, Mythes et Religions*, I, 383–92.
[6] Cecaumenus, *Strategicon*, 46, 75.

ing was becoming more widespread. Indeed, under Constantine VII the Court was almost an academy for the study of history. The Tenth-Century Saint born of upper- or middle-class parents was taught to ' hellenise his tongue ' as a matter of course : though piety would make him specialise at an early age in theology.   Yet at some time the University founded by Bardas was dissolved. Probably this was the doing of Basil II, who thought, like the author of the *Philopatris*, that too much learning did the State no good besides being an expensive extravagance. When Psellus and his contemporaries born in the early Eleventh Century wanted an education, they had to teach themselves or learn from private tutors or the Church schools.[1]

The Emperor Romanus III, who prided himself upon his culture, did nothing to remedy this. But Constantine IX, urged on by the dreadful condition of legal knowledge— barristers were almost all self-taught, and inadequately so— in 1045 founded a Law School, which all lawyers were obliged to attend before they might practise ; and at the same time he set up a Chair for Philosophy, comprising Theology and the Classics. The Law-Professor, the Nomophylax, was the Principal of this University. Constantine appointed a distinguished judge, John Xiphilin, to the post, while Psellus became the Philosophical Professor. It seems that this organisation lasted till 1204. Educational facilities were increased when Alexius I refounded the Orphanage schools. The State University and Schools were directly under the Emperor. He appointed, paid and dismissed the teachers and would frequently inspect the classes, asking test-questions and attending lectures [2]—there is a portrait extant of Michael VII listening to Psellus's lecturing.[3] Alexius himself advocated above all else the study of

[1] Psellus in *B.G.M.*, vol. 5, 14, 91, 147.
[2] Neumann, *Weltstellung des Byzantinischen Reichs*, 67.
[3] *Neos Hellenomnemon*, vol. 12, 241.

the Bible ; but under the Comneni classical learning was pursued as it never had been before. It is, however, difficult to tell how far down in society education reached. The penniless poet Prodromus studied Grammar, Rhetoric, Aristotle and Plato, but complained that the rough accents of the market-place have driven out elegant speech, and the poor had no libraries that they could use.[1] Indeed, the absence of libraries seems to have been a continuous difficulty. Since 476 there was no public library. The monasteries and churches often had their libraries, but if the collection of books at Saint Christodulus's establishment at Patmos was typical, they were mainly theological. Out of 330 books at Patmos, 129 were liturgical and only 15 secular.[2] There were certainly large private libraries, to which scholars were no doubt allowed access ; and there were numbers of scribes—chiefly lay, though a certain number of monks were copyers—copying out manuscripts ; fine books were one of the exports of Byzantium. But books remained expensive. In the early Tenth Century Arethas, the bibliophil Bishop of Cæsarea, paid 4 nomismata—nearly £12 of modern purchasing power—for a good edition of Euclid.[3]

The sack of 1204 upset the whole educational organisation. The Hellenic movement was at its height ; Michael Acominatus had just gone to Athens full of enthusiasm for its classical past, and the great Churchman Eustathius of Thessalonica had only recently finished his commentaries on Pindar. Now the scholars were scattered, their funds disappeared and their books had perished in the Latin flames. Nevertheless scholarship survived and soon centred itself round the exiled Court of Nicæa. There the learned Blemmydas established himself. His father had been a

---

[1] Prodromus, *M.P.G.*, vol. 133, 1291 *sqq.*, 1313 *sqq.*, 1419–22.
[2] Diehl, *Études Byzantines*, 307 *sqq.*
[3] Subscription on the MS. in the Bodleian.

doctor in Constantinople who retired to Brusa in 1204. In the chaos following on the crash Blemmydas had had difficulty in finding teachers and had finally learnt most from a recluse called Prodromus in the Bithynian mountains, who taught him Arithmetic, Geometry and Astronomy. In 1238 he toured the old Byzantine world collecting manuscripts, armed with introductions from the Nicæan Emperor.[1] Thanks largely to his efforts, education in Nicæa reached a high level ; Pachymer and Acropolita learnt and taught there ; and the Nicæan Court, especially under the Empress Irene, John Vatatzes's wife, and her son Theodore, devotedly patronised learning. Irene once called Acropolita a fool because he said that an eclipse was caused by the moon coming between the sun and the earth, but she apologised to him afterwards, saying to her husband, who told her not to worry—Acropolita was only a boy—' It is not right to apply such a word to anyone who advances scientific theories.' [2] But despite this attitude there was not, it seems, any organised school or university at Nicæa. The Government could not probably afford to endow one.

The days of the Palæologi when Byzantium was slowly but unmistakably dying were in contrast the most splendid period of Byzantine learning. Beset with troubles, the future dark before them, the Byzantines of the Fourteenth and Fifteenth Centuries looked back more eagerly than ever to the glories of the past. Writers like the statesman Theodore Metochites or Nicephorus Gregoras or the last great figures, Gemistus Plethon, Gennadius and Bessarion, were deeply imbued with classical lore besides all the studies of the Christian theologists. The Professors of the time, Planudes Moschopulus or Triclinius, had a fine knowledge of philology and literature. Chrysoloras, whose learning astounded his pupils in Italy, was an unworthy representative of

[1] Blemmydas, *Autobiography* (Teubner ed.), 27 *sqq.*, 35 *sqq.*
[2] Acropolita, 68.

Byzantine education at the time. Western thought too was studied ; Acyndinus and Cydones were both influenced by Thomic Scholasticism. Even at Thessalonica there were reading circles where the best works of literature were discussed ; and Trebizond was famous for its astronomic laboratories. Its learned doctors, such as George Choniades and George Chrysococces, studied in Persia and brought home the secrets of Oriental Knowledge.[1]

Whether there was any State school under the Palæologi we cannot tell. Greeks from all over the world, particularly Cypriots, still liked to come to Constantinople for their education ;[2] but they probably had to study in the private academies of the various teachers. The Church schools probably continued, but by now their curriculum was no doubt limited to theology. Nevertheless the range of education was certainly very wide ; and foreign travellers were deeply impressed by the purity of the Greek spoken by the dwindling inhabitants of the City on the very eve of its fall.

Of the facilities for female education we know nothing. There were many learned women in Byzantine history, ranging from the Professor Hypatia or Athenais the wife of Theodosius II, who studied all the sciences, wrote poetry and made speeches, to Casia, the witty hymnodist whose repartee cost her a throne, or to the great historian Anna Comnena and the other cultured princesses of the Houses of Comnenus and Palæologus. There were certainly women-doctors, and most of the lady correspondents of the great letter-writers seem to have been well-educated persons. But the mother of Psellus had not been taught anything, though she regarded that as a grievance and a handicap. There are no girls' schools mentioned anywhere in Byzantine

[1] Papadopoulos, *The School of Trebizond* (in Greek), in *Neos Poimên*, *1922.*

[2] E.g. *Vita S. Gregorii Sinaitis*, ed. Pomlyalovski, *passim.*

history. It is probably fair to say that girls of the richer
classes were given roughly the same education as their
brothers, though they would learn from private teachers at
home ; but in the middle classes they were usually literate
and no more.[1]

Learning was considered eminently desirable ; but a large
amount of Byzantine learning would seem to us either crude
or curious. The Greek language was, indeed, taught
thoroughly. Classical authors, both of prose and poetry,
were read and appreciated. Photius's *Bibliotheca*, his read-
ing-list of the former for a year, shows an extraordinarily
wide range, stretching from Herodotus to Synesius, with
intelligent comments : [2] while Anna Comnena knew the
poets well enough to quote the tragedians, though she
attributes to Sappho a line usually attributed to Alcæus.[3]
But the Byzantines had an unhappy passion for abridg-
ment, improvement and annotation. Cometas in the
Tenth Century amended and repunctuated Homer,[4] while
Constantine Hermoniacus in the Fifteenth abridged the
Iliad ; [5] and the Eleventh-Century Professor Nicetas would
see allegories in every line that Homer wrote.[6] Psellus
prided himself on restoring the science of Schedography, the
bugbear of Anna Comnena—it consisted of the minute
grammatical analysis of selected passages—exalting Grammar over Literature, in Anna's opinion—and was still highly
popular under the Palæologi. Moschopulus wrote a schedo-
graphical glossary.[7] The Byzantines found the study of
Classical Greek poetry difficult in that they pronounced
according to the written accent and they had to learn the old
pronunciation to appreciate its metre and rhythm.

[1] See Buckler, *op. cit.*, 184.   [2] In *M.P.G.*, vol. 103, 41 *sqq.*
[3] Anna Comnena, 415.
[4] *Greek Anthology* (Loeb Series), vol. 5, 142.
[5] Krumbacher, *Geschichte der Byzantinischen Litteratur*, 845 *sqq.*
[6] Psellus in *B.G.M.*, vol. 5, 92-3.
[7] See Krumbacher, *op. cit.*, 591.

The study of Latin was dying even under Justinian, though he himself was Latin-speaking. By the Eighth Century the 'language of the Romans' was Greek. Scarcely anyone in Constantinople spoke Latin, while no one in Rome even in Gregory the Great's day spoke Greek. In the Ninth Century the learned Photius himself knew no Latin. Latin letters however were still used on the coinage, even under Alexander ; and debased Latin acclamations were shouted in State ceremonies.[1] In the Tenth there was a revival of Latin studies, coinciding with a revival of Greek at Rome—Greek Christian names like Theophylact and Theodora became fashionable there. By the Eleventh Century a knowledge of Latin was not unusual at Constantinople. Romanus III spoke Latin ;[2] Psellus claimed to speak it ;[3] and a knowledge of it was obligatory for the Law Professor of Constantine IX's University.[4] Alexius I's letters to Monte Cassino are in amazingly bad Latin—possibly they were rough drafts. Anna Comnena apparently knew no Latin, nor certainly did her learned nephew Manuel I, though his mother was Hungarian. But his wife, a French princess from Antioch, knew both languages and caught out an interpreter who tried to deceive him.[5] The Latin conquest forcibly made a knowledge of Latin more usual ; and under the Palæologi several Greeks, such as Leo Corinthius, translated Greek works—chiefly hagiographical—into Latin.

Few other languages were studied.[6] There were probably several Hebrew scholars ; and the Court had its interpreters for its diplomatic needs. There were obviously numbers of Arabic linguists in Constantinople and

---

[1] E.g. Constantine Porphyrogennetus, *De Ceremoniis*, 1, 370.

[2] Psellus, *Chronographia*, 1, 32.   [3] Idem in *B.G.M.*, vol. 5, 492.

[4] Neumann, *op. cit.*, 67.   [5] Nicetas Choniates, 191.

[6] Anna mentions a Greek who knew Norman-French (Anna Comnena, 343).

Armenians who remembered their native tongue. But philologists like Saint Cyril the missionary, who certainly knew Hebrew, taught himself Chazar and was the founder of Slavonic studies, were without a doubt rare. Byzantium inherited the arrogance of ancient Greece about the barbarian world. Anna even apologises for inserting rough barbarian names into her history.[1] Passionately inquisitive though he was, the Byzantine could not bring himself to regard barbarian tongues as a subject fit for serious scholarship.

History too was hardly a subject for scholarship. On the contrary, to judge from the number of historians and still more of popular chroniclers and the frequent editions of the chronicles, it was a matter of widespread interest. The Byzantines loved to read of the past glories of the Empire ; and the best-liked of the chronicles even stretched back to the Creation and Adam and Eve, and included the Tale of Troy. Past Emperors and past saints were vivid before their eyes. One of the most stirring moments during the recovery of Constantinople in 1261 was when Michael Palæologus found in a little chapel before the walls the body of his great predecessor, Basil the Bulgar-slayer. The long-dead Emperor was reburied amidst enormous enthusiasm.[2] And Constantine XI, when the City was falling, could rouse his countrymen to their final effort, by talking of the prowess of their ancestors of ancient Greece and Rome.[3]

Philosophy was always a favourite Byzantine subject. The Fathers of the Church knew the pagan philosophers and owed much to Neoplatonism. In the Seventh and Eighth Centuries the decay of knowledge diminished philosophical study—though the monk Cosmas in 710 had read Aristotle and Plato [4]—but in the Ninth there was a

[1] Anna Comnena, 164.   [2] Pachymer, i, 125.   [3] Phrantzes, 271–8.
[4] *Vitæ S. Joannis Damasceni* in *M.P.G.*, vol. 94, 441.

revival. Leo the Philosopher was particularly fond of
Aristotle, but under his ægis Plato, Epicurus and the
Neoplatonists were all read.[1] In the Eleventh Century
there was a great revival of Platonism, led by Psellus :
though his claim to have entirely reintroduced it was a little
arrogant.[2] Romanus III and his courtiers did their best
to understand Plato—unsuccessfully, Psellus says, and the
Emperor's picture of himself as a second Marcus Aurelius
was pathetic. Psellus's contemporary John Mauropus,
Bishop of Euchaïta, was devoted to Platonism :[3] while
Psellus's pupil John Italus let Pythagoreanism tempt him
into gross heresy.[4] In the next century Michael Acominatus
preferred Stoicism to Aristotelianism.[5] By now the study of
Greek Philosophy was an accepted part of education ; and
under the Palæologi the study of Western Scholasticism was
often added. But none of the Byzantine philosophers produced any serious original work, except the last of them,
George Gemistus Plethon, the last great Neoplatonist—
whose free thought was helped by his indifference to Christianity. For though the Church did not disapprove of
philosophical learning, to combine a philosophical system
with orthodoxy was often somewhat difficult.

Theology remained a science apart, under the control of
the Church. But it was a very complicated science, and
the subtlety and learning of the great theologians, John
Damascene or Photius or Mark of Ephesus and Bessarion,
was enormous. Educated men liked to dabble in theology—
Photius must have acquired his vast knowledge as a layman
—particularly the Emperors as Supreme Heads of the
Church ; but these Imperial amateurs were seldom good

---

[1] Constantine's poem in *M.P.G.*, vol. 107, 61 *sqq.*
[2] Psellus, in *B.G.M.*, vol. 5, 508 *sqq.*
[3] Idem, *Chronographia*, I, 147 ; and see above, p. 130.
[4] Anna Comnena, 132 *sqq.*
[5] Michael Choniates, *Epistolae*, ed. Lambros, II, 120–1.

enough theologians. The Isaurians, indeed, involved the
Empire in horrible heresies. Justinian and Heraclius, for
all their admirable piety, were led astray, and Manuel I
attempted to be too clever over Holosphyrism,[1] while many
of the Palæologi were deluded by the errors of the Latins.
Even the learned Theodore Vatatzes displayed a sad ignorance between the two sorts of worship, *proskunêsis* and
latreia.[2] It was wiser to admire theology from afar.
Anna Comnena was deeply awe-struck to find that her
mother's favourite reading was the works of the Seventh-
Century mystic, Maximus the Confessor.[3]

The Byzantine knowledge of Mathematics, though it was
a source of pride to them, did not probably exceed that of
the Ancient Greeks. In Arithmetic they were handicapped
by their clumsy numbers. The Greeks had already advanced as far as it was possible when employing alphabetical
letters to stand for digits without a decimal system. It was
left to the Arabs to make the next contribution. In Geometry, though the Arabs too studied Euclid, the Byzantines
told stories to show that they understood geometrical reasoning better. The pupil of Leo the Philosopher who was a
slave in Baghdad astounded the savants of the Court of the
learned Calif Mamun by his mastery of the subject.[4] But
Euclid remained, as he did till recent times, the limit of
geometrical knowledge.

The ancient Greeks remained unsurpassed in other
branches of learning also. Ptolemy still dominated astronomy : while Anna Comnena apparently accepted the
doctrine of revolving spheres, with the earth the centre
of a concentric group of globes, to explain the universe—
a doctrine promulgated by Anaximander in the Fifth

[1] Nicetas Choniates, 278–284.
[2] Theodore Lascaris, *Opera*, ed. Festa, 99.
[3] Anna Comnena, 135.
[4] Theophanes Continuatus, 189 *sqq.*

Century B.C.[1] There were occasional revolts against
Ptolemaic theory. Cosmas Indicopleustes wrote his memoirs about the Indian trade to help himself to prove that
really the earth was rectangular and flat, like a ground-floor
room with the sky as its ceiling and Heaven on the first
floor—Moses had used the design for the Tabernacle. The
sun was much smaller than the earth and was hidden by
night by a high conical mountain at the west end. Round
the earth was the ocean, and, beyond, the land where men
lived beyond the Flood.[2]

The geographical knowledge of the Byzantines was good.
Their maps have not survived—it would be unfair to judge
them by the Sixth-Century mosaic map of Palestine at
Madaba, though that has its merits. Constantine Porphyrogennetus makes remarkably few geographical errors, though
he is often obscure. Anna Comnena is full of information, usually correct, about prevailing currents and winds ;
Alexius I, she tells us, had a map made of the Adriatic,
marking in the latter.[3] The phenomena of Nature were
imperfectly understood. Cecaumenus attempts to explain
thunder and realises that the clap and the lightning are
simultaneous ; [4] and Acropolita knew the cause of eclipses.[5]
But such things were so universally regarded as warnings or
punishments sent from on high—even Alexius I, who really
believed that a comet is ' dependent on some natural cause,'
yet consulted the soothsayers when one appeared—that the
right explanation seemed to be moral rather than physical.[6]

In Chemistry the one great contribution of Byzantium
was Greek Fire, that inflammable liquid that enabled her to
win her battles.[7] But the secret of its formula was kept so

---

[1] Buckler, *op. cit.*, 211 *sqq.*
[2] Cosmas, *passim* (see p. 165, note 1).
[3] Anna Comnena, 340.   [4] Cecaumenus, *Strategicon*, 83.
[5] Acropolita, 68.   [6] Anna Comnena, 308.
[7] See above, p. 153.

close that it could not become the starting-point for further experiments. In Mechanics the practical genius of the Byzantines had more scope. Their architectural achievements, notably the perfection of the dome, were considerable. They carried on and developed the Roman system of water supply and drainage, doing many fine pieces of engineering. The clocks and the toys, the roaring lions and the soaring throne, which made the Palace so impressive to barbarians, were all examples of their growing mechanical ingenuity.

Medicine was a subject that deeply interested the Byzantines. A medical education was by no means restricted to future doctors, with the result that amateurs like Psellus and Anna Comnena were convinced that they knew as much as members of the profession : while Manuel I was able to doctor his guest the Emperor Conrad.[1] It was a well-stocked profession. Hypochondriacs such as Romanus III would not do a thing without consulting the doctors ;[2] but Cecaumenus says that they are all a positive menace and induce illness to make themselves rich. Take pepper for the liver and be bled three times a year, and if you are ill rest, fast and keep warm, and then you can do without them, he says.[3] And certainly Theodore II's health and nerves were ruined by too many medical attentions.[4] But on the whole Byzantine medicine was admirable more for its common sense than for its theory. Theory had not advanced beyond Hippocrates. Its basis was the four humours of the body, blood, phlegm, yellow bile and black bile, and the four degrees, dry and moist, hot and cold ; and everything depended upon their proper proportion. All the great Byzantine medical writers, Oribasius, Aëtius, Paul of Ægina,

[1] Conrad, *Letter to Wibald*, in Wibald, *Epistolae*, 153.
[2] Psellus, *Chronographia*, 1, 50.
[3] Cecaumenus, *Strategicon*, 53.
[4] Theodore Vatatzes, *Epistola*, No. LXX.

Symeon Seth and Agapius of Crete, worked upon this basis ; and the popular Dietetic Calendars, advising as to what might be eaten at each season of the year, were evolved on a crude interpretation of the degrees. Their chief result was to create a tendency to gout, a disease regrettably prevalent in Byzantium.[1] But medical treatment seems to have been as sensible as anything known in Europe till comparatively recent times. Bleeding and cautery were perhaps rather drastic and not always happy, but in gout reasonable attempts were made to purge the acid ; massage was employed ; rest and an equable temperature were prescribed in all illnesses, and herbal drugs were usefully prescribed.[2] Anna Comnena recommends regular exercise as a preventive of illness, probably therein repeating the best opinion of the day—though her extraordinarily vivid and accurate description of her father's last illness and death shows an unusual interest and gift for medical matters.[3] But Byzantine medicine was at its best in the organisation of its hospitals. Not only had the army an efficient medical corps but the great charitable institutions had highly efficient wards attached to them. The hospital of the Pantocrator monastery endowed by John II in 1112 was attended by ten male and one female doctors, twelve male and four female assistants, eight supplementary male and two female helpers, eight male and two female servants, and three surgeons and two pathologists to do the diagnosis in a consulting-room. Lesser hospitals were similarly organised on a smaller scale. The nursing was actually done by the healthier inmates of the institution—for hospitals were always attached to monasteries, convents or homes for the poor. How many such hospitals there were we cannot tell, but pious Emperors and nobles often used to endow such institutions ; and though doubtless large numbers of the rabble suffered un-

---

[1] Jeanselme, *Les Calendriers de Régime*, in *Mélanges Schlumberger*, I, 217 *sqq.*
[2] Buckler, *op. cit.*, 215 *sqq.*   [3] *Ibid., loc. cit.*

heeded in their hovels, still everyone had a chance of entering the wards. The women doctors probably only worked in hospitals. Fashionable ladies were more usually treated by eunuchs ; and they too attended many of the convents.[1]

In all this, Medicine is typical of Byzantine learning. For the Byzantine love of theory and culture, great and highly vaunted though it was, was sterile. It was, unexpectedly, in practical efficiency that their genius lay.

[1] See Œconomus, *La Vie Religieuse dans l'Empire Byzantin*, 193 *sqq.* ; Petit in *V.V.*, vol. 11, supplement ; review of *Typikon* in *B.Z.*, vol. 8, 574.

CHAPTER X

Byzantine Literature [1]

Byzantine literature had something of the same limitations as Byzantine learning. It lacked a certain creative spontaneity. While the Byzantine genius found full and magnificent expression in art, in literature it flourished only in the two extremes of deep other-worldliness and practical common sense. Only in hymns and works of mystical devotion on one hand and in straightforward histories and biographies did Byzantine authors ever achieve greatness. But, though Byzantium produced few immortal literary triumphs, she could boast a long series of intelligent and able writers far outnumbering those of any contemporary nation.

From its early years Byzantine literature was handicapped by the difficulties of language. There were three forms of Greek known in Constantinople, Romaic, the demotic Greek of the market-place and the quay, a clipped careless language with a mongrel vocabulary and a childish grammar : the Greek spoken by the educated classes, the language in which they wrote their letters, where words were stressed according to the accent and most of the vowels and diphthongs were acquiring the sound of a broad *iota*. This language varied from time to time ; in the Eleventh and

[1] See Krumbacher, *Geschichte der Byzantinischen Litteratur*, the essential book on the subject. He gives the editions of Byzantine works published up to 1897. Later publications can be found in the bibliography to Dieterich's article on *Byzantine Literature* in the *Catholic Encyclopædia*, vol. 3, and in the bibliographies to the *Cambridge Medieval History*, vol. 4.

Twelfth Centuries it was far closer akin to Classical Greek than in the Eighth and Ninth, and an excellent Greek was spoken in Society under the Palæologi. Finally there was Classical Greek with its antiquely stressed pronunciation, which every educated person carefully learnt. The man of letters had to decide which language he would choose. Up till the Seventh Century in prose there was not much difficulty. Grammar and vocabulary were little enough debased for careful writing to be able to pass as Classical writing, but in poetry the new stressing involved new rules of prosody, which were followed by poets in the Sixth Century. But classical metres, notably iambics, written with a strict regard to classical quantities, were produced throughout the Empire's life. The chronicler Theophanes in the Ninth Century was the first writer definitely to use the spoken language, a simple but not very elegant language filled with words of mixed origin, Latin, Slav and Oriental. A century later Constantine VII compiled books in the spoken language, but it is a language that would have been slightly more comprehensible to an ancient Greek. After the great Classical revival of the mid-Eleventh Century, Classical Greek became almost the exclusive vehicle of a writer of any culture, to the detriment of his free individuality and self-expression; for he was continually writing in a language just slightly different from his own. Byzantium produced no Dante to legitimise the vernacular, because the true vernacular, the Romaic, was disowned by, and actually almost unintelligible to, the educated classes, and the educated vernacular was prevented by too many Classical revivals from cutting itself clear of its ancient model.

Prose suffered less than poetry. When Constantine founded the new Capital, the Church fathers and the last Neoplatonic philosophers were still producing works in the unbroken Classical tradition. The latter were growing misty or fantastic in their thought, but men like Proclus

Q

and Porphyry were still writers of elegance and vigour. The Christian fathers were in their hey-day. If nowadays only the historian or the theologian reads deep into Saint Basil, Saint Gregory of Nyssa or Saint Gregory Nazianzene, yet Greek literature can be proud of them ; for the practical wisdom of Saint Basil, the mystical thought of Saint Gregory of Nyssa, the fierce exaltation of Nazianzene are all expressed with a certain greatness. Compared to them Eusebius of Cæsarea, the theologian-biographer of Constantine, seems a little rough, though he was a writer of considerable merit ; but the sermons of John Chrysostom in the next century provide some of the finest rhetorical prose in the Greek language. In that same century there appeared the anonymous work claimed to be by Dionysius the Areopagite, a work with a vast influence upon Christianity ; it was an attempt to blend Neoplatonic mysticism with the Christian faith, admirably set down in Greek that might well be of the First Century.

In the Sixth and Seventh Centuries there were still great religious writers, such as Leontius of Byzantium and the mystic Maximus the Confessor, whose works were too difficult for Anna Comnena to comprehend, though her mother read little else. But already theology was becoming polemical, and somehow lost its old fullness. The great Iconodule theologians, John Damascene, Theodore of Studium and the Patriarch Nicephorus, and later the anti-Roman Photius were all too busily scoring argumentative points for their theological works to have the sweep of the early Fathers. After Photius theology in Byzantium lay dormant for over two centuries, till under the Comneni there flourished the great anti-Bogomil Euthymius Zigabenus, and the humanist theologians of the later Twelfth Century, Eustathius of Thessalonica and Michael Acominatus of Chonae. Under the Palæologi the Hesychast controversy and the Roman controversy gave a new impetus to theology. The participants in the latter, Mark of Ephesus and Gennadius on the one side and Bessarion on the other, were mainly barren controversialists ; but out of Hesychasm emerged some of the finest works of Eastern Mysticism, those of Palamas and of Nicholas Cabasilas.

The Sixth Century, which saw the decline of theology, saw the rise of lay history. The first great historian after the foundation of Constantinople was Constantine's biographer, the theologian Eusebius of Cæsarea ; but the historians of the Fifth Century were none of them of any distinction. With the age of Justinian a new era began. Procopius, though his Secret History is an embittered conglomeration of gossip, must, for his account of the Emperor's wars, rank as one of the great historians of all time. His language was vigorous, his judgment clear and his powers of description vivid. His later contemporary, Agathias, himself too an historian of merit, was a complete contrast ; he was a poet and his love of words at times befogs his sense. The reign of Justinian also saw the start of a new genre of historical writing. John Malalas of Antioch wrote the first of those simple chronicles, beginning usually with Adam and Eve, that were the delight of the humbler Byzantine reader. Malalas is bigoted, discursive and often inaccurate, yet he manages to give valuable and vivid sidelights on the daily life of his time, and his work shows the first concessions to the spoken tongue.

The chief historians of the late Sixth and early Seventh Centuries, the soldier Menander Protector, the superstitious Evagrius and the author of the *Paschal Chronicle* were worthy successors of the historians of Justinian. But after them Byzantine history is silent for two centuries : till in the early Ninth Century the monk Theophanes wrote his long chronicle in popular Greek. Theophanes wrote with a definite monkish bias, but he retained his judgment, and his work remains the one reliable authority for the previous

centuries.   His contemporary Nicephorus the Patriarch was
a less admirable historian.   He wished his chronicle to be
a best-seller and so definitely only inserted what he thought
would amuse the public or prejudice them in the right
direction.   Minor Ninth-Century works like the anonymous
fragment on Leo the Armenian show that history was not
neglected now ; and in the Tenth Century it received the
encouragement of Court patronage.   Constantine VII was
most anxious that Theophanes's chronicle should be brought
up to date ; and when his nominee Genesius failed to perform the task adequately, he himself edited the compilation
known as *Theophanes Continuatus*, and contributed to it a
tactful and well-written life of his own grandfather Basil I.
The authors of this compilation drew largely from the works
of a Ninth-Century monastic chronicler George the Monk
and of a secular chronicler of the early Tenth Century,
Symeon the Logothete—writers who both have provided
innumerable problems for modern Byzantinists.   Constantine's own works on the Administration and Ceremonies
of the Empire are, for all their vast historical value, hardly
in a finished-enough state to rank as literature.

Henceforward the sequence of historians and chroniclers
is unbroken, except during the reign of Basil II, an Emperor
who despised all forms of letters.   The most noteworthy of
these were Leo Diaconus in the late Tenth Century, whose
history of his own times is perhaps the best-written example
of Byzantine historiography—wise and vivid and written
in a direct unaffected Classical style (though he called
Bulgarians Moesians and Russians Scythians) : Michael
Psellus in the mid-Eleventh, the most modern of Byzantine
writers, cynical, amusing, cultured and sensible, but self-
laudatory, disingenuous and slightly affected : Michael
Attaliates, his contemporary, whose more honest narrative
is a useful corrective : the Cæsar Nicephorus Brýennius and
his portentous wife, the Porphyrogenneta Anna Comnena,

who for all her elaboration and self-consciousness remains the greatest of women historians : Cinnamus, less exuberant but scarcely less well-informed : the chroniclers Cedrenus, Zonaras and Glycas, the first embodying the earlier chronicle of Scylitzes, the second a chronicle written with a conscious effort at style, the third didactic and fond of natural history : and Nicetas Acominatus of Chonæ, the historian of the Fall of 1204, the most fair-minded of Byzantine historians. The sequence goes on under the Nicæan Emperors and the Palæologi—George Acropolita, whose work covered most of the Thirteenth Century till the recovery of the City ; George Pachymer, a passionate theologian, who carried on the Empire's history till 1308, and from under whose stilted language, a language obligatory on littérateurs at the time, real wit and spontaneity shone out : Nicephorus Gregoras, who began his history at 1204 but really concentrated on his own times (1320–1359) : the Emperor John Cantacuzenus whose apologia is, despite its bias, a reliable and well-written piece of work : and finally the historians of the Empire's death agony, Chalcondylas, Phrantzes, the loyal courtier, the homely Ducas, and Critobulus, Turkish in his sentiment and in his style an excellent imitator of his hero Thucydides.

The historians of Byzantium compare favourably with those of any other nation till modern times. In style, judgment, subtlety and critical ability they far outshone their contemporaries in the West. They compiled their information with care and studied their predecessors' works. Indeed, Scylitzes begins his chronicle with a criticism of all the historians since Theophanes—some are too biased, others too narrow in scope or in outlook.

Akin to the historians and even more numerous were the biographers. These were almost entirely hagiographical. Since Athanasius wrote his *Life of Saint Anthony*, scarcely a hermit, scarcely one eminent ecclesiastic was not the subject of a Life, usually varying in merit according to its hero's rank. There are few saints' lives from the earlier centuries except for several short lives written by Cyril of Scythopolis in the Sixth and Leontius of Neapolis in the Seventh, but it was the Iconoclastic persecution that produced the first large crop of biographies. Humble Iconodule martyrs, the orthodox Patriarchs, even the pious Empress Theodora herself had their deeds set down by devout admirers. Soon more and more lives appeared ; biographers told of Stylites, of women beaten by their husbands, as well as of bishops and patriarchs. Some of these works were of high literary value, such as the fragmentary life of the Patriarch Euthymius, or the Eleventh-Century life of Saint Symeon the Less by Nicetas Stethatus, who gave his authorities, the Abbess Anna or others of his friends, for the incidents that he related.[1] In the Tenth Century most of the hagiographical lives were collected by Symeon Metaphrastes and arranged as a menologium. He was not, however, always careful in his editing ; in the life of Saint Theoctiste he left in a passage saying that the glory of the Empire died with Leo VI : which so annoyed Basil II that he tried to destroy the whole edition.[2] After the Eleventh Century hagiography grows slightly more infrequent. Minor biographies were supplied in the funeral orations which friends spoke over the distinguished dead. Most of these that survive, such as Theodore of Studium's over his mother, that of the bibliophile bishop Arethas of Cæsarea over the Patriarch Euthymius, or the many delivered by Psellus, over his mother, over the jurist Xiphilin, the statesman Lichudes and the Patriarch Michael Cerularius, are fine works of rhetorical literature.

Autobiographies and memoirs are rarer. The one eminent autobiography is that of Nicephorus Blemmydas,

---

[1] E.g., *Vita S. Symeonis Novi Theologii*, 160, 162.
[2] Kekelidze, *Symeon Metaphrastes in Georgian Sources* (in Russian), in *Publications of Kiev Academy*, I, 172–91.

the great ill-tempered savant of the Nicæan Empire. The histories of Psellus and of John Cantacuzenus almost rank as memoirs ; and attached to them must be John Cameniates's description of his adventures at the Saracen sack of Thessalonica in 904, a well-written, vivid and terrible story, coming from an opinionated and ignorant priest : and the works of the old soldier Cecaumenus, a blunt vigorous jumble of advice and anecdotes taken from his own, his friends', and his ancestors' experience.

Outside of these categories there were few Byzantine prose works of importance. There were one or two semi-scientific, semi-descriptive treatises such as that of Cosmas Indicopleustes, and the various military, legal and administrative handbooks, all of them competently and clearly written. There were several descriptive works, such as the *De Aedificiis* of Procopius, the *Patria*, the account of the monuments of Constantinople, traditionally and wrongly attributed to Codinus, or the little book of Nicetas Acominatus on the statues destroyed by the Latins in 1204 ; there were encyclopædic works like the Lexicon of Suidas, frequent commentaries on the Classics, or Photius's valuable *Bibliotheke*, a collection of reviews of the Classical and Byzantine prose authors that he had read in a year. But all these works, though they were all written with some effort at style, were didactic rather than literary in their main intent. Even satire was rare. There are one or two pseudo-Lucianic dialogues, such as the *Philopatris*, and the more admirable *Timarion* and the *Visit of Mazaris to Hell*—the former a spirited production of the Twelfth Century containing a vivid description of the great annual Fair of Thessalonica, the latter a somewhat laboured work of the Fourteenth.

The Byzantine novel barely existed. There are one or two prose romances in the popular tongue, such as *Syntipas the Philosopher* which Michael Andreopulus translated from the Syrian in about the Twelfth Century and *Stephanites and Icnelates* translated by Symeon Seth a little earlier from the Arabic, both based on Indian stories—the *Book of the Seven Wise Masters* and the *Mirror of Princes*. But the one great Byzantine novel was the religious and moral romance of *Barlaam and Josaphet*—a story also of Indian origin, but with the Buddhist theology transformed to Christian. This well-written if rather lengthy story, which may well be the work of its traditional author, John Damascene, was, not undeservedly, one of the most-read books of the Eastern Middle Ages.

But the most prolific branch of Byzantine prose literature is letters. Copious collections exist, many still unpublished, of the correspondence of distinguished Late Romans, Emperors, Patriarchs, Bishops and statesmen, ranging from the great Fathers of the Fourth Century to the Court savants of the Fourteenth and Fifteenth—Saint Basil or Saint John Chrysostom to Nicephorus Gregoras or Gennadius. Amongst the letters are some that are virtual State papers, others that deal with Church administration, innumerable letters of condolence and exhortation and personal screeds of news and gossip. The longer letters are carefully written, usually in a rich rhetorical style, the short are often simple, direct and intimate. As great literature the letters are certainly unimportant, but they nearly all show the Byzantine gift of practical self-expression at its best ; and many of them, such as those of the Ambassador Leo Chœrosphacta in the late Ninth or Nicephorus Gregoras in the Fourteenth, are of great social interest, while for historical purposes the epistolary eagerness and care of the Byzantines has made posterity inestimably grateful.

In poetry the Byzantine lack of creative literary genius is more apparent. The number of Byzantine poets is comparatively small ; and though the taste and conscious culture of Byzantium kept the standard of their poems from falling really low, they also combined with the linguistic problem to sterilise spontaneity and freshness. Religious poetry alone managed, through the genuine intensity of Byzantine religious feeling, to break through this barrier and reach greatness. Its form, like the religion that it celebrated, comes from the Syrian East.

There were poets among the Fourth-Century Fathers, notably Gregory Nazianzene. In the Fifth Century the Empress Eudocia, the wife of Theodosius II, was a hymnodist of no mean attainments, but the Classical education given her by her father the pagan professor Leontius would break through to the detriment of her religious sincerity. The greatest of the Byzantine hymn-writers lived in the Sixth Century, the deacon Romanus, a converted Jew of Berytus· In acrostic stanzas whose varied rhythm, based on stress, appears more complicated than it is, often using dialogue, to be sung antiphonally, and refrains, Romanus achieves a combination of simplicity of language and magnificence of imagination unequalled in religious poetry. About the same time was written the *Acathistus*, a great anonymous hymn in praise of the Virgin. The second important religious poet of Byzantium, likewise a Syrian, John Damascene, was more mystical—Romanus had been mainly concerned with the glory of the Lord, the greatness of the contrast between His majesty and His suffering—but by his time simplicity is vanishing. Slightly before his day Andrew, Archbishop of Crete, had inaugurated a new form of religious poetry, the Canones, lyrics of varying metres strung together in one lengthy whole. John excelled at this art, to the detriment of his poetry ; and it ruined the work of his contemporary Cosmas of Jerusalem. The Ninth-Century nun Casia, the rejected candidate for the hand of the Emperor Theophilus, is typical of subsequent hymno-dists. A certain sense of beauty, of originality, and of real piety is present in her hymns, but they read more as set

pieces than as bursts of spontaneous feeling. The poets of
the later Empire, men such as John Mauropus in the
Eleventh and Theodore Metochites in the Fourteenth, all
similarly show an academic rather than an emotional
inspiration. But so many Byzantine hymns still lie unpublished in the libraries of Europe, that it is not impossible
that research may yet unearth another great religious poet.
The religious drama of *Christus Paschon*, ascribed once to
Gregory Nazianzene but whose date now varies between
the Fourth and Twelfth Centuries, is a somewhat tedious
work in iambics ; but at moments it reaches emotional
heights ; and some of its passages were copies from or were
copied by Romanus the Hymnodist.[1]

The Byzantine hymn-writers composed their own music,
which remains, except for traditional folk-tunes, the only
Byzantine music that has survived. But both the Palæo-
byzantine musical notation and the perfected round notation, introduced in the Thirteenth Century, are still to some
extent matters of controversy. The hymn music was modal
and antiphonal in form, and to be sung, like all Orthodox
Church music, unaccompanied.[2]

While Byzantine hymns took the form of Canones,
Byzantine lay poetry varied between three chief metres, the
classical iambic, usually restricted to epigrams, the twelve-
syllabled iambic trimeter, and the so-called Political verse,
fifteen-syllabled trochees, beginning off the stress. Owing
to what has been called the objective attitude of Byzantine
writers, the lyric did not flourish. The nearest approach to
the lyric was in the epigram, where the elegance and
sophistication of Byzantine secular sentiment found its most

[1] See Cottas, *Le Théâtre à Byzance*, 197 *sqq*. Mme Cottas believes in
the Nazianzene authorship.

[2] See articles by Tillyard in *B.Z.*, vols. 20, 24, 25, 31. The *Magna
Grecia Bizantina Society* of Rome is shortly going to publish an important
work on Byzantine music compiled by the monks of Grottaferrata.

suitable expression. George of Pisidia in the Seventh Century, the inaugurator of the iambic trimeter, wrote epigrams, some of them inordinately long, on the chief events of his day. Theodore of Studium wrote a vivid series of epigrams on the incidents of monastic life, and Casia several spirited semi-religious epigrams. But the heyday of the epigram was the Tenth and Eleventh Centuries. Not only was the Palatine Anthology compiled then, much of its contents being the work of Byzantine authors, but the epigrammatists of the time included many of the ablest Byzantine poets, Constantine of Rhodes, John Geometrus, Christopher of Mitylene and John Mauropus. Later the epigram declined ; neither Theodore Prodromus under the Comneni nor Manuel Philes under the early Palæologi wrote poems of more than historical merit. The epigram at times merged into descriptive poetry, a class where again the Byzantine poets found easy expression. In telling of the glories of Constantinople they felt something of the reverence that gave genuine feeling to their hymns. The description of Saint Sophia by Paul the Silentiary and the description of the mosaics of the Holy Apostles by Constantine of Rhodes were written with a real sense of magnificence and awe. Horror and sadness gave something of the same intensity to the poems of John Geometrus on the disasters that befell the Empire in the second half of the Tenth Century. But too many Byzantine poems are dreary productions of didactic intent, such as the philological works of John Tzetzes or the astrological works of John Camaterus, both writers of the Twelfth Century, or the scientific works of Manuel Philes : or Court poems, such as the begging verses that Theodore Prodromus addressed to various members of the Comnenian dynasty, the tactful epitaphs that Theodore Metochites wrote on various deceased princes of the Palæologi, or the fulsome description by Theodosius the Deacon of the wars of Nicephorus Phocas. Epic poetry

practically ceased with the Egyptian Nonnus, the last author
to use hexameters, who wrote early in the Fifth Century
a fantastic epic on the journeys of Dionysus in India and
after his conversion one that was decidedly staider para-
phrasing the Gospel of Saint John. In the Fourteenth
Century George Lapithes wrote a long allegorical epic, but
its moral and didactic tone and self-conscious, long-winded
style make it extremely hard to read.

The one really fine large-scale poem produced in Byzantium belongs to the category of popular Romance. Much of
Byzantine popular poetry is crude. The so-called Prophecies of Leo the Wise just merit the name of verse : the
doggerel chronicles of Manasses and Ephraëm (written
respectively in the Twelfth and Fourteenth Century) cannot
be so described. But the Romances sometimes show real
life and vigour. Some time in the Tenth Century there
appeared, written in political verse, a long popular epic in
ten books telling of the career of a warrior on the eastern
frontier, Digenis Akritas. It has been compared with the
Chanson de Roland. The Western epic is perhaps more
dramatic, but in the brilliance of its descriptions and in the
delicacy of its psychology, *Digenis Akritas* is infinitely the
greater work ; and it may well claim to be the most splendid
chanson de geste ever written. None of the later romances
achieved such heights. The Classical revival of the
Eleventh Century introduced the old Greek romances as a
model on one hand and on the other Western chivalrous
romances became known. The result was to make the
Byzantine *chanson de geste* self-conscious. The Twelfth
Century romances like *Callimachus and Chrysorrhoë* or
Belthandrus and Chrysantza are written on Western themes in
an artificial attempt at Classical language, while even poets
of Constantinople such as Theodore Prodromus and
Eustathius Macrebolites tried their hands, unsuccessfully,
at metrical love stories. There were popular adaptations

of French romances—*Flore et Blanche-fleur* appears as *Phlorius and Platziaphlora*, and *Reynard the Fox* produced a numerous progeny of animal poems in the East. But towards the last years of the Empire new types of popular poems arose. The Rhodian love-songs of the Fourteenth Century inaugurate a class of erotic poetry ; some of them have a spontaneous charm and beauty. There are also poems telling the great tragic stories of the decline of the Empire—threnodies of the fall of Constantinople, of Athens and of Trebizond. In their unpretentious sincerity they form a strange swan song to the sophisticated literature of Byzantium.

Byzantine literature stands a little removed from the main stream of the literature of the world. Its earlier theological works, up to John Damascene's, had a profound influence on Western thought ; and its historical works set a model for careful chronicling, that the Slavs, especially the Russians, long maintained. It is, however, for the conservative rather than the creative deeds of Byzantine letters that posterity is grateful. We owe the littérateurs of Byzantium a debt not so much for their own original triumphs as for having preserved lovingly so many treasures of the Classical past and the Classical tradition of philosophy, speculation and curiosity. Yet in hymns and in histories and one great popular epic these triumphs did exist.

CHAPTER XI

Byzantine Art [1]

In Literature the Byzantine genius might be lacking in creative power and originality. In Art it was very different ; both were present in plenty. It is in works of art that Byzantium has left her most magnificent and enduring legacy to the world.

Byzantine art is the truest mirror of the synthesis that made up Byzantine civilisation. There all the elements can be seen, Greek Roman, Aramaic and Iranian, in varying proportions, but always blended perfectly into a whole, into something unique and original for all its derivations. The name *Byzantine* has frightened modern historians of art. Just as the political historians tend nowadays carefully to call the Empire East Roman or Later Roman rather than Byzantine, so its art is veiled as East Christian or Early Christian. Such precautions are unnecessary, even misleading. The art was essentially the art of Imperial Constantinople, lasting in its fundamental characteristics so long as Emperors reigned on the Bosphorus. It was essentially a religious art, but not therefore Christian. Rather it was the product of that religious age in which Christianity triumphed. Its characteristics might be seen

[1] See Dalton, *Byzantine Art and Archæology* and *East Christian Art* ; Diehl, *Manuel d'Art Byzantin* ; Kondakov, *Histoire de l'Art Byzantin* ; Bréhier, *L'Art Byzantin* ; Bayet, *L'Art Byzantin* ; Millet, *L'Art Byzantin*, in Michel, *Histoire de l'Art*, vols. 1 and 3—all general works. For the early period see Strzygowski, *Origin of Christian Church Art*, and Tyler, *L'Art Byzantin*, vol. 1.

in Church art before Constantine, but they were also apparent in the art with which Diocletian sought to help the deification of Imperial Majesty. Constantine blended these two religions, making himself God's Viceroy, and henceforward the art that glorified the State therein glorified the Christian God ; but it was inspired by a deep, transcendental, almost mystical sense of worship rather than the particular symbolism of Christianity, which limited its influence to ecclesiastical art.

By the close of the Third Century Greco-Roman art could go no further. The old Greek naturalism, tastefully and gracefully arranged, had been embellished in the Hellenistic age, and still more under the Romans, with an elaboration of detail and usually an increase in size that made every work of art a colossal *tour de force*. The Fourth Century brought a reaction from the East. Religions of Syrian or Syro-Egyptian origin had been growing more popular throughout the world. Their votaries were fundamentally esoteric and fundamentally dissatisfied with the world, the complacency of Hellenistic naturalism was meaningless to them. Nature to them was often ugly and they were prepared to face its ugliness. They dispensed with delicacy of drawing and balance of composition ; they required an art that would speak to them directly without compromise, that would rouse them to an intensity of emotion rather than lull them in an æsthetic content. The triumph of Christianity inevitably meant the furthering of this Aramaic conception of art. Christ could not be depicted as Apollo had been. He was the God that suffered, the Great Judge, the Redeemer. His worshipper ought to feel Him at once in one of these rôles ; the lines of suffering, of sternness, or divine benevolence should be emphasised on His face. Religion demanded an impressionism unknown in the Greco-Roman world.

But the East contributed yet another element. The new

conception of sovereignty had come from Persia, from the
Sassanids, with a simpler and more direct majesty than the
elaborate magnificence of Rome. Its way had been paved
by Mithraism, the Iranian-born religion in worship of the
all-glorious Sun. Mithraism, or the Mazdaism from which
it derived, had its own art, not prettily naturalistic like
the Hellenistic, nor emotionally realistic like the Aramæan,
but a symbolical art of pattern coming originally, it seems
probable, from the highlands of Turkestan. This art of
pattern and design was already influencing the Aramæan
artists of the Near East, and in some way compensated
for their neglect of the Greek sense of composition.

The New Art, made up from these elements, showed at
the very beginning of the century. In the statues that
represent the Tetrarchy of Diocletian, the Imperial por-
traiture of the previous centuries, when the Emperor was
given only a magnificent physique to differentiate him
from the portrait of a subject, has given place to an impersonal symbolic art emphasising directly the stern majesty
of Rome face to face with the barbarians. Christianity
completed the movement. The Christian public demanded
art with a direct emotional appeal rather than technical
excellence, just as the Imperial authorities demanded the
portrayal of Roman sovereignty as a symbol rather than
capable likenesses of the various ephemeral Emperors.
The Hellenistic artists, having exhausted every technical
secret of their art, had a new problem to face, how to
adapt their technique to the new world. Probably, after
the manner of the sophisticated, they willingly threw over
their old elaborately life-like drawing with its careful if
exaggerated anatomies and brilliantly clever foreshortening
and all their wealth of detail, to experiment in the new
artistic point of view. Meanwhile the crude Eastern artist
found himself backed by the Court. He was unable to
supply any of the old technique, just as the sophisticated

artist reacted from it, and the demand for it was lessening. Thus during the Fourth Century a revolution took place ; and Constantinople emerged as the capital of the new æsthetic world.

Nevertheless, though Hellenism was beaten it did not die. Its conceptions were too deeply inherent in the blood of the Greek. At intervals throughout the lifetime of the Byzantine Empire, it would emerge to turn Byzantine art back towards the old naturalism.

The New Art was direct, but it was not simple. Worship, particularly Emperor-worship, must somehow be magnificent. It was by his materials that the Byzantine artist achieved the requisite sumptuousness. The Byzantine painter worked for choice in mosaic, rather than in dyes on a panel or a fresco. Even in his panel-painting he would use a background of gold ; and gold dominated the illuminated manuscript. Statues were carved in porphyry, in gilt or coloured bronze. In the stuffs, silks and brocades, gold threads played the largest part. This love of rich materials prevented mere size from providing the magnificence. They were too rare, too costly to procure. Unless the whole finances of the Empire were brought in to help, as when Justinian built Saint Sophia at the cost, it was said, of 320,000 lb. of gold,[1] the Byzantine artist usually worked on a small scale ; and it was often in the tiniest works, in little carvings of steatite or bas-reliefs in ivory or miniature enamel plaques, that his art achieved its most perfect balance, the richness of the texture or the colouring answering the simplicity of the line.

The various branches of Byzantine art reveal varying proportions of the Eastern and the Hellenistic elements. Painting and sculpture repeatedly were reinvaded by Hel-

---

[1] I.e. 345,600,000 gold francs (about £14,000,000)—obviously a vast exaggeration (*Scriptores Originum Constantinopolitani* (Teubner ed.), 102).

R

lenism. Architecture, however, early found its synthesis
and developed naturally along its own lines.

Byzantine architecture, indeed, stands apart. The painter
and the sculptor seem in the Fourth Century to have taken
a retrogressive step in technique ; the architect steadily
advanced in technical ingenuity.

The main contribution of Byzantium to architecture was
the secret of balancing the dome over a square, the outcome of the requirements of the new world. It is in Church
architecture that we can best watch the development ; for
churches alone have survived in any quantity. The great
secular buildings of the Empire have disappeared. To the
early Christian, as to the pagan, a simple hall was sufficient
for his worship. His basilica had an interior as plain as
that of a Classical temple. But gradually, especially in the
Fourth Century, the Church copied the ceremonious ritual
of the State. Just as the new dynasties of half-divine
Emperors required palaces with throne-rooms and robing-
rooms and a Gynæceum for the Empress, so Church ritual
grew dissatisfied with the unbroken interior. It demanded
a more complicated setting, without sacrificing the unity
of design. A dome placed over the centre of the basilica
had the effect of dividing off the interior ; it also gave a
greater impression of splendour. But the problem was how
to fix the dome. A dome over a rotunda, such as that of
the Pantheon at Rome, had long been known to architecture ; but here it had to be placed over a square. The
simplest method was corbelling, but that was crude and
apt to produce an ellipse. By the Fifth Century more
satisfactory processes were evolved.

Whether it is to the nomads of the Altai-Iran corner or
to the architects of Italy that the solutions were due is
a matter of controversy, in which neither side is entirely
convincing. The former theory is far-fetched, the latter
demonstrably improbable, for the dome left Italy with the

Court, following Imperial patronage to Constantinople. The source of the inspiration must remain as yet undecided ; the architects who perfected the technique were Greeks and Armenians, the former being the builders most sought by the Sassanids of Persia.[1] There were two processes. Either pendentives might be used, triangles rising from the corners of the square and bending in to join in a circle, or squinches, small apsidal vaults across the angles of the square, either in a square drum or on the level of the main supporting arches. The pendentive was known in pre-Constantinian times. An early example exists at Jerash in Transjordan and traces can be found in Asia Minor. In the Fifth Century its most famous example was the tomb of Galla Placidia at Ravenna, in the Sixth Saint Sophia at Constantinople. The squinch was a slightly later device. Probably it was Oriental in origin, though the first examples that can be dated with absolute certainty are Italian : the Baptistery at Naples and San Vitale at Ravenna (Sixth Century). But it is in the Tenth and Eleventh Centuries that it reached its pinnacle, in buildings such as the Great Church at the Monastery of Holy Luke in Phocis.

Meanwhile the basilica was undergoing modification. It had always shown two main divergencies. The Hellenistic basilica had a flat timbered roof, with three or five aisles and galleries and later a clerestory over the side aisles. The Oriental basilica was vaulted, with blind walls. But the dome enforced structural alterations. The thrust on the side-walls, the north and south walls of the orientated church, necessitated strengthening there, especially as, with the coming of the dome, height became more desirable

---

[1] Faustus of Byzantium, trans. Langlois, 281. The Persian general tells his troops, before a battle against the allied Greeks and Armenians, to capture as many Greeks as possible, so that they can build palaces for the Persians.

than length.   Buttresses such as Gothic architects used were alien to the Byzantine spirit, which remained Classical enough to insist on the design of the building being structurally adequate in itself.   Churches of a single square or polygonal chamber became, with the adaptation of the dome to the square, a fashionable design.   There the thrust was felt equally all round.   In the Octagonal Church of Saints Sergius and Bacchus at Constantinople (Kutchuk Aya Sofia), built early in Justinian's reign, this type can be seen at its best.   Already the piety or ingenuity of architects led them to attempt cruciform buildings.   There are catacomb churches of this shape, and the Tomb of Galla Placidia is a cross with arms of even length and a dome at the crossing.   Justinian's and Theodora's Church of the Holy Apostles at Constantinople with a central dome and a dome over each arm was accepted as the perfect example.   It was copied by the builders of Saint Mark's at Venice.   Finally these three types, the basilica, the square and the cruciform, were synthesised by the architects Anthemius of Tralles and Isidore of Miletus in the great Church of Saint Sophia.[1]   A long line of columns preserves the basilican interior, yet the external proportions are practically those of a square, while the side-stress is met with high-buttressed transepts crowned by a half-dome.   The first central dome collapsed during an earthquake in 558 and the second similarly in 989, when the present dome was built by an Armenian, Tiridates, the architect of the great Armenian cathedral of Ani.[2]

Saint Sophia remained the summit of Byzantine architectural achievement.   Even the Byzantines so regarded it and long used it as a model.   But Byzantine architecture was not unprogressive.   Gradually, almost certainly due to the same problem of thrust, the type of design known as

[1] See Lethaby and Swainson, *The Church of Saint Sophia*.
[2] Asoghic, *History*, trans. Dulaurier and Macler, II, 133.

the Greek Cross evolved. Here the transepts are high and
barrel-vaulted, roofed usually, like the nave and choir, with
a low gable ; the angles of the cross are occupied by lower
chambers, those at the west end being used as side aisles
to the nave, those at the east kept separate to serve as the
prothesis and diaconicon demanded by ritual. The simplicity and perfect structural balance of the design makes
it perhaps the most admirable in architecture.

The Greek Cross probably originated in Armenia. The
Arab conquests had enhanced the importance of Armenia.
Wars further south placed it upon the safest trade-route
between East and West, and Armenians in increasing
numbers sought their fortunes in the Empire. Their geographical position made them receptive to artistic ideas
coming from both East and West, and they were ingenious
enough to experiment with them. It appears in Greece
in the late Eighth Century, at Skiprou in Bœotia, a province in close touch with the East ; and its most celebrated
example was the New Church constructed by Basil I in
the Palace precincts.[1] That church, destroyed by the
Turks, was probably the only large building shaped in a
Greek Cross. As a rule, Byzantine churches now were
small. The tendency was all towards grace and lightness ;
height alone was increased. A triple apse at the east end,
the trichora or trefoil, had sometimes been used to lighten
the effect since the Sixth Century. Now it grew more
common. Columns replaced the piers that supported the
dome ; and the dome itself might be set on a high drum.
Half-domes might be placed on the arms of the cross ; the
straight lines of the gable were replaced by curves. Connections with the West introduced occasional belfry towers,
with bells to replace the *simandra*, the wooden gongs that
summoned the orthodox to prayer. The Greek Cross thus
elaborated or modified remained and still remains the basis

[1] Ebersolt, *Le Grand Palais*, 130–5.

of almost all orthodox ecclesiastical architecture, but it was
never quite so common in Constantinople as in the provinces, where the architects seem largely to have been
Armenian.

Of the forms of secular buildings it is hard to speak, as
so few have survived. The halls of the Palaces, such as
the Chrysotriclinus or the Triconchus in the Great Palace,
were formed like the contemporary churches with domes,
apses, narthexes and trefoils.[1] The ideal country-house of
Digenis Akritas had three cupolas, and its main reception-
room was cruciform ;[2] and in the old houses of the Phanar
to-day, many of the rooms have apses, often trefoil. But
a whole house cannot have the unity of a church. The
Great Palace, indeed, was a conglomeration, halls, galleries,
churches, baths, guard-rooms, an armoury, a library, and
suites of apartments, a museum, all set together with no
unity of design, in three main groups. Residential quarters were usually two-storied, the chief rooms being on the
first floor. The ground-floor rooms were lower and very
often opened off an arcade facing an inner courtyard.
Buildings were seldom more than two stories high, except
for military towers. The palace of Digenis Akritas boasted
four stories,[3] but then everything about him had to be remarkable. In fortifications, aqueducts and bridges Roman
models were copied and developed, and the Circus, though
it was longer than most Roman colossea, was equally Roman
in design. The underground cisterns of Constantinople,
built in the Fifth and Sixth Centuries, were more unique.
Their feature was the innumerable well-carved columns
that supported the roof.

Doors were almost all square-headed. Windows in secular buildings might be rectangular or arched. In halls and
churches they were almost all round-headed, elongated and

---

[1] Ebersolt, *Le Grand Palais*, 77 *sqq.*, 110 *sqq.*
[2] *Digenis Akritas*, 226 *sqq.*   [3] *Ibid.*, 226.

slender, to keep out the bright Eastern light. They were usually in threes set in a recess, with marble or wooden shutters at the foot, and often round lights of glass, mica or alabaster in stucco or in marble at the top.

The material employed varied according to the district. In stone-bearing countries, walls would be faced with worked stone with rubble inside. Constantinople was chiefly built in burnt brick, though stone was often used in alternate layers with the brick to decorate an exterior. The stone on outside walls would often be moulded or carved. This was particularly common in Armenia and in the districts where Oriental influence was predominant, such as Greece. The small Metropolis church at Athens is an example. The interior walls of important buildings were faced with decorative materials, slabs of marbles of various colours arranged in a pattern, and, higher up, mosaics. In poorer districts and in Constantinople under the Palæologi, when money was scarce, it was usual to decorate the walls entirely in frescoes. Columns, having more weight to carry than in Classical times, were solider, particularly as to their capitals. These were usually elaborately carved. Modifications of the Corinthian acanthus survived, but basket-work designs, animal sculpture or medallions of simple Christian monograms grew commoner.

In sculpture also, the East triumphed ; and there it was revolution rather than development. Classical three-dimensional sculpture was alien to the Aramæan. He saw things flat, in two dimensions, pictorially rather than sculpturally. Statuary had to be seen from one angle only ; shading alone could represent the third dimension. His attack coincided with the coming of pattern motives from Iran. Sculpted lines of drapery began to follow geometric patterns rather than the naturalistic curves of Hellenistic art. The statues of the New Art were often almost unpleasing. The features of the face were exaggerated by the Aramæan love of sensation ; the body was clothed geometrically. The whole was quite impersonal and for all its crudity very impressive. It suited the new conditions of the world. The late Fourth Century statue at Barletta is typical of the transition. There the figure has been visualised in the round and it is definitely a portrait ; but it is clearly intended to be seen from the front, there is no compromise with realism in the military costume, and the face is simple with the lines from the nose to the mouth intensified to make it appear a symbol of stern majesty. It is almost a work dedicated to the religion of Empire.

But soon any attempt at three-dimensional statuary was to become very rare. Christian artists never adopted it to any extent. It was an art unappreciated by the Oriental, and the Eastern Christian early began to identify it with the graven image anathematised by Jehovah. It survived almost entirely in somewhat impersonal Imperial portraits, made at Constantinople and sometimes set up there to celebrate Imperial majesty or sent out to vassal communities like Rome, so that the Emperor might be present at their deliberations. Sculpture quickly became an art of bas-relief, little more than a branch of painting, with shadows to take the place of colour effects. The panels of doors, the sides of church ambones or pulpits, or, in the earlier days, sarcophagi would be carved in wood or stone with a pictorial two-dimensional technique. But at first the artist tried to retain the power of showing a background by heaping it up vertically behind the main subject with an almost Chinese perspective. Later he gave up the unsuccessful attempt.

The most successful bas-reliefs were on a smaller scale, carvings in metals, in steatite and still more in ivory.[1] Carved ivory, jewel-caskets or relic-caskets, consular diptychs, book-covers, devotional diptychs and triptychs were

[1] See Ebersolt, *Les Arts Somptuaires de Byzance.*

made throughout the Empire's history. In the first five hundred years till the Ninth Century the Oriental influences predominated—figures had great expressive heads, ill-proportioned and often ill-drawn ; but with the Classical revival of the Ninth and Tenth Centuries a sense of composition and of grace was introduced without destroying the simplicity and strength of the Oriental School. The best small Byzantine carvings, the Veroli casket at the Victoria and Albert Museum and the Romanus and Eudocia panel at the Cabinet de Médailles, belong to this period. The latter is indeed one of the triumphs of Byzantine craftsmanship, composed with feeling and with skill, well drawn and admirably executed. After the Eleventh Century, ivory carving declined ; the carvers seem to have lost taste and technical ability ; and soon the growing poverty of the Empire made so costly a material too expensive to procure. Ivory carvings were usually ornamented with gilt and, it seems, often coloured.

Architectural decorative sculpture, door-moulding, and column capitals, showed in its variety of design its mixed origin. The acanthus-leaf and the naturalistic drawing of animals were of pure Hellenism ; geometric design, often flowing with a Hellenistic grace, recalled the patterns of Iran ; a bare surface would be adorned, with the stern drama of the Aramæans, by a stark monogram of Christ. From the Fifth Century onwards all these types can be found, with a technique that remained on a fairly even level. The method, however, slightly changed. The first means of treating this decorative sculpture was by drilled work, which reached its climax in the Fifth Century. The ' Theodosian ' or acanthus capital is typical of it, the leaf standing out pale against a deeply drilled black background. In the Sixth Century drilled work was succeeded by pierced work in which the design stood out as a sort of lacework, apparently separated from the background. The ' basket ' capitals of Saint Sophia were thus formed, and all the capitals of Saints Sergius and Bacchus. After the Seventh Century pierced sculpture lost its popularity, though it was never entirely discarded, and can be seen with *cabochons* in Fourteenth-Century work at Mistra. ' Embroidery' sculpture was the most employed in later centuries, from the Seventh onwards. Here the design is applied on to the flat stone in ribbons and interlacing bands, often surrounding geometric figures, or panels with animals or rosettes. Capitals with animal carvings were of this work. The fourth form was *Champlevé*, in which the holes forming the background were filled up with a brown-red composition, made largely of wax, which set off the design. This came into fashion in about the Tenth Century. It can be seen well exemplified in the small Church of Saint Theodore at Athens.

Where free sculpture lost by the triumph of the East, painting somewhat gained.[1] Hellenistic painting had degenerated into graceful prettiness. The Aramæan brought a new force, his directness of vision and intensity of feeling. The shock was salutary, particularly as the Hellenistic influence was never utterly crushed. The two styles existed side by side, each checking the faults of the other. The careless drawing of the Aramæans could not satisfy the public, but it demanded more emotion than the Hellenists could give, it liked to feel at once the spiritual import of the picture. And the material in which the more important works were now painted helped on the Aramæan victory. Mosaics by their splendour outclassed any other pictorial medium, and in mosaics a delicate chiaroscuro is almost impossible. Drawing must be bold, colours contrasting and the design without any fussy complication. Frescoes naturally followed the lead of mosaics. It was

---

[1] See Muratov, *La Peinture Byzantine* ; Ebersolt, *La Miniature Byzantine* ; van Berchem and Clouzot, *Mosaïques Chrétiennes*.

only in miniatures, in the illuminated manuscripts, that Hellenistic technique had the advantage, and it is consequently in the manuscripts that the continuity of Hellenistic influence is seen and through the manuscripts that it made itself felt, for mosaic and fresco artists largely relied for their inspiration on thin, small and easily portable miniatures.

But even in mosaics, the Hellenistic School, possessing as it did the best artists, long held the field, only slightly adapting itself to the demands of the day. In the Fifth-Century buildings, such as the Mausoleum of Galla Placidia or the Church of Saint George at Thessalonica, the subjects are treated in a flowing naturalistic manner. The background is sometimes built up behind, for the artists, like the artists in bas-relief, could not bear to leave it unfilled. But already, their naturalism was being blended with the naturalism of Iran. The peacocks and gryphons that were creeping into their art were inspired from the distant East ; and Iran, working through Armenian artists, was teaching how to use animals as a decorative pattern rather than as a picture without sacrificing accuracy in the drawing. By the Sixth Century the Semitic influence was stronger. The figures of Justinian and Theodora and their suites in San Vitale at Ravenna are stylised and stiff, but effective. The mosaics at Saint Sophia are probably of the same style. At Thessalonica, however, Hellenistic ideas lingered longer. The Sixth-Century decorations in Saint Demetrius retain much of the old naturalism, though the figure panels are drawn full face with the same hard, bold lines as those in San Vitale.

Meanwhile floor mosaics, which by their nature involved a more patterned style of decoration, followed the same movement away from Hellenism. Birds and trees remained naturalistic, but regular motives of a decorative nature surrounded them and gradually superseded them. They are most common in Syria and Palestine and seem to have been made mainly by Alexandrians and Armenians. The former naturally retained Hellenistic tendencies. The Fifth-Century mosaic map of Alexandria at Jerash is distinctly Hellenistic; the map of Palestine and Egypt at Madaba in Moab, made in the Sixth Century, is more formless, though a certain delicacy of drawing still remains. The Armenians worked according to their own Iranian synthesis of pattern and naturalism. After the Sixth Century floor mosaics are rare. The floors are covered instead with bold geometrical designs in coloured marbles.

Manuscript illumination was, it seems, originally an Alexandrian art. Alexandrian models went out and were copied all over the Greco-Roman world. These remained Classical till the Sixth Century. The Fifth-Century Joshua Roll,[1] of which we only have a Tenth-Century copy, attempts perspective and figures in all sorts of attitude ; the pictures are merely tinted and gracefully graduated. The Iliad at the Ambrosiana,[2] of about the same date, is perfectly Classical in treatment. In the Sixth-Century works, particularly secular works, still follow the Alexandrian tradition. The Dioscorides illuminated for Juliana Anicia in about 512 only shows Eastern influence in having ornamental borders to the page : [3] and even the manuscripts of the Christian topographer Cosmas Indicopleustes, the moralist merchant, all probably copied from a Sixth-Century original, have the non-religious illustrations executed in a Classical manner, while the religious pictures are monumentally Oriental.[4] Indeed, religious illumination was now given over to Orientalism. The productions were often magnificent. The Rossano gospel [5] and the Vienna Genesis [6] each have a background of pure purple, and

---

[1] *Vatican, Palat. Gr.*, No. 431.   [2] *Milan, Ambrosiana*, No. F205.
[3] *Vienna, National Library, Med. Gr.*, No. 1.
[4] E.g. *Vatican, Gr.*, No. 699.   [5] At Rossano in Calabria.
[6] *Vienna, ibid., Theol. Gr.*, No. 31.

the latter's lettering is entirely silver. Decorative patterns were often both delicate and sumptuous. But the figure drawing was crude and ungainly ; and vertical perspective was usually and unsuccessfully attempted for the backgrounds.

Thus in the Sixth Century Byzantine pictorial art had reached an uneasy synthesis, in which the Oriental contribution was dominant. In the Seventh the Arab conquests caused a revolution. The Semitic provinces were lopped off the Empire, the Armenian influence grew. Meanwhile the Moslems, disliking all representational art, found in Iran, as they advanced eastward, an ornamental art admirably suited to them. They adopted it and revitalised it. Aramæan art, with its stark intense figures, became the sole property of the monks of Byzantium. The Seventh Century was too turgid to produce many works of art. The only important sets of mosaics were set up in Moslem lands, in the Dome of the Rock at Jerusalem and in the courtyard of the Ommayad Mosque at Damascus. The early Califs employed Greek artists and architects, but these both seem rather the work of natives. The former consists of rich foliate and geometrical ornament, obviously Iranian in inspiration ; the latter is a magnificent series of landscape, trees, hills and houses, arranged in flowing design, richly coloured and gracefully drawn. But the naturalism is not Hellenistic ; pattern not composition is the basic intent. The two series represent the height to which Syrian art had attained, before the sterilising force of Islam had time to work.[1]

The Iconoclastic movement of the Eighth Century had an even profounder effect on pictorial art. Artistically it was a struggle between the Aramæan and the Iranian, with the Hellenist intervening and emerging victorious, but having learnt much from both his rivals. The edict for-

[1] See Mlle van Berchem's detailed analysis of these mosaics in Creswell, *Early Muslem Architecture*, 149–252.

bidding the worship of icons meant that religious representational art lost its lay patronage and became the
surreptitious property of the persecuted monks. Under
such circumstances it could hardly prosper. In its place the
Imperial authorities encouraged an art of patterns, geometric figures and still more those flowing designs of birds
and leaves in which the Iranian and Armenian delighted.
But figure painting could not be suppressed ; it merely
secularised itself. The artists developed the decorative
birds and animals and trees into hunting scenes which the
impiety of the Iconoclast emperors considered suitable as
Church ornament. But the Byzantine was Oriental enough
to like a story. If he might not tell religious stories, might
not depict Christ on the Cross or the Saints awaiting
martyrdom, he fell back to his other source of legend,
Classical mythology. The Ninth Century brought a
Classical renaissance. In art it was eagerly received. But
it inevitably brought out all the old Hellenistic theories of
painting. Figures no longer stood stiffly full face but bent
in graceful attitudes ; perspective again entered the picture.
But this neo-Hellenism was enriched by the patterns of the
East, the peacocks and the twining foliage. Of this secular
art nothing of importance survives. We know it only from
descriptions, as of the halls that Theophilus built and
decorated in the Great Palace [1] or of the mosaics in Digenis
Akritas's chief chamber—though that was erected after the
fall of Iconoclasm, and pictures of Moses and Samson
jostled against those of Achilles or Alexander. [2] The Tenth-
Century manuscript of Oppian's Cynegetica at Venice
probably give a fair idea of the style. There the subjects
are almost similar to those recorded in Digenis, and they are
enriched by hunting scenes in decorative medallions.

[1] Theophanes Continuatus, 140 *sqq.* ; Ebersolt, *Le Grand Palais*,
110 *sqq.*
[2] *Digenis Akritas*, 230–2.

The victory of the Images brought back religion into art. But the patrons, especially in Constantinople, now liked the neo-Hellenistic style. The religious painters had to adapt themselves to a Hellenistic public, as the Hellenistic painters had four centuries before to a religious public. The synthesis was remarkably successful ; the Tenth and Eleventh Centuries are the finest period of Byzantine pictorial art, as they were in Byzantine carving. The two strains, Hellenistic and Aramæan, can still be seen, but they had come close together. Religious painters, such as the artists that decorated the late Tenth-Century Church of Holy Luke in Phocis, have all the fervour and intensity of the earlier centuries, the drawing and colouring are just as bold, but they have lost the old crudeness, their attitudes vary and the former stiffness is now dignity. The Psalter now in the British Museum, completed in 1066 by Theodore of Cæsarea,[1] is of the same type. The figures are well drawn, but are deeply felt and have not been given the distraction of a background. But Constantinople itself favoured a more Hellenistic flavour in the synthesis. The Tenth-Century Psalter at the Bibliothèque Nationale [2] and Basil II's Psalter at Venice [3] both go back almost to Fifth-Century Hellenism, possibly being derived from an early Alexandrian model. Only a certain directness in the composition implies the influence of the Church. The famous Menologium of Basil II at the Vatican [4] shows a slightly greater mixture of origin—a mixture that is more successful, though a certain monotony in the pictures spoils the effect. There the main figure stands prominent and at times intense against a simple background of formal architecture or landscape. The drawing is simple but elegant and effec-

---

[1] *British Museum, Add.* No. 19352.
[2] *Paris, Bibliothèque Nationale, Gr.,* No. 20.
[3] *Venice, Marcian Library, Gr.,* No. 17.
[4] *Vatican, Gr.,* No. 1613.

tive ; the colouring is rich but graduated.   Each picture is framed in an elaborate border of varying design.   The same synthesis can be seen in mosaics in the Church of the Nea Moni in Chios and in a more perfect state in the Church of Daphni in Attica, both buildings of the Eleventh Century. Both lack the strength and feeling of the mosaics of Holy Luke ; and at Daphni the drooping figures and gentle faces of the saints appear all the more graceful and all the weaker in contrast to the Christ Pantocrator in the dome, where some able monastic artist has given full rein to his conception of the awful majesty of God, without any conciliation to the taste of Constantinople.

In the Twelfth Century the Hellenising influence continued, but it was at the expense of strength and unity. The mosaics executed by Greek artists for Manuel in the Church of the Nativity at Bethlehem are decorative but weak ; those made by Byzantine masters for the Norman rulers of Sicily are magnificently rich and splendid, but they are strangely without spiritual force ; the great Christ at Monreale fails to have half the significance of the Christ at Daphni.   In the mosaics of Venice and Torcello there is the same defect.   Skill and decorative value are present, but not the intensity of earlier Byzantine art.

The Latin Conquest did not have the deadly effect on Byzantine art that sometimes is pretended.   The fall of the City caused a diaspora ; the work of the schools and their traditions were interrupted.   Moreover, during the Thirteenth Century political conditions were too unsettled for art to flourish ; and henceforward the Empire, even after the recovery of Constantinople, was too poor to indulge in the old materials.   Mosaics, the favourite medium of earlier days, were expensive now.   Frescoes emerged to the fore in their place.   Fresco-painting had been practised since the earliest times, but they had been used as a substitute for mosaics among poorer communities or in parts of a church

or palace that were less important. Their style followed that
of the contemporary mosaics, except in remote corners such
as the rock churches of Cappadocia, where an austere but
effective monastic Aramæan tradition lasted unbroken.
Now frescoes became the most important branch of painting.
Fresco technique introduced new possibilities. It allowed a
certain pathos, almost sentimentality, that was practically
impossible in mosaics. The Byzantines of the Palæologan
epoch were eager Classicists ; Hellenism renewed its vitality once more. Perspective, complicated figure-draw-
ing and backgrounds all reappeared. But it was Hellenism
without its joy in life. Vigour was there, but it was often a
wistful vigour, and still the fierce mysticism of the Orthodox
would show through in a certain tenseness. The result was
to produce an art closely akin to that of the Sienese painters.
Possibly even it was influenced by them, for East and West
were now in close touch. But the dates marked on some
frescoes of the type in the side-chapels of Saint Demetrius at
Thessalonica are almost too early for such to be the case.[1]
It is perhaps possible to see the common origin of Italian
and late Byzantine painting in Cilician Armenia, whose
illuminated manuscripts of the Thirteenth Century combine
richness and power with a graceful human pathos such
as Byzantium never knew. The Byzantine illuminations
meanwhile reverted to old Hellenistic models, the Alexandrian style of the Fourth and Fifth Centuries, lightened
by a little of the later decoration.

The pathos even crept into the rare mosaics erected. In
the Church of the Chora at Constantinople the great series
of mosaics set up by Theodore Metochites, for all their
magnificence, not only have the weakness of Hellenism, but
also they express human emotions rather than the spiritual
force of former days.

The quality of pathos lasted ; but gradually the old battle

[1] A.D. 1304, Dalton, *East Christian Art*, 255.

S

between the Hellenist and the Oriental broke out again. The Capital kept on its composite art, but provincial Byzantine painting divided into two schools, called usually the Macedonian and the Cretan. The former, emanating from the Holy Mountain, Athos, though by 1300 it was feeling the Sienese or quasi-Sienese influence, developed along the lines of monastic directness and austerity. Though it showed a sense of human tragedy, its boldness and freedom made it suited to large spaces and impersonal. The Cretan School was in closer touch with Italy, particularly Venice. Still basically Byzantine, and Hellenistic in its colour gradations and its restraint, it acquired a certain charm and intimacy. It was vigorous enough in the Sixteenth Century to oust the Macedonian School on Athos itself. But by then the Empire had fallen, secular art was dead, and the Church had taken to itself the control of ecclesiastical art, ordaining how and where every saint or holy scene should be painted.

Panel icons alone allowed the artist any latitude, and few of them now survive of a date earlier than the Sixteenth Century.[1] There must have been many painted from the earliest days of the Empire, and a few miniature mosaic panels survive. But the wooden and the rarer canvas panel was probably too destructible.

The minor arts of Byzantium [2] followed, as far as their nature permitted, the fashions of painting and bas-relief. The Byzantines excelled at all the decorative arts. To work in a rich material, gold, enamel or silk was admirably suitable for them, for both their Classical restraint and their religious bold simplicity gave the texture its full decorative value and kept the object sumptuous without overloading

---

[1] There are several pictures of the Virgin extant, the best being perhaps the Twelfth-Century Our Lady of Vladimir, now in Moscow. The majority of these portraits were attributed to the brush of St. Luke.

[2] Ebersolt, *Les Arts Somptuaires de Byzance.*

it. Metal-work carvings form more a part of sculpture. The silks, woven brocades and purple or appliqué embroideries rich with gold thread, were usually patterned with a formal figure or animal in a medallion, repeated close afterwards by a similar medallion facing the other direction. Silk had come first through Persia. It was therefore natural that designs based on Persian Sassanid motives should soon predominate, particularly as they were suited for the genre. Byzantine brocades always remained faithful to Iranian pattern-art, though Classical grace occasionally modified the drawing.

In the art of enamelling also the East triumphed. Byzantium here was a pioneer ; rare examples of Roman-Egyptian times have been found, but the art of *cloisonné* was practically created by the Byzantine craftsmen. The technique is troublesome ; the lines of the base—almost invariably gold, which was the metal best suited to high-temperature smelting—coming between the various plaques of colour, prevented drawing of any delicacy, particularly as the whole could never be more than a few inches in length or breadth. Patterns inevitably made the most effective decoration. But the religious Byzantine could not bear not to put the art to Christian purposes. He introduced figures, usually as simply drawn as possible, on a plain background. A Hellenistic style was impossible. However, by the Eleventh Century, when Byzantine art was in its heyday, craftsmen had so perfected their technique that they could reproduce in *cloisonné* not only portraits with a rough likeness but, as on the crown that Constantine IX gave to King Andrew of Hungary, dancing figures of extraordinary delicacy and vigour.[1] In the latter years of the Empire, enamel, like the other more sumptuous artistic materials, was too costly to be freely used.

[1] In the Museum at Buda-pest. One plaque is in London at the Victoria and Albert Museum.

Niello and Damascene work were both made in Constantinople. Their designs were similar to the contemporary designs on enamel.

Of Byzantine glass and pottery it is difficult to speak.[1] So few examples, particularly of the latter, have survived. The technique seems to have been surprisingly low, the ornament mainly Iranian or Saracen in inspiration. There was found in the Tenth-Century Church of Patleina in Bulgaria a ceramic icon of Saint Theodore, made of various tiles. The inspiration is clearly Byzantine, but we know no similar ceramic icon of Byzantine origin.

It is difficult to do justice to Byzantine art in so short a space. Long neglected and despised, it is coming at last to receive its due appreciation ; and the energy of modern research is widening the field of its understanding. Unknown frescoes are being discovered, long-hidden mosaics being stripped of whitewash. Historians and writers on æsthetics both are concentrating attention on it, as they never have done before. In a few years we shall be better able to estimate how vast a debt the world of beauty owes to the artists of Byzantium.

[1] See Rice, *Byzantine Glazed Pottery*.

CHAPTER XII

Byzantium and the Neighbouring World

Often it is assumed that the part played by Byzantium in history was passive, to be for nearly a thousand years the bulwark of Christendom against the Eastern infidel, Persian, Arab and Turk, and to preserve for the Western Renaissance the treasures of Classical literature and thought. It is forgotten that throughout its whole existence the Empire continually exercised an active influence on the civilisation of the world : that Eastern Europe owed almost its whole civilisation to the missionaries and statesmen of Constantinople, and, further, that Western Europe was perpetually in debt to her, long before her scholars on her death-bed carried off their manuscripts and their Neoplatonism to Italy, while even Islam was subject to a constant flow of ideas from the Bosphorus.

Up till the Latin capture, Constantinople was the unquestioned capital of European civilisation. The Westerner might affect to despise the Byzantine as sodden with luxury and unchivalrously clever, but the wealth and comforts of Constantinople made it a fairy-tale city, of which men dreamed in France, in Scandinavia, in England. In Eastern Europe, closer to the very gates of the City, the effect was immeasurably greater. Eastern Europe lay near to those dark plains of Asia which poured people after people of barbarians into the civilised world. Even in the Balkan peninsula, the shock of Gothic, Hunnic and Avar invasions wiped out the traces of the old Roman civilisation. When

eventually the country was filled by the Slavs, they found
no local traditions and they brought no native memories.
They only saw in the corner of the peninsula a vast brilliant
invincible city, whose age, comparatively little in reality,
seemed to them measureless, stretching back into a past
before their consciousness. Tsarigrad, the city of the
Emperors, became to them synonymous with civilisation.

Early in the Seventh Century the Slavs of the Balkans
acknowledged the suzerainty of the Emperor Heraclius.
But during the next two centuries the Empire was distracted
by chaos, the great attacks of the Saracens and the great
persecutions of the Iconoclasts. It was only in the Ninth
Century that Byzantium was able to turn a more than
pragmatical attention to the Slavs. Meanwhile various
changes had taken place amongst the Slavs. Late in the
Seventh Century a Hunno-Ugrian tribe called the Bulgars
crossed the Danube.[1] They were not probably very
numerous, but they possessed powers of organisation in
which the Slavs were lacking. Gradually they built up a
strong kingdom that occupied the whole hinterland of the
peninsula, and by the year 800 they controlled Transylvania
and the Wallachian plain. They had met the Imperial
troops in several wars ; in 811 their Khan Krum slew the
Emperor Nicephorus I in battle. But hitherto they had
been too unsettled for civilisation to reach them. The Khan
Krum (c. 797–814) and his son Omortag (815–833) were,
however, administrators of ability. Under their orderly
rule Greeks and Armenians began to penetrate into the
country. The Khans desired royal residences ; Greeks and
Armenians came to build them. The country offered openings for commerce, which the traders of the Emperor eagerly
took up. In the wars the great fortresses of Adrianople and

---

[1] For the Bulgarians, see Zlatarski, *History of the Bulgarian Realm* (in
Bulgarian) and Runciman, *The First Bulgarian Empire*, where full references are given.

Mesembria were for a time in Bulgar hands ; captives and captured goods taught the resources and wealth of Byzantine civilisation. But the Khans were suspicious at first, and showed their alarm by persecuting any signs of Christianity that appeared. Gradually the Bulgar element mixed more with the Slav ; and the united Bulgarian Kingdom found the attraction of Constantinople irresistible. Finally, in 865 the Khan Boris, Omortag's grandson, decided, half from immediate diplomatic needs, half from far-sighted policy, to become a Christian convert. Eagerly the Imperial Government sent out missionaries. Byzantines flocked to the Palace of Pliska. Boris after his baptism—under the name of Michael, with Michael III as his godfather—toyed for a while with Rome, to see if he could find there a more convenient form of Christianity ; but Roman intransigence and discipline disgusted him. He reverted to the allegiance of the Church of Constantinople ; and the Patriarch Photius encouraged him to set up an autonomous vassal-church, using a liturgy in the vernacular.

The final establishment of the Bulgarian Church was helped by a contemporary missionary movement that Byzantium inaugurated.[1] At the very close of the Eighth Century Charlemagne, with the Bulgarians helping on the other flank, destroyed the Kingdom that the Avars had set up in the Central Danubian plain rather more than a century before. But the Franks gained little from the victory. Half a century later the plain was dominated by the great Slav Kingdom of the Moravians. In 862 Rostislav, the Moravian King, decided that so great a monarch should be a Christian, and sent to Constantinople for instruction. The Regent, Bardas, and the Patriarch Photius chose as missionary a friend of theirs, the Macedonian Constantine or Cyril, a distinguished linguist who had been experi-

[1] See Dvornik, *Les Slaves, Byzance et Rome, passim* ; Runciman, *op. cit.*, 99 *sqq.*

menting with Slavonic philology and had invented an
alphabet to satisfy the phonetic requirements of the Slavonic
tongues. Cyril and his brother Methodius set out for
Moravia and founded there a Church which had the Bible
and the Liturgy both in the vernacular. But the Moravian
Church was too young to stand alone. Constantinople was
far off and the Bulgarian Kingdom lay in between. Cyril,
finding Latin Christians in the neighbouring countries,
decided to place it under the see of Rome. The great Pope
Nicholas I accepted the gift with gladness. But Rome never
liked a vernacular liturgy. After Cyril's and Nicholas's
death later Popes put so many difficulties in the way
of Methodius, and the Latin bishops of Germany intrigued
so indefatigably against him, that the Moravian monarch Svatopulk, Rostislav's successor, was discouraged.
Methodius died with his work failing. On Latin advice
his chief disciples were thereupon banished from Moravia,
while less important followers were sold in the slave markets
of Venice, where the Byzantine ambassador bought them
and sent them to Constantinople. There Photius received
them gladly and used them to found a seminary for Slavonic
missionaries. Meanwhile the exiled disciples arrived in
Bulgaria, where they were no less well received by Boris, who
employed them to Slavise his Church. With his help and
the patronage of the Emperor and the Patriarch the autonomous native-speaking Church of Bulgaria began.

Thus Moravia lost the fruits of the work of the Macedonian brothers. Soon afterwards it was punished for its
ingratitude. At the close of the century the heathen Magyars invaded the Danubian plain and extinguished the
Moravian Kingdom. It was Bulgaria that kept Cyril's work
from perishing, and the Bulgarians, Finno-Ugrian in
origin, have the glory of being the first great civilised state
amongst the Slavs.

It was a very Byzantine civilisation, for all that it had an alphabet of its own. Boris's son Symeon, self-styled Tsar, and chief patron of the new culture, had been educated at Constantinople, where he read deep in Demosthenes and in John Chrysostom. At his court translators flocked to render Greek chronicles, homilies and romances into the Slavonic ; his buildings in his vast capital of Preslav the glorious copied and ambitiously emulated the splendours of Constantinople —though recent excavations show work rather Iranian in design, like most of early Bulgarian art. This is doubtless due largely to Armenian craftsmen, for Armenians had already come in large numbers to Bulgaria : though modern Bulgarian historians see in it traces of a native proto-Bulgar art carried by the nomad Bulgars round the north of the Black Sea during their migrations.

Tsar Symeon inaugurated another fashion, copied by his successors and their Serbian neighbours down to the days of the Coburger Ferdinand. He dreamed of reigning at Constantinople as the heir of all the Cæsars. He crowned himself Emperor and gave his Church a Patriarch, and hurled himself against the walls of Constantinople. It was in vain. His son Peter (927–969), though the Imperial and Patriarchal title were kept, married a Byzantine princess ; and the government like the culture fell under Byzantine influence.

When Byzantium recovered her full strength at the close of the Tenth Century, she made it her business to crush the upstart Empire of the Bulgars. It was a slow labour, for the Bulgars under Tsar Samuel fought hard ; but in the end Basil II, the Bulgar-slayer, completed the conquest. But though Bulgaria sank now to be a province, she was left with her language and her church organisation—the nucleus for a new independent realm when the occasion should come. Moreover, she had inaugurated a new civilisation, owing everything, literature and art, to Constantinople or the Armenians, but in itself Slavonic.

Serbia had been converted in the course of the Macedonian brothers' missions. As the inevitable enemy of
Bulgaria she fell early under the influence of Constantinople,
but she was too poor at first to have any settled civilisation.
The Serbo-Croatian states further to the west looked rather
towards the Adriatic. They too were the spiritual children
of Cyril ; but only Rascia (Montenegro) kept to the Cyrillic
allegiance. Croatia, emerging as a great military power at
the close of the Ninth Century, decided under her King
Tomislav that her ambitions in Dalmatia made the goodwill
of Rome essential. At the Synods of Spalato in 924 and 927
Croatia and the countries within her sphere went over to the
Latin liturgy. Their civilisation therefore had a Latin-
Dalmatian colour, Byzantine only at secondhand.

The fall of the first Bulgarian Empire had been helped
by the appearance in Bulgaria of the Bogomil heresy,
started by the priest Bogomil and undoubtedly influenced
by the Armenian Paulician heretics. It was a dualist creed,
disapproving alike of labour and procreation and adopting
an attitude of passive resistance fatal to a state. It produced a native literature of legends and fairy-tales, some
indigenous, but more of Greek, Armenian or Eastern origin.
In Bulgaria the Imperial authorities stamped it out within
a century of the conquest. But it spread westward to
Serbia and settled firmly in Bosnia and Croatia. In
Bosnia it was the dominant religion till the coming of the
Turks.

The Tenth Century saw a second great missionary movement. The Russians like the Bulgarians were a Slav people
organised by an alien aristocracy.[1] Byzantium had for

[1] For the Russians, see Soloviev, *History of Russia* (in Russian) ;
Uspenski, *Russia and Byzantium* (in Russian) ; Kluchevsky, *History of
Russia*, trans. Hogarth ; Golubinski, *History of the Russian Church* (in
Russian) ; Leib, *Kiev, Rome et Byzance* ; Vasiliev, *Was Old Russia a
Vassal-State of Byzantium?* in *Speculum*, vol. 7, 350 *sqq.*

some time been in touch with the Norse Grand Dukes of Novgorod and Kiev, who yearly sent flotillas to Constantinople to trade and occasionally to raid, and had acquired certain commercial rights at the Capital. In the middle of the century the Dowager Grand Duchess Olga had become a convert to Christianity and paid a visit to Constantinople. Some fifty years later, in 989, her grandson Vladimir the Great agreed to baptise himself and his subjects in return for the hand of the Emperor's sister, Anna. Henceforward Byzantine influence spread rapidly in Russia. The Russians were given the Cyrillic liturgy and alphabet ; and they made good use of both. Alone of the Slavonic peoples they produced a literature not merely of translations. Their chronicles, such as the so-called Nestor and the Novgorod Chronicles, are creditable historical works ; their art, Byzantine in its origin, acquired features of its own, largely due to the play of influences from the East. The great Church of Saint Sophia at Kiev, Byzantine in its main design and its mosaics, has features that relate it closely to the churches of Georgia, like the small Abasgian church of Mokvi ; and this interplay of ideas gradually produced a native Russian style. How far the mediæval Russian civilisation might have developed it is hard to say. The country was very wide and diffuse ; and too early, in the Thirteenth Century, the Mongols came, stunting the country's growth and upsetting its orientation. When Russia re-emerged it was as an Oriental country. Even the Church, no longer inspired by the active thought of Byzantium, sank into passivity. The women were hidden in the terem ; ignorance and illiteracy invaded even the aristocracy. Little more than empty forms and usages and Cyril's alphabet reminded Russia of her Byzantine sponsorship. The Romanovs introduced a hybrid Byzantine Western veneer and gave the country a superficial greatness ; but the East was to triumph again. The same ruthless impersonal autocracy enables Stalin as it enabled Genghis Khan to rule from the Baltic to the Pacific Ocean.

Indeed, none of Byzantium's god-children were allowed to reach maturity in peace. Bulgaria and Serbia revived in the late Twelfth Century, and each founded Empires, the first to last nearly two centuries till it fell before the Turk, the latter to linger a century longer till the field of Kossovo reduced it to a vassaldom that soon became slavery.[1] Both developed their Byzantine civilisation. The history of Bulgaria under the Asen dynasty is obscure ; of its literature little has survived, and external records are scrappy and confused. More than once the Tsars threatened Constantinople during the Latin Empire. But the Palæologan recovery and the rival growth of Serbia overshadowed the Bulgars. Influential Byzantine-born or Serbian Tsaritsas weakened their independence. Nevertheless they produced an art, illustrated in the churches of Trnovo and the frescoes of Boiana, Byzantine basically but in simplicity of form and warmth of colouring acquiring a character of its own.

The Serbian Empire was more splendid. Indeed, in the Fourteenth Century the Tsar Stephen Dušan was probably the most powerful monarch in Europe ; and Constantinople seemed indubitably within his grasp. The disciplined Bulgar system of government lent itself easily to Imperialisation. Serbia, however, had a native system that might almost be called feudal ; the Serbian monarch was by no means absolute over his vassals. Thus Serbia was never so Byzantine. But there was a constant stream of Byzantine influence. Several Byzantine princesses made Serbian marriages, many Byzantine embassies travelled to the Serbian Court—which princesses and ambassadors alike represented

[1] See Miller, in *Cambridge Medieval History*, vol. 4, 517–93, and bibliography, 871–6 ; *L'Art Byzantin chez les Slaves, Premier Recueil Uspenski*.

as fiendishly uncomfortable and austere.[1]   When Stephen
Dušan issued a code of laws, though the basis was largely
Serbian feudalism, the bulk of it was certainly culled from
the law-books of Byzantium.   Serbian pictorial art was
very Byzantine ;   Serbian architecture developed national
characteristics.   The proximity of Dalmatia and a Latin
queen Helena, daughter of the Latin Emperor and wife of
Stephen Uroš I, gave it in the Thirteenth Century an
Italo-Gothic tinge.   In the Fourteenth, the golden age of
Serbia, Byzantine ideals and Byzantine queens dominated
again ;   but Serbian architects kept certain ideas of their
own.   But, like Russia, neither Bulgaria nor Serbia was
given time to pursue its career to full maturity.   The
Turks reduced them too soon to slavery and their civilisation crumbled—save what the Church, struggling humbly
against innumerable difficulties, managed by tenacity to
preserve.

It is therefore unfair to judge Byzantine mission-work on
the present state of the Balkan countries.   For the Balkan
countries have only recently emerged from four centuries'
black night.   Rather we should compare them as they were
before the Turkish conquest with the Fourteenth-Century
West—compare Salisbury Cathedral with the great Serbian Church of Gratchenitsa.   The former may soar gracefully heavenward ;   the latter with the simplicity of its
design, the comprehensive economy of its balance and its
stresses and the rich restrained decoration of its interior,
is the work of a people no less spiritual but far more
sophisticated and cultured.

In the other neighbouring countries of Europe Byzantine
influence never reached full fruition.   In Hungary as in
Croatia its early successes gave place to those of the West

---

[1] See Lascaris, *Byzantine Princesses in Medieval Serbia* (in Serbian),
passim, esp. 132-5, quoting Gregoras's account of his embassy ;   and
Metochites's account of his embassy in *B.G.M.*, vol. 1, 154-93.

and of Rome. In Wallachia and Moldavia settled states only appeared during the decline of Byzantium. There it worked indirectly, through the Bulgars and the Serbs and possibly more lengthily through the Russians to the Lithuanians and so back to the Danube—but the question of the Lithuanian influence and its origin is still a matter of discussion. It was only under the Turks that Phanariot governors of the principalities gave them their complexion of superficial and perverted Byzantinism.[1]

Byzantium inaugurated other missions that failed. The Chazars obstinately decided that Judaism was a better creed than Christianity, and not all the labours of Saint Cyril, who learnt Chazar and Hebrew for the task, could quite dissuade them.[2] The Alans on the northern slopes of the Caucasus were converted for a short while in the early Tenth Century. But they soon found the Christian faith insipid and exiled all the priests.[3]

With the nations just south of the Caucasus, the various Armenian, Georgian and Albanian peoples, the relations of Byzantium were somewhat strange. Indeed, Armenian influence on Byzantium was probably greater than Byzantine influence on Armenia.[4] Christianity had been brought to Armenia from the Greek East by Saint Gregory the Illuminator in the Third Century. Before the Victory of the Church or the foundation of Constantinople it was the official Armenian faith, though it suffered certain early set-backs. The Armenians were extremely proud of their ancient Christianity ; and when they were not fully con-

---

[1] See Iorga, *Geschichte des Rumänischen Volkes.*

[2] *Vita Constantini* (Slavonic), ed. Miklosich-Dümmler, 219, 224–5.

[3] Maçoudi, *Prairies d'Or,* II, 43.

[4] For Armenia, see Chamich, *History of Armenia* ; Adonts, *History of Armenia* (in Russian. MS. translation of portions by Conybeare in London Library) ; Laurent, *l'Arménie entre Byzance et l'Islam* ; Strzygowski, *Baukunst der Armenier und Europa* ; Macler, in *Cambridge Medieval History,* vol. 4, 153–83 and bibliography, 814–18.

sulted at the Fourth Œcumenical Council at Chalcedon, they rejected its decrees. Henceforward they were schismatic and associated in Orthodox minds with the Monophysites. There was therefore mutual suspicion between the Empire and Armenia, and it was enhanced by Armenia's liaison with Persian civilisation—the first great Armenian royal dynasty, the Arsacids, was a branch of the Parthian royal family ; and during the Imperial wars against the Sassanids Armenia was the usual battleground, and continually overrun by either side. From the Persian connection Armenian art and architecture in particular acquired Sassanid traits, which simmered and developed there, and at intervals were carried westward to give new life to the art of the Empire.

After the fall of the Sassanids, the Arabs dominated Armenia for two centuries. The Armenians gained nothing from Arab civilisation, and little from Constantinople. Many Armenians went now to seek their fortunes in the Empire, but few returned home. It was in the Ninth Century that the connection between the Capital and Armenia became close again. A great native dynasty arose on the slopes of Ararat, the Bagratids, who traced their descent from David and Bathsheba and called the Virgin Mary their cousin. They established a certain hegemony over the lesser principalities that filled the Armenian valleys ; their title of King of Kings was recognised both at Baghdad and at Constantinople ; and gradually, after a set-back early in the Tenth Century, they freed themselves from Arab domination. In the task they were greatly helped by the growing power of the Empire under the Macedonian dynasty that itself claimed Bagratid ancestry.

The Tenth Century was the golden age of Armenia. It was then that her finest buildings, in Akhthamar and in Ani, were built, that her best historians, John the Catholicus and Thomas Ardzruni, wrote. But how far this civilisation was affected by Byzantium it is difficult to say. Armenians still flocked into the Empire ; but those that remained in Armenia were strongly nationalistic, hating the schismatic Greeks and all their works. Their literature, after the Fourth Century, owed nothing to the Greek. An Armenian, Saint Mesrob, had invented their alphabet—on a Greek basis, it is true—their early historians, such as Faustus of Byzantium and Ananias of Shirak, in their style and matter were native and naïve. Their Church had its own organisation with its Primate, the Catholicus, a prelate usually succeeded by his nephew. Even the writers of the Golden Age clearly knew no Greek. Nevertheless, Constantinople exercised an irresistible attraction. In a crisis it was to Constantinople that they appealed. It was in Constantinople that their adventurous sons hoped to grow rich. To Constantinople came their princes, acquiring prestige from being received at Court. The princes of the provinces nearest to the Empire, such as of Taron, even kept up a palace at Constantinople and many of them married Byzantine wives. Among such princes and adventurers the idiosyncrasies of the Armenian Church were quickly discarded.

But in the valleys of Ararat the Armenians were obstinately nationalistic. Byzantium tried every device to establish its influence ; the Emperor Romanus III even married his niece Zoe to the Bagratid king John Sembat. But the Armenians remained untrustworthy ; and eventually the Imperial Government decided that Armenia must be annexed as a precaution against the coming attack of the Seljuks. Already the princes of Taron were the Byzantine family of Taronites ; the Ardzruni principality of Vaspurakan on the shores of Lake Van had been taken over in 1023. In 1044 the Bagratid King Gagic II was deposed and his country became an Imperial theme. Gagic was given a house in Constantinople and large estates in Asia Minor, where he caused a scandal by inviting Bishop Mark of Cæsarea to dinner and murdering him by tying him up in a sack with his dog, all because the Bishop, feeling about the Armenians much as Eighteenth-Century Englishmen felt about Scots, had called that dog ' Armenian.' [1]

The Byzantine rule was conciliatory. The Armenians kept their Church and their language. Basil II had already indicated the policy. When he was in Trebizond in 1022 he invited the Catholicus to come and preside at the Blessing of the Waters at Epiphany. After the annexation, when Constantine IX summoned the Catholicus to Constantinople, he appointed his nephew as the Syncellus for the Armenian Church, thus giving it an official recognition. [2]

But the annexation was in vain. In three decades Armenia along with much of Asia Minor had passed into Turkish hands. Like the Balkan peoples a few centuries later, only more lastingly, the people of Ararat were given over to servitude, and their Church alone kept their spirit alive, ruling them from the metropolitan Church of Etchmiadzan, where are still the bones of their martyrs, a piece of the Cross and a plank from Noah's Ark.

Nevertheless, Armenian vitality was uncrushed. Out of the chaos they built up in Cilicia a new kingdom, vassal in the Twelfth Century to the Empire, but in the Thirteenth an independent state of considerable power and wealth. Of the mutual influence of the Empire and this Armenia it is hard to give an estimate. Probably it was less than the mutual influence of Armenia and the Crusaders from the West. Indeed, in its last days the kingdom was an appanage of the French rulers of Cyprus. On both Byzantine and Italian painting Cilician-Armenian influence was probably considerable.

With the peoples beyond Armenia, the Albanians, the

---

[1] Matthew of Edessa, trans. Dulaurier, 153–4.
[2] See above, p. 93.

Circassians, and the tribes of the Caucasus of whom, said
the Tenth-Century Arab geographer Mas'udi, God alone
knows the number,[1] Byzantium had few dealings, though
most of their names were inserted in the Imperial diplomatic registers. It was only the Georgians that played
much part in the Byzantine world.[2] The Georgians, with
their various offshoots, Abasgians, Mingrelians and Iberians,
had been converted soon after the Armenians ; and the
same inventive Saint Mesrob had given them an alphabet.
But, unlike the Armenians, they remained in full communion with the Orthodox Church. Early Georgian history is obscure. Early in the Eighth Century Leo the
Isaurian as a young man led a diplomatic mission into the
Georgian hills and underwent incredible adventures there.[3]
Probably this was largely for recruiting purposes ; for the
main function of the Caucasus in Byzantine eyes was to
provide mercenaries. Georgia emerged as a civilised nation
in the late Ninth Century, when an Abasgian dynasty ruled
the country from their strongholds on the Black Sea coast,
winning its power first by a Byzantinophil policy, but towards the close of the Tenth Century interfering, not
always helpfully, in Imperial civil wars. In the early
Eleventh Century the Abasgians merged with a Georgian
branch of the Bagratid dynasty, a dynasty which reached
its zenith in Queen Thamar (1184-1212) and lasted on
till the Nineteenth Century. The Georgians were always
receptive to Byzantine influences, particularly after the
foundation of the Empire of Trebizond ; and Byzantine
ideas can be found in their architecture and their illuminations. But the Sassanid-Armenian share was as strong
in moulding their style. Their churches, tall, wider than
they were long, with attenuated windows and domes under

---

[1] Maçoudi, *Prairies d'Or*, II, 2-3. He estimated it at 72.
[2] See Brosset, *Histoire de la Géorgie* ; Allen, *History of the Georgian People*.
[3] Theophanes, 391-5.

steep conical roofs, belonged uniquely to their country, though they had some influence on the architecture of early Russia.[1] The spiritual prestige of Byzantium was, however, so great that the biographer of the martyr Constantine of Iberia, who was actually an Armenian heretic, wishing to enhance his hero's glory, forged a letter of condolence from the Empress-Regent Theodora to his relatives after his death, copying the one that she in fact wrote to her sister Sophia when Sophia's husband Constantine Babutzicus was martyred at Amorium in 838.[2]

The part played by Byzantium in building up the civilisation of Islam was enormous. The Arabs that came out of the desert were simple people, few of them literate, breathing asceticism. Almost all the refinements that they subsequently acquired, they borrowed from their subject peoples, some from the Persian but far more from the Hellenistic Semitic Christian civilisation of Syria and Egypt. This civilisation, already Byzantine, was continually, even after the Conquest, being revictualled from Byzantium. Not only did Christians living in Syria, like the late Seventh-Century author of the *Trophies of Damascus*, often regard themselves as subjects of the Emperor,[3] but the Ommayad Califs at Damascus found themselves obliged to employ Greek architects, Greek artists and even Greek statesmen, Christians as pronounced as John Damascene himself. Not only were the early Moslem buildings, the Mosque of the Ommayads at Damascus or the country palace of Q'alat, Byzantine in design and, as far as religion would allow, in decoration, but actually the State accounts of the Califate were kept in Greek till the early Eighth Century.[4]

[1] See Baltrusaïtis, *L'Art Mediéval en Géorgie.*
[2] Peeters, introduction to *Vita S. Constantini Iberi, A.S.Boll.,* November 10, 542–5.
[3] *Trophées de Damas* in *Patrologia Orientalis,* vol. 15, 173 *sqq.*
[4] Theophanes, 375–6.

The removal of the Moslem capital to Baghdad increased the Persian at the expense of the Byzantine influence on Islam, though even Baghdad was built partly by Greek architects and masons. The Iconoclastic movement showed rather the effect of Islam on Byzantium ; and in the Ninth Century the Emperor Theophilus was undoubtedly stimulated by stories of the magnificence of the Court of the Abbasids. But his reign was also the epoch of an intellectual revival at Constantinople which was eagerly copied at Baghdad. The great Byzantine geometricians, such as John the Grammarian, were vainly begged to go to instruct the Moslem savants.[1] Henceforward the schools of Constantinople were the cynosure of the intelligentsia of Islam. Two centuries later Psellus numbered amongst his pupils several Arabs and even a Babylonian.[2]

On the frontiers there was a continual interplay of ideas. Intermarriage was not uncommon, as the story of Digenis Akritas showed : while John Tzimisces was said to have had a liaison with a Moslem lady of Amida.[3] In these connections it was probably Christian rather than Arab civilisation that dominated.

The unofficial Imperial protectorate over the Christian subjects of the Calif continued unbroken. Harun al-Raschid might send the keys of the Holy Sepulchre to Charlemagne, but that was more to annoy the Emperor Nicephorus than in admiration of the Frank ; and its implications were soon forgotten. Indeed, it became a habit of Baghdad to put pressure upon Constantinople by persecuting these Christians. The Christians themselves whenever possible paid visits to the Imperial Court. The Patriarch Theophilus of Alexandria spent several weeks with Basil II in 1016, and acted as mediator between him and the Patriarch Sergius.[4]

---

[1] Theophanes Continuatus, 189.
[2] Psellus in *B.G.M.*, vol. 5, 508.   [3] Matthew of Edessa, 15–16.
[4] Dositheus, *The Patriarchs of Jerusalem* (in Greek), 746.

The Eastern Patriarchs followed Cerularius as their predecessors followed Photius in his schism with Rome. In
1042 Constantine IX saw to the rebuilding of the Church of
the Holy Sepulchre, destroyed by the mad Calif Hakim.[1]
The Crusades made such patronage no longer easy. Syria
became now a country under Christian government, Latin
heretics indeed but indubitably Christian. The Comnenian
Emperors did their best ; Manuel I as a gesture provided
mosaics for the choir of the Church of the Nativity at
Bethlehem and gilt ornament for the Holy Sepulchre, and
sent artists to paint the little Gothic church of Abu Gosch.[2]
But the Latin Christians had won too deep a hold on the
land, and after 1204 the Church of Constantinople, along
with the Empire, was too weak for the old patronage to
survive. Henceforward Byzantine influence on the former
lands of the Califate was indirect and very rare.

In the Turks, however, it found a new field. The Seljuks
were barbarous and destructive.[3] They had become
Moslems and acquired a thin veneer of Persian culture, but
that was all. Like the early Arabs they had to accept the
help of Greeks in all the more complicated processes of their
life. Unlike the Arabs they never developed much culture
of their own. Their art only produced a few mosques in
Konia, of Greek or imitation Greek work with Persian traits.
They did not persecute much ; indeed, Christians often
preferred their rule to the Emperor's because of the lighter
taxation. By the close of the Thirteenth Century, Christian
proselytisers were having many successes amongst them,
even in their princely families. It is possible that had the
Ottomans not come to revitalise them they might have

[1] See Duckworth, *Church of the Holy Sepulchre*, 203 *sqq.*

[2] *Corpus Inscriptionum Graecarum*, 8736 ; Phocas, *Descriptio Terrae Sanctae*,
M.P.G., vol. 133, 957 ; the frescoes of Abu Gosch are clearly Greek
Twelfth-Century work, though they are never mentioned.

[3] See article ' Seljuks ' in *Encyclopedia Britannica* (11th edition) with
bibliography.

become Christian subjects of a poor but renascent Byzantine Empire.

The Empire of the Ottoman Sultans has often been called Byzantine, erroneously, for though both were Empires governed through the army, the Ottomans all along had nothing beside their magnificent military organisation. Their bureaucracy was a farce. From Byzantium they borrowed little except the Capital. Even their theocratic autocracy was derived not from Constantine the Thirteenth Apostle but from the Califs of Islam.

The influence exercised by the Byzantines on Italian learning in the Fifteenth Century is well recognised. The part played by such men as Chrysoloras and Gemistus Plethon in furthering the study of Greek and of Platonism in the West put the whole Renaissance in debt to the Byzantines. But the influence did not begin solely then. It had been playing on Western Europe at intervals throughout the history of the Empire.

It came through various channels. Justinian's conquests, though they were short-lived, did not utterly disappear. Not only did the Exarchate of Ravenna provide a district in Italy where Byzantine civilisation, Byzantine art and Roman law could be studied, but also the revived connection with Constantinople stimulated interest in Greek affairs. Many of the Irish monks of the Seventh Century spoke Greek ; and the Bishop of Rouen thought that far too much Greek was studied in his diocese : while King Ina of Wessex invited two Greek scholars from Athens.[1] The Iconoclastic struggle broke the connection. At first the rush of refugee religious artists from the Empire to Rome bore fruit in mosaics and frescoes in many Roman churches ; [2] but apart from the refugees and their works, Byzantine things were

---

[1] Bury, *Later Roman Empire from Arcadius to Irene*, II, 392–3 ; James, *Learning and Literature*, in *Cambridge Medieval History*, vol. 3, 502 *sqq.*
[2] E.g. in the Church of S. Maria in Cosmedin.

greeted with disapproval in the West : where indeed there was little civilisation now. The Carolingian Renaissance brought a renewed interest in the Near East. The eunuch Elissæus, who went to Aachen to prepare the Princess Rotrud to be the bride of Constantine V by teaching her Greek, found a class of eager pupils ; [1] and Ravenna provided most of the models for Carolingian art. The Exarchate was extinct now : but there was a new channel. Venice had already started on her rôle as intermediary between East and West.[2] Her language was demotic Latin and she kept a close connection with the Western Emperors ; but with Constantinople her connection was rather closer. Her art was Byzantine—Saint Mark's was the replica of the Holy Apostles ;—she kept an almost permanent commercial mission on the Bosphorus ; and until well into the Eleventh Century her doges would send their eldest sons to finish their education under the ægis of the Emperor.

There was a connection, too, further south. Even in Theodore of Studium's lifetime his hymns were quoted in Sardinia ; [3] and the reconquest of Southern Italy under Basil I enlarged this channel. The commercial cities of the south, Naples, Amalfi and Gaeta seized hold of the commercial opportunities that it offered. They too sent missions to Constantinople, who brought back Byzantine ideas. Their chief magistrates too sent their sons to be finished at the Imperial Court ; and the Lombard princes of the south followed suit. In Rome Greek Christian names became all the fashion ; and further north King Hugh of Italy wooed the Emperor with frequent embassies. The thrill of the ambassador Liudprand at visiting Constantinople, his pride in his knowledge of Greek, his admiration for everything

[1] Theophanes, 455.
[2] For Venice, see bibliography in *Cambridge Medieval History*, vol. 4, 846–9.
[3] *Vita S. Theodori Studitae*, M.P.G., vol. 99, 215.

Byzantine are illustrative of the times : while Desiderius, Abbot of Monte Cassino, sent to Constantinople to have the abbey's gold plate manufactured there.[1] But the fashion did not spread much outside of Italy ; and later in the century it was altered by the Saxon Conquest. Time-serving Italians found it wiser to divert their admiration to the Emperor at their gates. When Liudprand visited Constantinople again, as Otto I's envoy, on an occasion chosen without tact, he found a chilly reception, and came back declaring that everything was done much better at home : though he did his best to smuggle pieces of imperial silk brocades through the customs. A few years later the old fashion returned when Otto II married the purple-born princess Theophano. In the train of this strong-minded lady Greeks from the East and from Southern Italy flocked northward and followed the Court to Germany. There she scandalised the inhabitants by taking baths and wearing silk —horrible habits that sent her to hell (a nun in a vision saw her there [2])—just as her cousin Maria Argyra a few years later shocked good Saint Peter Damian by introducing forks to Venice.[3]

Theophano's son, Otto III, was fantastically proud of his Greek blood ; he loved to speak Greek and to surround himself with what he thought was the true Imperial ceremonial. Under his patronage many more Greeks came to Germany. Greek monks were established at Reichenau on Constance well before the end of the Tenth Century. About the same time a certain Gregory, related, it was said, to the Empress Theophano, founded the religious house of Burtscheid near Aachen ; and Greek monks built the chapel of Saint Bartholomew in the Cathedral of Paderborn. A little later, Greek monks, probably earning their living as

---

[1] *Chronicon Monasterii Casinensus*, in Muratori, *Rerum Italicarum Scriptores*.
[2] *Vita Bernwardi*, addenda, in *M.G.H.Ss.*, vol. 4, 888.
[3] Peter Damian, *Epistolae*, *M.P.L.*, vol. 175, 744.

craftsmen, were so numerous that Bishop Godehard of Hildesheim, announced that they might only stay two nights at his hospices—he disapproved of wandering monks.[1] The mark of these Byzantine artists can be seen in the rich ornament of German Romanesque architecture.

In France the influence was more indirect. The great Byzantine cathedrals of Aquitaine probably owe their nature to Venetian rather than to first-hand Byzantine models. Saint Front at Perigueux has a strong resemblance to Saint Mark's. Hugh Capet of France was so much impressed by Otto II's marriage that he asked for a Byzantine bride for his son Robert.[2] The request was not granted. Intercourse between the two courts continued to be extremely rare.

With England points of contact were few.[3] The Northumbrian sculptured stones of the Seventh Century are extraordinarily Byzantine in feeling and execution, and the English coronation service has a curiously Byzantine ritual. Probably both facts are explicable by the unbroken connection that Anglo-Saxon England kept with Rome, and Rome with the East.

The Crusades brought the West and Byzantium in closer touch than ever before. But Saracen civilisation was more of a novelty to the West and it impinged on it more directly in Syria. The later Byzantine princesses that married in Germany, Comnenian ladies or the lovely tragic Irene Angela, Queen of the Romans, were none of them missionaries like Theophano or the early Dogissæ. The Westerner merely regarded the Byzantine with a scornful dislike now, as a *rusé* schismatic. He preferred to receive the works of Classical Greece, of Aristotle or of Galen from the Saracens rather than directly from the mediæval Greeks. Even after the conquest of 1204 the Latin masters learnt

---

[1] See Muntz, *Les Artistes Grecs dans l'Europe Latine, Revue de l'Art Chrétien,* May 1893, *passim* ; Schlumberger, *Epopée Byzantine,* ii, 260 *sqq.*

[2] Gerbert, *Epistolae,* ed. Havet, 101–2. [3] Dalton, *East Christian Art,* 66–7.

little from their more civilised subjects. They had come to plunder and destroy, not to be educated. Only Frederick II, restlessly alien to the complacency that has usually beset Western Europe, borrowed, through his friendship with the Court of Nicæa, some of the ideas and methods of the old Imperial form of government.

It was only in the Fourteenth Century that Western scholars began to realise what treasures of learning were stored up at Constantinople. Petrarch tried, in vain, to learn Greek—his master was the Calabrian Barlaam, who later provoked the Hesychast controversy.[1] But in the Fifteenth Century the savants that accompanied the begging Palæologan Emperors to the West were equal to the task of teaching. The crowds that hung on the lips of even that somewhat indifferent scholar Chrysoloras were proof of the new state of affairs. A few years later the fall of the City brought new learned refugees to Italy. Bessarion of Trebizond himself, a Cardinal now, was their patron, and with his aid men such as Lascaris, a pioneer of printing, Argyropulus and Chalcocondylas settled in the Western universities. At last the Byzantine work of conservation, so nearly ruined in 1204, was appreciated in the West.

To the Christian East, whoever were its masters, Constantinople remained the capital to the last. Even the subjects of the Emperor of Trebizond came when they could to settle there, the Russians would go on pilgrimage there, the Cypriots sent their sons there to be educated. Indeed, even the wealthiest Cypriots, little though they minded their Lusignan Kings, felt themselves somehow in exile. Lepenthrenus wrote from there to his friend Nicephorus Gregoras a long letter about the sad state of the old Greek world in the Fourteenth Century. A tactful fear of the Censor made him evade answering Gregoras's question how he endured the insolence of the Latins; but his true opinion shows

[1] See Gibbon, *Decline and Fall*, ed. Bury, vol. 7, 317–20.

sadly through every line.[1] Even the humble chronicler
Machæras, the friend of the Lusignans, was appalled at the
fall of Constantinople and sympathised with the Greek
Queen Helena Palæologæna, niece of the Emperor, in her
horror at the final tragedy.[2]

For the tragedy was final. On May the twenty-ninth,
1453, a civilisation was wiped out irrevocably. It had left a
glorious legacy in learning and in art ; it had raised whole
countries from barbarism and had given refinement to
others ; its strength and its intelligence for centuries had been
the protection of Christendom. For eleven centuries Constantinople had been the centre of the world of light. The
quick brilliance, the interest and the æstheticism of the Greek,
the proud stability and the administrative competence of the
Roman, the transcendental intensity of the Christian from
the East, welded together into a fluid sensitive mass, were
put now to sleep. Constantinople was become the seat of
brutal force, of ignorance, of magnificent tastelessness.
Only in the Russian palaces, over which flew the two-headed
eagle, the crest of the House of Palæologus, did some vestige
of Byzantium linger for a few more centuries—only there,
and in dark halls by the Golden Horn, hidden amongst the
houses of the Phanar, where the Patriarch kept up his
shadowy Court, allowed by the statesmanship of the Con-
quering Sultan and the labour of George Gennadius
Scholarius to rule over the subject Christian people and give
them some measure of security. . . . But the Two-headed
Eagle no longer flies in Russia, and the Phanar is lost in
uncertainty and fear. The last remains are dying or are
dead.

It is as the seers of Byzantium foretold, the prophets that
spoke incessantly of the fate that was coming, of the final
days of the City. The weary Byzantine knew that the doom

---

[1] Gregoras, *Correspondence*, ed. Guilland, 1285–9.
[2] Makhairas, 682.

so often threatened must some day surely envelop him. And what did it matter? It was needless to complain. This world was a foolish travesty, haunted with pain and with sorrowful memories and foreboding. Peace and true happiness lay beyond. What was the Emperor, the Peer of the Apostles, what even was Constantinople itself, the great City dear to God and to His Mother, compared to Christ Pantocrator and the glorious Courts of Heaven?

A LIST OF ROMAN EMPERORS FROM CONSTANTINE I TO CONSTANTINE XI

(Emperors of the East till 480, except when otherwise stated)

Constantinian Dynasty

CONSTANTINE I, the Great	died 337	
CONSTANTIUS	337–361	sole Emperor after 351.
JULIAN, the Apostate	361–363	sole Emperor.
JOVIAN	363–364	sole Emperor.
VALENS	364–378	

Theodosian Dynasty

THEODOSIUS I, the Great	379–395	sole Emperor after 392.
ARCADIUS	395–408	
THEODOSIUS II	408–450	Anthemius, Regent 408–414.
MARCIAN	450–457	

Leonine Dynasty

LEO I	457–474	
LEO II	474	
ZENO	474–491	Basiliscus, Usurper 475–6.
ANASTASIUS I	491–518	

Justinian Dynasty

JUSTIN I	518–527	
JUSTINIAN I	527–565	
JUSTIN II	565–578	Sophia, Regent 573–574. Tiberius, Regent 574–578.
TIBERIUS II	578–582	
MAURICE	582–602	
Theodosius, Co-Emperor	590–602	
PHOCAS	602–610	

301

Heraclian Dynasty

HERACLIUS I	610–641	
Constantine III . . .	613–641	
Heracleonas	638–641	
CONSTANTINE III . . .	641	
HERACLEONAS	641	Martina, Regent 641.
CONSTANS II	641–668	
Constantine IV . . .	659–668	
Heraclius	659–681	
Tiberius	659–681	
CONSTANTINE IV, Pogonatus .	668–685	
JUSTINIAN II, Rhinotmetus .	685–695	
LEONTIUS	695–698	
TIBERIUS III, Apsimar . .	698–705	
JUSTINIAN II, Rhinotmetus .	705–711	
Tiberius	706–711	
PHILIPPICUS, Bardanes . .	711–713	
ANASTASIUS II, Artemius . .	713–715	
THEODOSIUS III . . .	715–717	

Isaurian Dynasty

LEO III, the Isaurian . .	717–740	
Constantine V . . .	720–740	
CONSTANTINE V, Copronymus .	740–775	
Leo IV	750–775	
LEO IV, the Chazar . .	775–780	
Constantine VI . . .	776–780	
CONSTANTINE VI . . .	780–797	Irene, Regent 780–790, 792–797.
IRENE	797–802	
NICEPHORUS I. . . .	802–811	
STAURACIUS	811	
MICHAEL I, Rhangabe . .	811–813	
LEO V, the Armenian . .	813–820	

Amorian Dynasty

MICHAEL II, the Amorian .	820–829	
Theophilus	821–829	
THEOPHILUS	829–842	
MICHAEL III, the Drunkard .	842–867	Theodora, Regent 842–856. Bardas, Regent 862–866.
Basil I	866–867	

Macedonian Dynasty

BASIL I, the Macedonian. .	867–886	
Constantine . . .	869–880	
Leo VI	870–886	
Alexander	871–912	
LEO VI, the Wise . . .	886–912	
Constantine VII . . .	911–913	
ALEXANDER	912–913	
CONSTANTINE VII, Porphyrogennetus	913–919	Regency Council 913. Zoe Carbopsina, Regent 913–919.
ROMANUS I, Lecapenus . .	919–944	
Constantine VII . . .	919–944	
Christopher Lecapenus . .	921–931	
Stephen Lecapenus . .	924–945	
Constantine Lecapenus .	924–945	
CONSTANTINE VII, Porphyrogennetus	944–959	
Romanus II . . .	c. 950–959	
ROMANUS II	959–963	
Basil II	960–963	
Constantine VIII. . .	961–1025	
BASIL II, Bulgaroctonus . .	963	Theophano, Regent 963.
NICEPHORUS II, Phocas . .	963–969	
Basil II	963–976	
JOHN I, Tzimisces . . .	969–976	
BASIL II, Bulgaroctonus . .	976–1025	
CONSTANTINE VIII . . .	1025–1028	
ROMANUS III, Argyrus . .	1028–1034	
MICHAEL IV, the Paphlagonian	1034–1041	
MICHAEL V, the Calfat . .	1041–1042	
ZOE and THEODORA, Porphyrogennetæ	1042	
CONSTANTINE IX, Monomachus	1042–1055	
THEODORA, Porphyrogenneta .	1055–1056	
MICHAEL VI, Stratioticus. .	1056–1057	
ISAAC I, Comnenus. . .	1057–1059	

Ducas Dynasty

CONSTANTINE X, Ducas .	.	1059–1067
Michael VII . .	c.	1060–1067
MICHAEL VII, Parapinaces	.	1067–1068 Eudocia Macrembolitissa, Regent 1067–1068.
ROMANUS IV, Diogenes .	.	1068–1071
Michael VII . .	.	1068–1071
MICHAEL VII, Parapinaces	.	1071–1078
NICEPHORUS III, Botaniates	.	1078–1081

Comnenian Dynasty

ALEXIUS I, Comnenus	.	1081–1118
Constantine Ducas	.	1081–c. 1090
John II . .	.	1092–1118
JOHN II, Calojohannes	.	1118–1143
Alexius . .	.	1119–1142
MANUEL I . .	.	1143–1180
Alexius II . .	.	1172–1180
ALEXIUS II . .	.	1180–1183 Maria of Antioch, Regent 1180–1182.
Andronicus I .	.	1182–1183
ANDRONICUS I. .	.	1183–1185

Angelus Dynasty

ISAAC II, Angelus .	.	1185–1195
ALEXIUS III . .	.	1195–1203
ALEXIUS IV . .	.	1203–1204
Isaac II . .	.	1203–1204
ALEXIUS V, Murtzuphlus .	.	1204

Lascarid Dynasty

(Nicæan Empire, 1204–1261)

THEODORE I, Lascaris .	1204–1222
JOHN III, Ducas Vatatzes	1222–1254
THEODORE II, Lascaris Vatatzes	1254–1258
JOHN IV, Ducas Vatatzes	1258

Palæologan Dynasty

MICHAEL VIII, Palæologus .	1258–1282	
Andronicus II . . .	1272–1282	
ANDRONICUS II . . .	1282–1328	
Michael	1295–1320	
Andronicus III .	1325–1328	
ANDRONICUS III . . .	1328–1341	
JOHN V	1341–1347	Anne of Savoy, Regent 1341–1347.
JOHN VI, Cantacuzene . .	1347–1355	
John V	1347–1355	
Matthew Cantacuzene .	1348–1355	
JOHN V	1355–1376	
ANDRONICUS IV . . .	1376–1379	
John VII	1376–1390	
JOHN V	1379–1390	
Andronicus IV . . .	1379–1385	
Manuel II	1386–1391	
JOHN VII	1390	
JOHN V	1390–1391	
MANUEL II	1391–1425	
John VII	1399–1412	
John VIII	1423–1425	
JOHN VIII	1425–1448	
CONSTANTINE XI, Dragases .	1448–1453	

Note : The *Basileus Autocrator's* name is given always in capitals. Constantine II and Constans I are not included in the list as they never exercised effective power in the East.

U

BIBLIOGRAPHICAL NOTE

The best bibliographies on Byzantine civilisation can be found in the *Cambridge Medieval History*, vol. IV, in Leclercq's article ' Byzance,' in Cabrol's *Dictionnaire d'Archéologie Chrétienne et de Liturgie*, and, especially for modern works, in Vasiliev's *Histoire de l'Empire Byzantin*. For the general reader the various works of Diehl and Schlumberger can be recommended. For the student Krumbacher's *Geschichte der Byzantinischen Litteratur*, Ramsay's *Historical Geography of Asia Minor*, and Bury's various works are fundamentally essential.

The figures given after the sources cited in the footnotes refer to the relevant page. For Greek authorities I have used the editions in the Bonn *Corpus Scriptorum Historiae Byzantinorum*, except where I have stated otherwise on the first mention of the work.

I have made use of the following abbreviations :

A.S.Boll.	for	*Acta Sanctorum Bollandiana.*
B.G.M.	,,	*Sathas, Bibliotheca Graeca Medii Aevi.*
Byz. Arch.	,,	*Byzantinische Archiv.*
B.Z.	,,	*Byzantinische Zeitschrift.*
J.H.S.	,,	*Journal of Hellenic Studies.*
H.Z.	,,	*Historische Zeitschrift.*
M.G.H.Ss.	,,	*Monumenta Germaniae Historica, scriptores.*
M.P.G.	,,	*Migne, Patrologiae cursus completus, series Graeco-Latina.*
M.P.L.	,,	*Migne, Patrologiae cursus completus, series Latina.*

The dates and places of publication of the various books that I cite can be found in the bibliographies given above.

INDEX OF PROPER NAMES

Note.—Except in the case of Emperors, persons will be found under their surnames whenever they are known : e.g. for Bardas Sclerus, *see* Sclerus not Bardas.

Aachen, 296
Abasgia, 161, 283, 290
Abbasid Califs, 45, 46, 292
Abu Gosch, church at, 293
Abydos, 99, 170, 172, 199
Abyssinia, 62, 165–6
Acathistus, hymn, 249
Achilles, 270
Acominatus, Michael, of Chonae, 125, 134, 228, 234, 242
—, Nicetas, of Chonae, 98, 125, 245, 247
Acropolita, George, 229, 236, 245
Acyndinus, Gregory, 230
Adelchis, Lombard prince, 162
Adhoud ed-Dauleh, 158
Adrianople, 46, 59, 194, 211, 278
—, battle of, 32, 138
Adriatic Sea, 151, 152, 168, 236
Adulis, 165
Ægean Sea, 11, 13, 209–10
— theme, 150, 153
Ægina, 209
Aëtius, doctor, 237
Africa, province of, 17, 21, 40, 41, 42, 84, 88, 140, 150, 166, 167, 173
Agapius of Crete, doctor, 238
Agathias, 243
Akthamar, 287
Alania, Alans, 147, 160, 286
Albania (in Asia), 286, 289–90
— (in Europe), 94, 206
Alcæus, 231
Aleppo, 48, 167
Alexander, Emperor, 47, 70, 212, 217, 218
— the Great, King of Macedonia, 13, 270
Alexandria, 34, 41, 76, 109–10, 115–16, 120, 171, 183, 206, 225, 268, 271, 273

Alexius I, Comnenus, Emperor, 52–3, 68, 74, 83, 84, 101, 105, 118, 133, 145, 147, 152, 159, 177, 189, 198, 200, 212, 217, 227–8, 232, 236
— II, Emperor, 54
— III, Emperor, 54–5
— IV, Emperor, 54
Alypius, St., of Paphlagonia, 213
Amalfi, 168, 295
Amida, 292
Amorian dynasty, 45–6
Amorium, 291
Ananias of Shirak, 225, 288
Anastasius I, Emperor, 34, 35, 38, 65, 69, 96, 164, 192
— II (Artemius), Emperor, 43
—, Patriarch of Constantinople, 95
Anatolic theme, 88, 89, 100, 141, 142
Ancyra, 211
Andreopulus, Michael, 247
Andrew, St., Apostle, 215
—, King of Hungary, 275
—, Archbishop of Crete, 249
Andronicus I, Emperor, 54, 63, 169, 215, 219
— II, Emperor, 57–8, 79, 95
— III, Emperor, 58, 79
— IV, Emperor, 58
Angela, Irene, Queen of the Romans, 297
Angelus dynasty, 54, 148
Angora, battle of, 59
Ani, 161, 260, 287
Anna, Porphyrogenneta, Grand-Duchess of Russia, 160
—, Abbess, 246
Anne, St., 215
— of Savoy, Empress, 58
Anselm, Bishop of Havelberg, 128

Anthemius, regent, 35
—, of Tralles, 260
Anthimus, Patriarch of Constantinople, 191
Anthony, St., 245
Antichrist, 121
Antioch, 34, 48, 93, 109–11, 120, 167, 183–4, 206, 213, 225, 232
Aphthartocathartism, 37
Apollo, 18, 23, 26, 28, 255
Apollonius of Tyana, 20, 217
Apostles, Holy, Church of the, 185, 186, 187, 225, 251, 260, 295
Apsimar, see Tiberius III
Apuleius, 20
Arabia, 15, 180
Arabs, 41 sqq., 76, 88–9, 140, 142, 143, 144, 150–1, 154, 156, 157, 159, 162, 166–7, 172, 182, 200, 205, 206, 215, 221, 226, 232, 233, 277, 278, 287, 291–3, 297 ; see Islam
Aramæan, Aramaïc, 254, 255, 256, 263–6
Ararat, Mt., 287, 288, 289
Arcadius, Emperor, 32, 180, 215
—, Forum of, 186
Ardzruni, Armenian dynasty, 288
—, Thomas, 287
Arethas, Bishop of Cæsarea, 228, 246
Argyra, Maria, Dogissa of Venice, 296
Argyropulus, scholar, 298
Argyrus family, 194
Ariadne, Empress, 33–4, 69, 192
Aristotle, 228, 233–4, 297
Arius, Arian heresy, 26, 115
Ark, Noah's, 289
Armenia, Armenians, 15, 31, 32, 35, 50, 51, 52, 87, 102, 118, 138, 161, 163, 167, 180–1, 183, 205, 206, 210, 233, 259, 260–2, 263, 267, 268, 270, 273, 278, 281, 282, 286–7
—, Cilician, 273, 289
Armenian theme, 100
Arsacid dynasty, 16, 287
Arsenius, Patriarch of Constantinople, 113, 119, 131, 133

Arsenius, monk, 131
Arsinus, St., 213
Artemius, see Anastasius II
—, St., 216
Asen dynasty, 58, 284
Asia, province of, 21, 84
Aspar, 33, 63
Athanasia, St., of Ægina, 209
Athanasius, Patriarch of Alexandria, 115, 245
Athenaïs, see Eudocia-Athinaïs
Athene, 218
Athens, 12, 45, 125, 194, 225, 228, 253, 263, 266, 294
Athos, Mt., 80, 111, 133, 221, 274
Attaliates, Michael, 244
Attica, 125, 272
Attila, King of the Huns, 138
Augustus, Emperor, 14, 20, 22, 98
Aurelian, Emperor, 22
Avars, 39–40, 277, 279
Axum, 164–5, 167

Babutzicus, Constantine, 291
Baghdad, 45, 48, 134, 143, 157, 158, 162, 167, 235, 287, 292
Bagrat, King of Abasgia, 161
Bagratid dynasty, 287
Baldwin I, Latin Emperor, 56
— II, Latin Emperor, 56–7, 190
Balsamon, Theodore, Patriarch of Antioch, 78
Baradæus, Jacob, 116
Bardanes, see Philippicus
Bardas, Cæsar, 46, 79, 83, 119, 218, 226, 227, 279
Bari, 51, 52, 159, 167–8, 206
Barlaam and Josaphat, 248
Barlaam of Calabria, 298
Barletta, 264
Basil I, the Macedonian, Emperor, 46–7, 66, 67, 74, 77–8, 92, 97, 102, 113, 142, 151, 168, 181, 187, 189, 193, 195, 197, 210, 218, 244, 261
— II, Bulgaroctonus, Emperor, 48–9, 93, 96, 97, 103–4, 114, 128, 148, 152, 159, 160, 168, 196, 198, 218, 227, 233, 244, 246, 271, 281, 289, 292
—, St., 111, 242, 248
—, St., the Less, 195, 214

Basil I, Patriarch of Constanti-
   nople, 113
— the Paracoemomenus, 92, 102,
   149, 195, 203
Basilica, code, 47, 77–8
Basiliscus, rebel, 225
Bathsheba, 287
Belgrade, 205, 211
Belisarius, 36, 139
Benedict, Cardinal, 125
Benjamin of Tudela, 96
Bertha of Sulzbach, Empress, 217
Berytus, 76, 165, 171, 225, 249
Bessarion, Cardinal, 229, 234, 243,
   298
Bethlehem, 272, 293
Bithynia, 141, 229
Bizya, 202–3
Blachernae, 105, 185, 186, 215
—, Palace of, 189–90
Blastares, Matthew, 78
Blemmydas, Nicephorus, 133,
   228–9, 246–7
Blood, the Holy, 215
Blues, the, Circus-faction, 71–2,
   192
Bœotia, 261
Bogas, John, 156
Bogomil heresy, 101, 114, 118, 282
Bohemond, Prince of Antioch, 148
Boiana, 284
Boris (Michael), Prince of Bul-
   garia, 279–81
Bosnia, 282
Bosphorus, 11–12, 99, 170, 184,
   187, 190, 206, 254, 295
Brocquière, Bertrandon La, 132,
   188
Brusa, 58, 206, 229
Bryennius, family, 194
—, Nicephorus, Cæsar, 28, 244
Bucellarian theme, 88, 100, 139,
   140
Bucoleon, harbour, 189
Bulgaria, Bulgars, 42, 49, 50, 54,
   56, 58, 59, 82, 93–4, 118, 123,
   128, 147, 156, 157, 158, 160,
   161, 180, 206, 221, 244, 276,
   278–82, 284–6
—, Black, 159
Bull, Forum of the, 186
Burtscheid, 296

Cabasilas, Nicholas, 243
Cæsar, Julius, 16
Cæsarea, 211
Calabria, 44, 89, 93, 121, 153, 212
Calliana, 165
Callinicus of Heliopolis, 154
Calvary, 26
Camaterus, John, 251
Cameniates, John, 247
Cantacuzenus family, 70, 194
—, John, *see* John VI
Cappadocia, 87, 140, 273
Caracalla, Emperor, 13
Caria, 87
Carolingian dynasty, 295
Carthage, 33, 42, 183
Casia, poetess, 191, 230, 249
Cassino, Monte, Abbey of, 232,
   296
Catanances, fortune-teller, 217
Caucasus, Mts., 128, 129, 157,
   161, 170, 286, 290
Cecaumenus, 81, 82, 83, 145, 146,
   155, 198, 226, 236, 237, 247
Cedrenus, George, 245
Cephallonia, 151
Cerularius, Michael, Patriarch of
   Constantinople, 50, 113, 124,
   218, 246, 293
Ceylon, 165, 178
Chœrosphacta, Leo, 156, 248
Chalcedon, 11–12, 187, 205
—, Council of (Fourth Œcu-
   menical Council), 34–5, 37,
   40, 102, 116, 181, 287
Chalcondylas, Laonicus, 245, 298
Chalcopratia, 215, 225
Charisian Gate, 186
Charles the Great (Charlemagne),
   Western Emperor, 45, 122,
   162, 279, 292
— of Anjou, King of the Two
   Sicilies, 57, 126
Charon family, 194
Charsianian theme, 140
Chazaria, Chazars, 44, 156, 159,
   167, 182, 233, 286
Cherson, 43, 89, 153, 155–6, 160,
   164, 167
Children, the Three, 215
China, 15, 116, 163–5, 188
Chios, 272

Chonæ, 216
Choniades, George, 230
Choniates, see Acominatus
Chora, Church of the, 273
Christodulus, St., of Patmos, 133, 228
Christopher Lecapenus, Emperor, 180
— of Mitylene, 251
Christos Paschon, 250
Chrysococcus, George, 230
Chrysolaras, 229–30, 294, 298
Chrysopolis, 13, 24
Chrysostom, St. John, Patriarch of Constantinople, 34, 113, 133, 187, 242, 248, 281
Chytri, 134
Cibyrrhæot theme, 89, 150, 153
Cilicia, 48 ; see Armenia
Cilician Gates, 211
Cinnamus, 215, 245
Circassia, 290
Circus, see Hippodrome
Claudius II, Gothicus, Emperor, 16
Clement, Patriarch of Alexandria, 19
Cluny, Cluniac movement, 123
Clysma, 165
Codinus, 82, 247
Cometas, poet, 231
Commagene, 211
Comnena, Anna, 132, 137, 145, 149, 194, 220, 223, 224, 230, 231, 232, 233, 235, 236, 237, 238, 242, 244–5
—, Maria, Queen of Jerusalem, 161
—, Theodora, Queen of Jerusalem, 161
Comnenus dynasty, 52–4, 78, 84, 92, 94, 99, 100, 104, 124, 133, 148, 152, 160, 169, 171, 189, 199, 228, 297
— dynasty, of Trebizond, 55, 60, 170 ; see Trebizond
— family, 30, 31, 194, 196, 214, 230
Conrad III, Western Emperor, 237
Constans I, Emperor, 31
— II, Emperor, 42, 73
—, Patriarch of Constantinople, 157
Constantine I, the Great, Emperor, 13–14, 22, 24–8, 108,

109, 137, 174, 176, 177, 224, 241, 242, 243, 255, 294
Constantine II, Emperor, 31
— III, Emperor, 42
— IV, Pogonatus, Emperor, 42, 64, 121
— V, Copronymus, Emperor, 44, 81, 83, 159, 166, 212, 295
— VI, Emperor, 45, 66, 161, 191, 198
— VII, Porphyrogennetus, Emperor, 47–8, 49, 63, 66, 67, 78, 81, 93–4, 100, 103, 106, 149, 159, 160, 189, 192, 223, 227, 236, 241, 244
— VIII, Emperor, 48, 49–50, 219
— IX, Monomachus, Emperor, 50, 79, 93, 227, 232, 275
— X, Ducas, Emperor, 51
— XI, Dragases, Emperor, 60, 65, 160, 198, 233, 289
— Lecapenus, Emperor, 48
—, St., of Iberia, 291
— of Rhodes, 251
—, a monk, 226
—, see Cyril
—, Forum of, 186
Constantinople, First Council of (Second Œcumenical Council), 32, 34, 115
—, Second Council of (Fifth Œcumenical Council), 37, 109, 116
—, Third Council of (Sixth Œcumenical Council), 42, 116
—, University of, 76, 78, 100–1, 224–5, 226, 227
Constantius I, Emperor, 23, 24, 26
— II, Emperor, 30–1, 215, 224
Corfu, 98
Corinth, 169, 171
Corinthius, Leo, 232
Cosmas, Patriarch of Constantinople, 217
— Indicopleustes, 165, 176, 236, 247, 268
— of Jerusalem, 249
—, a monk, 233
Councils, Œcumenical, 65, 114 *sqq.*, *see* Nicæa, Constantinople and Chalcedon, Councils of

Cretan School of painting, 274
Crete, 45, 48, 150–1, 153, 210
Critobulus of Imbros, 245
Croatia, 282
Cross, the True, 26, 161, 215, 289
Crown of Thorns, the, 26, 215
Crusades, the, 51, 52–5, 124, 154, 159, 169, 190, 206, 289, 293, 297–8
Curcuas, John, 48, 181
Cyclades, 87
Cyprus, Cypriots, 48, 54, 87, 98, 111, 128, 134, 230, 289, 298–9
Cyril, St., Patriarch of Alexandria, 34, 116
— (Constantine), St., Apostle to the Slavs, 129, 233, 279–80, 282, 283
Cyrus, Prefect, 35
Cyzicus, 82

Dalassena, Anna, 194, 198, 199
Dalassenus family, 194
Dalmatia, 89, 151, 282, 285
Damascus, 213, 269, 291
Damian, St., 132, 216
—, St. Peter, 296
Daniel, the Prophet, 215
— the Stylite, St., 213
Danielis, 195, 204
Daphni, 272
Dara, 164
David, King of Israel, 287
Demes, 71–2
Demetrian, Bishop of Chytri, 134
Demetrius, St., 42, 205, 216
—, St., Church of Thessalonica, 267, 273
— of Lampe, 117
Demosthenes, 224, 281
Desiderius, Abbot of Monte Cassino, 296
Digenis Akritas, 141, 182, 195, 198, 221, 252, 262, 270, 292
Diocletian, Emperor, 13, 20–5, 61, 64, 74, 83, 87, 92, 109, 137, 201, 255, 256
Diomede, St., 216
Dionysius the Areopagite, 117, 242
Dioscorus, Patriarch of Alexandria, 116
Dnieper, R., 167

Dome of the Rock, at Jerusalem, 269
Domitian, Emperor, 23
Dorylæum, 211
Ducas, chronicler, 245
— family and dynasty, 28, 51, 52, 194
—, Constantine, rebel, 199, 219
Dyrrhachium, 148, 206, 211

East, Prefecture of the, 21
Ecloga, 76–7, 107, 176
Edessa, 216 .
—, Image of, 215
Egypt, 34–5, 41, 102, 140, 153, 166, 167, 173, 180, 268, 291
Ekthesis, 40
Elijah, the Prophet, 215
Elissaeus, eunuch, 295
El-Mahdia, 156
England, English, 147, 148, 182, 277, 289, 297
Epanagoge, 77
Ephesus, 12
—, Council of (Third Œcumenical Council), 34, 115–16, 128
Ephraïm, chronicler, 252
Epicurus, 234
Etchmiadzan, 289
Eubœa, 210
Euchaïta, 130
Euclid, 228, 235
Eudocia (Athenaïs), Empress, 230, 249
— Macrembolitissa, Empress, 51
— Porphyrogenneta, nun, 50
Eudoxia, Empress, 67, 180
Eugenius, usurper, 32
Euphrates, R., 118
Euphrosyne, Empress, 46
Eusebius, Bishop of Cæsarea, 242, 243
Eustathius, Patriarch of Constantinople, 123
—, Archbishop of Thessalonica, 201, 228, 242
Euthymius, Patriarch of Constantinople, 119, 246
—, St., the Young, 146
Eutyches, heretic, 34 ; see Monophysitism
Evagrius, 243

Farmers' Code, 77, 208
Faustus of Byzantium, 288
Febronia, St., 216
Filioque clause, 122–3, 125–6, 127
Flanders, 182
Florence, Council of, 60, 127
Forty Martyrs, Church of the, 225, 226
France, French, 277, 289, 297
Franks, 44, 121, 144, 147, 158–9, 182, 183, 279
Frederick II, Western Emperor, 125, 298
Fréjus, 151

Gaeta, 168, 295
Gagic II, King of Armenia, 288–9
Gainas, 138
Galata, 187
Galen, 297
Galla Placidia, Mausoleum of, 259, 267
Gallienus, Emperor, 13
Garigliano, R., 151
Gauls, the, Prefecture, 16, 36
Gemistus, *see* Plethon
Genesius, 244
Geneviève, St., 166
Genghis Khan, 284
Gennadius, George Scholarius, Patriarch of Constantinople, 19, 129, 130, 229, 243, 248, 299
Genoa, Genoese, 54, 57, 152, 168–70, 178
Geometrus, John, 251
George, St., Church of, at Thessalonica, 267
—, Bishop of Pisidia, 134, 251
—, a monk, 244
Georgia, Georgians, 147, 283, 286, 290–1
Germanus, Patriarch of Constantinople, 113, 121
Germany, Germans, 31, 117, 138, 147, 168, 280, 296, 297
Glycas, 245
Gnosticism, 19
Godehard, Bishop of Hildesheim, 297
Golden Gate, 186
— Horn, 12, 35, 170, 184–5, 187, 190, 299

Gothia, 156
Goths, 16, 115, 138, 149, 180, 277; *see* Ostrogoths *and* Visigoths
Gratchenitsa, 285
Gratian, Emperor, 32
Great Mother, the, 18
Greek Fire, 145, 153–4, 160, 236–7
Greens, the, Circus-faction, 71–2, 192
Gregoras, Nicephorus, 229, 245, 248, 298–9
Gregory, St., of Nyssa, 242
—, St., the Illuminator, 286
— the Great, Pope, 120–1, 232
—, lawyer, 75
Grimoald, Prince of Benevento, 161

Hakim, Calif, 293
Halys, R., 142
Hamites, 180
Harmenopulus, Constantine, 78
Harun al-Raschid, Calif, 167, 292
Hebdomon, 66, 187
Hebrew language, 232, 233
Helena, St., Empress, 26–7, 215
— Dragases, Empress, 198, 214
— Lecapena, Empress, 214
—, Queen of Serbia, 285
Heliogabalus, Emperor, 23, 180
Hellas, theme, 94, 151, 153
Hellespont, 11, 19, 170
Henoticon, 35
Henry, Latin Emperor, 56, 125
— VII, King of England, 103, 198
Heraclea, 109
Heracleonas, Emperor, 42
Heraclian dynasty, 30, 40–3, 116, 150
Heraclius I, Emperor, 40–1, 49, 62, 73, 83, 102, 131, 140, 175, 199, 205, 215, 235, 278
Hercules, 23, 26
Hermogenianus, 75
Hermoniacus, Constantine, 231
Herodotus, 231
Hesychast controversy, 118, 242–3, 298
Hieron on the Bosphorus, 99, 170 172
— on the Marmora, 187
Hippocrates, 237

Hippodrome, 71–2, 81, 184, 185, 187, 189, 192–3, 199, 219, 262
Holospyrism, 235
Homer, 223–4, 231
Honorius, Emperor, 32
— I, Pope, 40, 120
Hugh of Provence, King of Italy, 295
— Capet, King of France, 297
Hungary, Hungarians, 127, 147, 158, 159, 205, 232 ; see Magyars
Huns, 31–2, 188, 221, 277
Hypatia, 225, 230

Iamblichus, 20
Iberia, 84, 290–1
Ibn-Haugal, 98
Iconoclasm, 44–6, 47, 112, 116–17, 118, 121, 133, 150–1, 200, 216, 226, 269–70, 294
Ida, Mt., 11
Ignatia, Via, 211
Ignatius, Patriarch of Constantinople, 119, 203
Illyricum, 21, 86, 180
Ina, King of Wessex, 294
India, 15, 163–5, 167, 248, 252
Innocent III, Pope, 124–5
Iran, Iranian, 17, 180, 254, 258, 263–5, 267–70, 275
Ireland, 294
Irenæus, St., 19
Irene, Empress, 45, 69, 94, 97, 98, 99, 172, 183, 191, 206, 218
— Lascarid, Empress, 229
Isaac I, Commenus, Emperor, 51
— II, Angelus, Emperor, 54, 63, 68
Isaiah, the Prophet, 215
Isaurian dynasty, 30, 43–5, 46, 48, 72, 140, 150, 174, 208, 235
— tribes, 33, 138
Isidore of Miletus, 260
Isis, 18
Islam, 117, 131, 182, 226, 269, 277, 291–2, 294 ; see Arabs and Mahomet
Italus, John, 101, 114, 130, 223, 234
Italy, Italians, 21, 39, 42, 44, 47, 124, 134, 172, 173, 182, 185, 229, 258, 274, 277, 285, 294

Italy, Southern, 50–1, 88, 123, 124, 151, 159, 161, 295, 296

Jerash, 258, 268
Jerusalem, 26, 41, 48, 109, 161, 215, 269
—, Sixty Martyrs of, 195
Jews, 131, 183
John the Baptist, St., 215
— the Evangelist, St., 252
— I, Tzimisces, Emperor, 48, 69, 70, 113, 143, 157, 181, 215, 292
— II, Comnenus, Emperor, 53–4, 106, 147, 189, 218, 238
— III, Vatatzes, Emperor, 55, 125, 133, 172, 204, 209
— IV, Emperor, 55–6, 119
— V, Emperor, 58–9
— VI, Cantacuzenus, Emperor, 58, 70, 99, 104, 126, 218, 245, 247
— VII, Emperor, 58
— VIII, Emperor, 59–60, 127
— XIX, Pope, 123
— the Faster, Patriarch of Constantinople, 120
— the Grammarian, Patriarch of Constantinople, 216, 226, 292
— Catholicus of Armenia, 287
— of Brienne, King of Jerusalem, 56
— -Sembat, King of Armenia, 288
— Damascene, St., 234, 242, 248, 249
— the Cappadocian, 38
— the Orphanotrophus, 201
Joseph, Patriarch of Constantinople, 119, 126, 134
Jotabe, 165
Jovian, Emperor, 31
Julian, the Apostate, Emperor, 30–1, 138, 224
Juliana Anicia, 268
Julius Nepos, Emperor, 32
Justin I, Emperor, 35–6, 71, 73, 165, 218
— II, Emperor, 39, 69, 71–2, 73, 79, 83, 166
Justinian I, Emperor, 35–9, 62, 66–7, 68, 71, 72, 73, 74, 75–6, 82, 86–8, 90, 96, 98, 105, 116, 132, 139, 150, 166, 174,

Justinian I, Emperor (*continued*):
181, 189, 191, 192, 195, 216,
225, 232, 235, 243, 257, 260,
267, 294
— II, Rhinotmetus, Emperor,
42–3, 73, 139, 150, 153, 156,
159, 182, 193

Kadisaya, battle of, 41
Kiev, 283
Konia, 293
Kossovo, battle of, 284
Krum, Khan of Bulgaria, 154, 278

Labarum, the, 25
Lance, the Holy, 26, 215
Lapithas, John, 252
Lascarid dynasty, 55–7
Lascaris, scholar, 298
Latin Empire, 55–7
— language, 21, 35, 121, 139,
232, 241
Lazarus, St., 215
—, St., the Galisiote, 213
Lebanon, Mt., 102
Lecapena, Maria-Irene, Tsaritsa
of Bulgaria, 160
Lecapenus family, 70
—, Theophylact, *see* Theophylact
Leo I, Emperor, 33, 63, 65, 138,
215
— II, Emperor, 33
— III, the Isaurian, Emperor,
43–4, 63, 66, 73, 74, 76–7,
88–9, 99, 106–7, 108, 110,
116–17, 176, 291
— IV, the Chazar, Emperor, 44,
196
— V, the Armenian, Emperor,
45, 63, 181, 217, 218, 219, 244
— VI, the Wise, Emperor, 47, 61,
67, 68, 73, 77–8, 81, 84, 92,
98, 100, 114, 119, 123, 137,
141, 143, 149, 154–5, 156,
158, 173, 189, 204, 215, 217,
218, 246, 252
— the Great, Pope, 34, 120
— III, Pope, 45, 122
— XI, Pope, 124
— Diaconus, 244
— the Philosopher, professor, 217,
226, 235

Leo of Tripoli, 151
Leontius, Emperor, 43, 150
— of Byzantium, 242
— of Neapolis, 246
—, professor, 249
Lepenthrenus, George, 298–9
Libanius, 225
Lichudes, Constantine, 246
Licinius, Emperor, 13, 24–6
Lithuania, 286
Liudprand, Bishop of Cremona,
100, 151, 168, 171, 214, 295–6
Lombards, 39, 121, 161, 162, 168,
295
London, 59
Longobardia, theme, 93
Louis II, Western Emperor, 159
Luke the Evangelist, St., 215, 274
— the Less, St., 134, 212
— the Stylite, St., 114, 213–14
— Holy, Church of, in Phocis,
259, 271, 272
Lusignan dynasty, 298–9
Lycus, R., 185
Lyons, Council of, 126

Macedonia, 58, 89, 102, 146
Macedonian dynasty, 30, 46–51,
177, 200, 208, 287
— school of painting, 274
Macrembolites, Eustathius, 252
Madaba, 236, 268
Magnaura, 226
Magnentius, usurper, 31
Magyars, 144, 280 ; *see* Hungary
Mahomet, 41 ; *see* Islam
Maïna, 57
Malabar, 165
Malalas, John, 243
Maleïnus, Eustathius, 198
Mamas, St., suburb, 173
Mamun, Calif, 235
Manasses, chronicler, 252
Mani, Manichæans, 19–20, 118
Manuel I, Emperor, 53–4, 78, 96,
97, 131, 148, 152, 190, 193,
232, 235, 237, 272
— II, Emperor, 59, 127
Manzikert, battle of, 52, 54, 147,
203
Marcian, Emperor, 33, 34, 65, 69
Marcus Aurelius, Emperor, 20, 234

Mardaïtes, Syrian tribe, 202
Margarites, Constantine, 220, 223
Maria of Alania, Empress, 160
— of Antioch, Empress, 54, 148
— of Trebizond, Empress, 188
—, daughter of Theophilus, 83
Maritsa, R., 59
Mark the Evangelist, St., 120
—, St., Church of, at Venice, 260, 295, 297
—, Archbishop of Ephesus, 234, 243
—, Bishop of Cæsarea, 289–90
— the Greek, 154
Marmora, Sea of, 11–12, 35, 41, 184
Martina, Empress, 42, 73
Mary, Virgin, Mother of God, 29, 115, 117, 132, 187, 190, 215, 299, 300
— Magadalene, St., 215
— St., of Egypt, 210
— the Younger, St., 202–3
Mas'udi, chronicler, 290
Matrakha, 170
Maurice, Emperor, 39–40, 72, 137, 139–40
Mauropus, John, Bishop of Euchaïta, 130, 134, 234, 250, 251
Maxentius, Emperor, 24–5
Maximian, Emperor, 25
Maximin, Emperor, 24–5
Maximus the Confessor, 117, 235, 242
Mazaris's Visit to Hell, 247
Mazdaïsm, 256
Melissenus family, 193
Menander Protector, 243
Mesê Street, 185–6
Mesembria, 82, 154, 206, 279
Mesrob, St., 288, 290
Metaphrastes, Symeon, 246
Metochites, Theodore, 196, 197, 229, 250, 251, 273
Michael, Archangel, 132, 216
— I, Rhangabe, Emperor, 45, 63, 82, 203
— II, the Amorian, Emperor, 45–6, 97, 98, 217, 218, 219, 223
— III, the Drunkard, Emperor, 46, 81, 83, 92, 119, 151, 197, 212, 226, 279

Michael, IV, the Paplagonian, Emperor, 50
— V, the Calfat, Emperor, 50, 219
— VI, Stratioticus, Emperor, 51
— VII, Emperor, 51–2, 227
— VIII, Palæologus, Emperor, 56–7, 58, 104, 119, 126, 152, 190, 233
—, Prince of Bulgaria, 162
—, see Boris
Milan, 13, 23, 183
—, Edict of, 25
Military Code, 77
Milvian Bridge, 24
Mingrelia, 290
Mistra, 57, 59, 65, 95, 266
Mithras, Mithraism, 18–19, 23, 25, 28, 256
Moab, 288
Moesia, Lower, 87
Mokvi, 283
Moldavia, 286
Monemvasia, 57, 166
Mongols, 59, 90, 283–4
Monophysitism, Monophysites, 34–40, 102, 116, 117, 120, 287
Monotheletism, Monotheletes, 40, 42, 102, 120, 242
Monreale, 272
Montanism, 19
Montenegro, 282
Morava, R., 205
Moravia, Moravians, 279–80
Morea, see Peloponnese
Moschopulus, Planudes, 229, 231
Moses, 236, 270
Murad II, Ottoman Sultan, 162
Musele, Alexius, Cæsar, 83
Muzalon, George, 56
Myriocephelum, battle of, 54, 147

Naïssus, 13
Naples, 168, 259, 295
Narses, 36, 139, 181, 203
Nativity, Church of the, at Bethlehem, 272, 293
Nazianzene, St. Gregory, 132, 242, 249, 250
Nea Moni, Church of, 272
Neopatras, 215
Neoplatonism, 20, 233, 234, 242, 277

Nestor, Russian chronicle, 283
Nestorian heresy, 34, 116–17, 165, 167
Nestorius, Patriarch of Constantinople, 34, 115–16, 117
New Basilica Church, 187, 261
Nicæa, 53, 58, 82, 206
—, First Council of (First Œcumenical Council), 26, 115
—, Second Council of (Seventh Œcumenical Council), 45, 117
Nicæan Empire, 55–7, 94, 104, 125, 148, 152, 160, 228–9, 298
Nicephorus I, Emperor, 45, 63, 97–9, 141, 172, 177, 182, 278
— II, Phocas, Emperor, 48, 70, 78, 81, 83, 84, 99, 104, 123, 137, 142, 143, 151, 158, 175, 177, 189, 194, 204, 206, 213, 214, 215, 251
— III, Botaniates, Emperor, 52, 176, 177
—, Patriarch of Constantinople, 225, 226, 242, 244
—, St., of Miletus, 213
— the Logothete, 147, 203
Nicetas, Patriarch of Constantinople, 180, 220
—, Bishop of Nicomedia, 128
— the Young, St., 214
—, Magister, 210
—, Patrician, 223
—, professor, 231
—, see Ignatius
Nicholas I, Pope, 46, 122, 124, 280
— Mysticus, Patriarch of Constantinople, 47–8, 63, 113, 119
Nicomedia, 13, 23, 58
Nicon, St., Metanoeite, 134, 212
Nicopolis, battle of, 59
Nihawand, battle of, 41
Nika riot, 38, 71, 192
Nilus, St., of Calabria, 134, 212
Nisibin, 164
Nonnus, poet, 252
Normans, 50–1, 52, 98, 100, 147, 169
Northumbria, 297
Notaras, Lucas, 127, 196
Novgorod, 283

Odoacer, 33, 138
Olga, Grand Duchess of Russia, 283
Olympus, Bithynian, Mt., 11
Omar, Arab general, 142
Ommayad dynasty, 44, 269, 291
Omortag, Khan of Bulgaria, 278
Ooryphas, Nicetas, 151
Opsician theme, 88, 100
Optimatian theme, 139, 140
Oribasus, doctor, 237
Origen, 19
Orseolo, John, Doge of Venice, 161
Osman, Ottoman chieftain, 58
Ostrogoths, 32–3, 36
Otranto, 156
Otto I, Western Emperor, 296
— II, Western Emperor, 159, 296, 297
— III, Western Emperor, 296
Ottoman Turks, 55, 58–60, 127, 135, 152, 190, 221, 284, 285, 293–4 ; see Turks

Pachymer, George, 229, 245
Pachomius, 226
Paderborn, 296
Palace, the Great, 184, 187, 188, 189–90, 262, 270
Palæologæna, Eulogia, 126
—, Helena, Queen of Cyprus, 299
Palæologan dynasty, 30, 56–60, 65, 66, 94–5, 99, 105, 148, 152, 160, 170, 177, 178, 188, 190, 193, 196, 205, 229, 230, 231, 232, 234, 235, 251, 273, 299
Palamas, Gregory, 118, 243
Palatine Anthology, 251
Palestine, 41, 143, 236, 267–8
Pantaleon, St., of Nicomedia, 161
—, Amalfitan noble, 168
Papacy, 34–5, 44–5, 46, 50, 67, 93, 109–10, 116, 119 sqq., 158, 243, 279, 282
Paris, 59
Paristrion, theme, 93
Paros, 210
Parthenius, Bishop of Lampsacus, 216
Parthia, Parthians, 16
Patleïna, 276

Patmos, 133, 228
Patras, 112, 206
Paul, St., the Apostle, 19, 76, 129
—, Patriarch of Constantinople, 121
— of Ægina, doctor, 237
— the Silentiary, 251
Paulicians, 102, 118, 282
Pavia, 158
Pegæ, 186
Pelagius, Cardinal, 125
Pelagonia, 57
Peloponnese, 57, 58, 59, 60, 80, 84, 95, 140, 151, 172, 195, 212
Peloponnesian War, 12
Pera, 170, 178
Périgueux, 297
Persia, Persians, 16, 23, 31, 36, 39–41, 64, 73, 116, 140, 164–6, 167, 170, 172, 205, 206, 215, 221, 230, 256, 259, 277, 287, 291, 292–3 ; see Iran
Pescennius Niger, 13
Petchenegs, 146, 147, 156, 159
Peter, St., the Apostle, 66, 108, 119, 120
—, Latin Emperor, 56
—, Tsar of Bulgaria, 162, 281
—, nephew of the King of Germany, 148
Petrarch, 298
Phanar, Phanariot, 286, 299
Philaretes, agriculturalist, 195–6, 198, 209
Philes, Manuel, 251
Philip, Emperor, 180
Philippicus, Emperor, 43
Philocales, Protovestiary, 197
Philopatris, 226, 227, 247
Philoræus, stable-boy, 193, 195
Philotheus, author, 82
Phocas, Emperor, 40, 63, 65, 193, 225
— family, 49, 194, 196
—, Bardas, 49, 147, 199
—, Leo, 176
—, Nicephorus, Emperor, *see* Nicephorus II
—, Nicephorus, general, 47, 196
Phocis, 259, 271
Photius, Patriarch of Constantinople, 46, 47, 78, 113, 119, 122–3, 124, 129, 197, 216–17, 226, 231, 232, 235, 242, 247, 279–80
Phrantzes, 220, 245
Phrygia, Phrygians, 180
Pindar, 228
Pisa, Pisans, 54, 152, 168–9
Plato, Platonism, 20, 80, 130, 226, 228, 233–4
—, St., Abbot of Saccudium, 133
Plethon, George Gemistus, 80, 130, 229, 234, 294
Pliny, 15
Plutarch, Neoplatonist, 130
Polyeuct, Patriarch of Constantinople, 113, 134
Porphyrius, charioteer, 192
Porphyry, 20, 242
Preslav, 162, 281
Procheiros Nomos, 77
Proclus, 241
Procopius of Cæsarea, 137, 138, 243, 247
Prodromus, Theodore, 228, 251, 252
—, a recluse, 229
Psellus, Michael, 51, 130, 194, 202, 211, 220, 223, 227, 230, 232, 234, 237, 244, 246, 247, 292
Ptolemy, geographer, 235–6
Pulcheria, Empress, 33, 68, 69, 197
Purgatory, 130
Purple Chamber, in the Great Palace, 70, 84
Pythagoras, Pythagoreanism, 234

Q'alat, 291

Rascia, 282
Ravenna, 39, 44, 259, 267, 295
—, Exarchate of, 67, 121, 294
Red Sea, 165, 167
Reichenau, 296
Rhodian Code, 77, 174
— Love-songs, 253
Ricimer, 138
Robert, Latin Emperor, 56
—, King of France, 297
Roger II, King of Sicily, 169
Roman Church, *see* Papacy
Romanov dynasty, 283

Romanus I, Lecapenus, Emperor,
48, 49, 64, 70, 74, 83, 92, 94,
103, 105, 113, 131, 151, 152,
157, 159, 160, 162, 181, 195,
197, 203, 208, 210, 212, 218,
220
— II, Emperor, 48, 60, 265
— III, Argyrus, Emperor, 50, 161,
200, 227, 232, 234, 237, 288
— IV, Diogenes, Emperor, 51-2,
70, 147
—, hymnodist, 249, 250
Rome, city of, 13, 17, 23, 27, 39,
42, 85, 109, 119, 183, 184,
213, 225, 232, 258, 264, 294,
295, 297
Romulus Augustulus, Emperor, 32
Rosia, 170
Rossano, 268
Rostislav, King of Moravia, 279-
80
Rotrud, daughter of Charles the
Great, 294
Rouen, 294
Russia, Russians, 48, 129, 153,
158, 159, 160, 161, 167, 172-3,
200, 221, 244, 282-4, 285,
286, 291, 298

Samonas, 92, 204
Samos, Samian theme, 89, 151,
153
Samson, 270
Samuel, the Prophet, 215
—, Tsar of Bulgaria, 49, 281
Sappho, 231
Saracens, see Arabs
Sarah, 226
Sarantopechys, 183
Sardinia, 295
Saronites, Romanus, 194-5
Sassanid dynasty and culture, 16,
23, 40, 41, 62, 259, 275, 287,
290
Saxa Rubra, battle of, 24-5
Scandinavia, 182, 277
Scholarius, see Gennadius
Scholasticism, 130, 230
Sclerus family, 194
—, Bardas, 49
Scotland, Scots, 181, 289
Scylitzes, John, 245

Scythia, 87, 180
Seamless Coat, the, 215
Sebaste, 114
Seleucia, 140, 141
— of Antioch, 167
Seljuk Turks, 51-4, 94, 100, 131,
152, 159, 168-9, 173, 177, 181,
214, 288, 293-4 ; see Turks
Selvio, Domenico, Doge of Venice,
161
Semites, 17, 180, 291
Senate, 14, 22, 61, 63, 66, 70,
72-4, 82
Sepulchre, Holy, Church of, at
Jerusalem, 292, 293
Serbia, Serbs, 58, 59, 161, 281,
282, 284-6
Sergius, Patriarch of Constanti-
nople, 292
—, St., and St. Bacchus, Church of,
184, 260, 266
Seth, Symeon, 238, 248
Severus, Emperor, 13
Sicidites, Michael, 217
Sicilian Vespers, 126
Sicily, Sicilians, 41, 42, 47, 50,
57, 89, 121, 150, 151, 161
Siena, Sienese, 273, 274
Skiprou, 261
Slavs, 40, 94, 102, 128, 144, 160,
168, 180-1, 182, 206, 210,
232, 241, 253, 278-85
Smyrna, 12, 151, 206
Socotra, 165
Sofia, 211
Solomon, King of Israel, 36
Sophia, Empress, 39, 69
—, wife of Christopher Lecapenus,
Empress, 180, 214
—, sister-in-law of Theophilus, 291
—, St., Church of, 36, 66, 127,
184, 187, 192, 221, 251, 257,
259, 260, 266
Spain, 36, 39
Spalato, Synods of, 282
Sparta, 172
Stauracius, Emperor, 45, 62, 69,
191
Stephen Uroš I, King of Serbia,
285
— Uroš IV, Dušan, King of
Serbia, 58, 284-5

Stethatus, Nicetas, 246
Stilo, battle of, 159
Stoïcism, 20, 234
Strasburg, battle of, 138
Strymon, theme, 89
Studium, 82, 185, 186, 219, 225
Suez, Isthmus of, 164–5, 167
Suidas, lexicographer, 247
Svatopulk, King of Moravia, 280
Symeon, Tsar of Bulgaria, 48, 24, 218, 281
—, St., Stylites, 166
—, St., the Young, 213
—, St., the New Theologian, 114, 117, 131, 246
— the Logothete, 244
Synesius, 223, 231
Syracuse, 42
Syria, Syrians, 34–5, 40, 41, 53, 102, 116, 124, 140, 164–6, 169, 178, 180, 206, 211, 248, 249, 255, 267–8, 269, 291–3

Tabor, Mt., 118
Taman peninsula, 170
Tarasicodissa, see Zeno
Taron, 161, 288
Taurus Mts., 41, 43
Tertullian, 19
Thamar, Queen of Georgia, 290
Thebes, 169, 171, 206
Thecla, Empress, 83
Themes, system of, 88 sqq.
Theoctiste, St., of Lesbos, 210, 246
—, mother of Theodore of Studium, 195, 198
Theodora, Empress, 36–7, 38, 68–9, 73, 76, 82, 86, 187, 191, 193, 201, 260, 267
—, wife of Theophilus, Empress, 46, 70, 73–4, 96, 151, 191, 246, 291
—, Porphyrogenneta, Empress, 50–1, 63, 69
—, St., of Thessalonica, 209
Theodore I, Lascaris, Emperor, 55
— II, Emperor, 55–6, 229, 235, 237
—, St., Church of, at Thessalonica, 266
—, St., icon of, at Preslav, 276

Theodore, St., Abbot of Studium, 82, 112, 121–2, 195, 200, 213, 225, 242, 246, 251, 295
—, St., the Siceote, 202, 213
— of Cæsarea, 271
Theodoric the Ostrogoth, 33
Theodosia, Empress, 219
Theodosius I, the Great, Emperor, 32–3, 86, 109, 138
— II, Emperor, 33, 35, 69, 75, 180, 184, 189, 213, 215, 224
— III, Emperor, 43
— the Deacon, 251
—, Forum of, 186
Theodote, mother of Psellus, 202
Theodulus, St., 213
Theophanes, St., chronicler, 196, 241, 243–4, 245
— the Paracoemomenus, 92, 218
Theophano, wife of Stauracius, Empress, 69
—, wife of Romanus II, Empress, 48, 70, 201, 214
—, Porphyrogenneta, Western Empress, 160, 161, 296, 297
Theophilus, Emperor, 46, 67–8, 69, 70, 83, 105, 189, 190, 191, 218, 249, 270, 292
—, Patriarch of Alexandria (in Fifth Century), 34
—, Patriarch of Alexandria (in Eleventh Century), 292
Theophylact, Patriarch of Constantinople, 113–14, 181, 203, 214
— Abestactus, the Unbearable, 197
Thessalonica, 42, 47, 59, 80, 95, 104, 151, 167, 173, 176, 204, 205, 206, 211, 216, 247, 267, 273
—, Empire of, 55
Thessaly, 29
Thomaïs, St., of Lesbos, 205
Thomas, rebel, 180, 217
Thrace, 11–12, 89, 141, 146, 173, 207
Thracesian theme, 88, 100
Three Chapters, heresy, 37
Thucydides, 245
Tiberias, 183

Tiberius II, Emperor, 39, 72, 83, 139-40
— III, Emperor, 43, 150
Timarion, 205, 247
Timothy, St., 215
Timur the Tartar, Mongol king, 59
Tiridates, architect, 260
Tomislav, King of Croatia, 282
Torcello, 272
Tornices family, 194
Transjordan, 258
Transylvania, 278
Trebizond, 165, 167, 169, 170, 225, 230, 253, 289
—, Empire of, 55, 60, 160, 188, 290, 298 ; *see* Comnenus of Trebizond
Tribonian, 38, 75
Trnovo, 284
Troy, 13, 233
Trullo, Synod *in*, 42, 111
Turkestan, 164, 169, 256
Turks, 144, 147, 165, 183, 277, 293 ; *see* Ottoman *and* Seljuk
Tyana, 211
Tychicus of Byzantium, 225
Tyre, 165, 171
Tyriæum, 199
Tzetzes, John, 251
Tzimisces, John, *see* John I

Uranus, Nicephorus, 158, 203
Urbicius, military writer, 137
Uroš dynasty, 58

Valens, Emperor, 31-2
Valentinian I, Emperor, 31-2, 65
— II, Emperor, 32
Valerian, Emperor, 16
Van, Lake, 288
Vandals, 33, 36, 87, 150
Varangian Guard, 147, 148, 182

Vardar, R., 205
Varna, battle of, 60, 127
Vaspurakan, 93, 288
Vegetius, military writer, 137
Venice, Venetians, 53, 54, 57, 59, 152, 161, 168-70, 172, 178, 221, 260, 270, 271, 272, 274, 295, 296
Vespasian, Emperor, 13, 22
Vigilius, Pope, 37, 120
Villehardouin, Geoffrey de, 190
Virgin, *see* Mary
Visigoths, 32-3, 36, 39
Vitale, St., Church of, at Ravenna, 259, 267
Vlachs, 133, 206
Vladimir, Grand Duke of Russia, 160, 282
—, Our Lady of, icon, 274
Vlattus, Archbishop of Otranto, 156
Volga, R., 164
Vutelinus, Senator, 107

Wallachia, 278, 286

Xiphilin, John, 227, 246

Yarmak, R., battle of the, 41
Yolande, Latin Empress, 56

Zealots of Thessalonica, 80, 104
Zeno, Emperor, 33, 35, 138, 186
Zeugma, district in Constantinople, 187
Zeuxippus, Baths of, 186
Zigabenus, Euthymius, 242
Zoe, Carbopsina, Empress, 48, 70, 151, 156
—, Porphyrogenneta, Empress, 50, 63, 64, 69, 192, 201, 220-1
Zonaras, John, 245
Zoroaster, Zoroastrians, 16, 19